PROBLEMS AND PERSPECTIVES IN HISTORY

EDITOR: H. F. KEARNEY, M A, PH D

Social Change and Revolution in England
1540 – 1640

PROBLEMS AND PERSPECTIVES IN HISTORY

EDITOR: H. F. KEARNEY, M A, PH D

Titles already published:

In Preparation:

Social Change and Revolution in England 1540 - 1640

Lawrence Stone

DODGE PROFESSOR OF HISTORY
PRINCETON UNIVERSITY

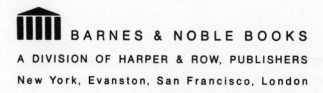
BARNES & NOBLE BOOKS
A DIVISION OF HARPER & ROW, PUBLISHERS
New York, Evanston, San Francisco, London

Published in the United States
by Barnes & Noble, Inc.
through special arrangement with
Longmans, Green & Co. Limited

SBN 389 03557 2

Printed in the United States of America

Editor's Foreword

'Study problems in preference to periods' was the excellent advice given by Lord Acton in his inaugural lecture at Cambridge. To accept it is one thing, to put it into practice is another. In fact, in both schools and universities the teaching of history, in depth, is often hindered by certain difficulties of a technical nature, chiefly to do with the availability of sources. In this respect, history tends to be badly off in comparison with literature or the sciences. The historical equivalents of set texts, readings, or experiments, in which the student is encouraged to use his own mind, are the so-called 'special periods'. If these are to be fruitful, the student must be encouraged to deal in his own way with the problems raised by historical documents and the historiography of the issues in question and he must be made aware of the wider perspectives of history. Thus, if the enclosure movement of the sixteenth century is studied, the student might examine the historiographical explanations stretching from More's *Utopia* and Cobbett to Beresford's *Lost Villages of England*. At the same time he might also be dealing with selected documents raising important problems. Finally he might be encouraged to realize the problems of peasantries at other periods of time, including Russia and China in the nineteenth and twentieth centuries. In this particular instance, thanks to Tawney and Power, *Tudor Economic Documents*, the history teacher is comparatively well off. For other special periods the situation is much more difficult. If, however, the study of history is to encourage the development of the critical faculties as well as the memory, this approach offers the best hope. The object of this series is to go some way towards meeting these difficulties.

The general plan of each volume in the series will be similar, with a threefold approach from aspects of historiography, documents and editorial consideration of wider issues, though the structure and balance between the three aspects may vary.

A broad view is being taken of the limits of history. Political history will not be excluded, but a good deal of emphasis will be placed on economic, intellectual and social history. The idea has in fact grown out of the experience of a group of historians at the University of Sussex, where the student is encouraged to investigate the frontier areas between his own and related disciplines.

H. KEARNEY

TO ROBERT

Contents

CONTENTS

Acknowledgements

I am grateful to the authors of the books and articles which I have used for their good nature in allowing me to carve up their works in order to make my selections. I should emphasize that the cutting is my responsibility, not theirs, although I had their permission. In the extracts from primary sources, spelling and punctuation have been modernized.

For help in the exacting and laborious task of making the extracts, checking their accuracy and checking the bibliography, I am indebted to my wife and to my research assistant, Mr John Godich. The book owes much to them.

We are grateful to the following for permission to reproduce copyright material:

George Allen & Unwin Ltd for material from *Members of the Long Parliament* by D. Brunton and D. H. Pennington; the author for material from 'Office-Holding as a Factor in English History' by Professor F. E. Aylmer, first published in *History*, XLIV, 1959; The Bristol and Gloucestershire Archaeological Society for material from *Lives of the Berkeleys* by T. Smyth, ed. J. McLean; the Keeper of Manuscripts at The British Museum for material from *Additional Mss. No 29442*; Cambridge University Press for material from *De Republica Anglorum* by T. Smith, ed. A. Alston; Cambridge University Press and Melbourne University Press for material from *The Independents in the English Civil War* by G. Yule; The Clarendon Press for material from *History of the Rebellion* by the Earl of Clarendon, and *The Crisis of the Aristocracy 1558-1641* by L. Stone; Constable & Co. Ltd. for material from *A Royalist's Notebook* by J. Oglander, ed. Francis Bamford; the author for material from *Marx and Engels: Basic Writings on Politics and Philosophy* by Professor Lewis S. Feuer; *Encounter* (London) for material from 'Storm Over the Gentry' by Professor J. H. Hexter; The Historical Association for material from 'Recent Interpretations of the Civil War' by Professor C. Hill, published in *History* XLI, 1956; Leicester University Press for material from 'The County Committee of Kent in the Civil War, 1957' by Dr A. M. Everitt; John Murray (Publishers) Ltd for material from *The Breviary of Suffolk* by Robert Reyce, ed. Francis Lord Hervey; The Economic History Association for material from 'The Social Interpretation of the English Revolution'

ACKNOWLEDGEMENTS

by Professor P. Zagorin, published in *Journal of Economic History* XIX, 1959; *Revue Historique* for material from 'La Revolution Anglaise du XVII! Siècle' by Professor C. Hill; Royal Historical Society for material from 'T. Wilson's State of England in 1600' ed. F. J. Fisher, and 'Memorials of the Holles Family' ed. A. C. Wood, published in *Camden Third Series*, Vols. 52 and 55 respectively; the author and The American Political Science Association for material from 'Ideology Hunting: The Case of James Harrington' by Judith N. Shklar, published in *The Americal Political Science Review*, LIII, 1959; the Literary Executors of the late Professor R. H. Tawney for material from 'The Rise of the Gentry' by Professor R. H. Tawney, published in *Economic History Review*, XI, 1941; the author for material from 'The Gentry' by Professor H. R. Trevor-Roper, published in *Economic History Review, Supp. I*, 1956, and the author for material from 'The Independants Reconsidered' by Professor D. Underdown, published in *Journal of British Studies*, III, 1964.

Introduction

The problem of the social origins of the English Revolution in the seventeenth century was first brought to the attention of historians at large by R. H. Tawney in 1940. He saw a change in the ownership of property occurring in the century before the civil war, by which the old-fashioned landowners decayed and a new class of gentry rose to the top. He attributed this change mainly to different degrees of adaptability in estate management to rising prices, new agricultural techniques and new market outlets, partly to the presence or absence of non-agricultural sources of wealth. The events of 1640 he interpreted as a shift in the political structure to accommodate the power of the new class of risen gentry. His thesis of social change was supported by two sets of statistics, the one purporting to show a dramatic fall in the manorial holdings of the aristocracy compared with the gentry, and the other a shift in the size of manorial holdings away from the large and towards the medium-sized landowner.

Between 1940 and 1945 English scholars were otherwise engaged, and the issue lay dormant until 1948, when I inadvertently triggered off the controversy by publishing an article on the Elizabethan aristocracy. In this I picked up one element in Tawney's thesis, that of the decline of the aristocracy, pushed it very much further, assigned the cause of decay not to inefficient land management but to overexpenditure and produced some impressive-looking statistical data, particularly about indebtedness, to support my startling conclusion that 'over two-thirds of the earls and barons were thus swiftly approaching or poised on the brink of financial ruin in the last few years of Queen Elizabeth'. If this ruin was in most cases averted, I attributed it primarily to the largesse of King James.

Three years later this article was subjected to devastating criticism by H. R. Trevor-Roper, who pointed out the extravagance of the language used, the very serious mistakes made in interpreting the statistical evidence for debt, and the unscholarly treatment of much of the ancillary evidence. I replied, withdrawing from my previous exposed position, admitting many errors of statistical interpretation and of fact, but maintaining the general position by the use of some revised statistics of manorial holdings.[1]

[1] These three articles by myself and H. R. Trevor-Roper (items 67, 83, 70 in the bibliography) have been omitted from this collection owing to shortage of

Two years later, in 1953, H. R. Trevor-Roper published a full-scale assault on the Tawney thesis itself. So far from seeing the characteristic feature of the age as a rise of the gentry, he postulated instead a massive decline of the 'mere gentry': small or middling landowners, hard-pressed by inflation and lacking alternative sources of income to main-tain their accustomed way of life. Those who rose, according to Trevor-Roper, were, first, the yeomanry, who flourished on the profits of direct farming, rigorous austerity in spending, and systematic saving, and secondly, those gentry and nobility who had access to the cornucopia of gifts at the disposal of the Crown, or who practised trade or the law. The rising gentry were thus almost exclusively courtiers, court lawyers, and monopoly merchants. The 'mere gentry', who paid for all this largesse, were the 'country party', who in the 1640s overthrew the court system, who fought and defeated the King, and who finally emerged as the radical leaders of the New Model Army, the Independents. Their policy was decentralization, reduction of the costs of litigation, elimination of the detested Court, and destruction of its financial buttresses of state trading and manufacturing monopolies, sale of offices, wards and the like.

This brilliantly formulated argument at first swept all before it. Tawney attempted to defend some of his statistical methods, but he now lacked the vigour to take up the gage of battle which had been thrown down. In 1956 the way seemed to be cleared for general accept-ance of the Trevor-Roper thesis, after J. P. Cooper had marshalled a battery of facts and arguments to demonstrate the worthlessness of the statistical methods of both Tawney and myself and had discredited the whole idea that somehow or other the counting of manors could be made to provide a useful indicator of social mobility.

It was not until 1958 and 1959 that the Trevor-Roper thesis in turn came under serious criticism. Both J. E. C. Hill and P. Zagorin pointed

space. They are of considerable interest to students of historical method and academic controversy, since they demonstrate the serious mistakes in the use of evidence which even reputable scholars can commit, and the ferocity with which they can, on occasion, attack each other's work. For a full appreciation of the issues at stake in the controversy, however, it seemed more useful to devote the space to my revised views of 1965, which are designed to meet the valid objections raised against my earlier formulations. Since I was the target for attack in the articles which I have decided to omit, it is hoped that only my enemies will believe that my motive was merely a desire to suppress the evidence of youthful misdemeanours.

out the extreme fragility – indeed, in some cases the non-existence – of certain key links in the chain of argument: the equation of 'mere gentry' with small gentry, and small gentry with declining gentry; the assertion that profit could not be made from agriculture in an inflationary era; the assumption that the Court was a smooth highway to riches; the explanation of religious radicalism as a refuge from economic decay; the failure to discuss the Parliamentary leaders of 1642; the identification of the Independents with the 'mere gentry' class; and the description of the policy of the Independents as one of decentralisation.

At about the same moment J. H. Hexter published a vigorous attack on both the Tawney and the Trevor-Roper theses; he asserted that Tawney was hypnotized by the Marxist theory of the rise of the bourgeoisie and the decline of feudalism and was trying to cram the events of seventeenth-century England into this procrustean mould; that Trevor-Roper was obsessed with economic motivation at the expense of ideals and ideology, and saw politics merely as a struggle of the Ins versus the Outs, the Court versus the Country, a version of the model set up by Sir Lewis Namier for mid-eighteenth-century England twenty years before. Hexter's own explanation of the social changes prior to 1640 was a new version of my thesis of the decline of the aristocracy. He rejected my concept of financial decay, but argued that there had been a collapse of the military control by the aristocracy over the greater gentry. This meant that political leadership had shifted from the House of Lords to the House of Commons, though the immediate causes of the political breakdown of the 1640s he ascribed to the traditional religious and constitutional factors.

By now it was all too clear that fertility of hypothesis was running far ahead of factual research. What was needed was a massive assault upon the surviving records, economic and personal, of the landed classes of the period, and an examination of the footnotes to the various articles showed that no one had yet done very much work on these lines. Yet as it happened the material had just become available in bewildering profusion. After 1945 the rapid decline of the old landowning classes caused a flood of private family papers to pour into the newly constituted County Record Offices, where they were catalogued and listed and made available for inspection. As a result the decade 1955–65 saw a crop of doctoral theses upon the finances either of individual families such as the Percys or Hastings, or of a group of well-documented families in certain areas such as Northamptonshire

or East Anglia, or of the gentry of a single county such as Yorkshire.[1]
In 1965 I published a book on the aristocracy, based on a lengthy study
of private and public archives. In it I developed a new interpretation,
an amalgam of some of my earlier ideas and those of J. H. Hexter.
I argued that the aristocracy lost military power, territorial possessions
and prestige; that their income declined sharply under Elizabeth,
largely due to conspicuous consumption, but recovered equally
strongly in the early seventeenth century, largely due to buoyant
landed incomes and lavish royal favours. These propositions I supported with a good deal of statistical evidence, some of it based on
reformulations of the previously discredited method of counting
manors. In my view, what had changed was the power and wealth
and prestige of the magnates relative to the greater gentry. I argued
that the change left the King and the Church in a dangerously exposed
position when they started adopting highly unpopular religious and
constitutional policies, and that the debacle of 1640 was therefore
made possible by this prior decline in the power and authority of the
peerage. This hypothesis will no doubt in its turn be the subject of
vigorous criticism, but at least it begins to look as if some areas of
disagreement are being slowly narrowed. On the other hand, many
important questions are still not settled. It is not clear whether the rise
of the gentry meant an increase in the numbers of the class or a rise in
relative power and wealth of the upper levels of it; what political
significance should be attached to the undeniable phenomenon of
declining gentry; whether efficient estate administration or court and
business profits were the more important in creating the new wealth;
who were the leaders of Parliament in 1642; whether or not the
Independents represented the interest of the smaller 'mere gentry'
excluded from the Court; what were the respective roles of ideas and
social forces in creating the political crisis of the 1640s. The debate
continues.

It is safe to say that no historical controversy in the last fifty years
has attracted so much attention. Why is this? In the first place the
area of disagreement appeared to be all-embracing: disagreement over
the definition of terms by which to explain the phenomena under
discussion; disagreement over what had happened; disagreement over
the way it had happened; disagreement over the consequences of what
had happened. Such total lack of common ground is very unusual,

[1] See items 8, 16, 19, 22, 62 in the Bibliography.

and its appearance seemed to cast doubt upon the right of the historian to be regarded as an empiricist who bases his enquiries upon reason and proof. Secondly, the protagonists mustered a prodigious array of talent. The three main contestants, R. H. Tawney, H. R. Trevor-Roper and J. H. Hexter, are all, in their different ways, very distinguished stylists; they are also that very rare thing, men who are capable of dealing in broad and original conceptual generalizations about the past. Thirdly, the dispute soon developed into a kind of academic gladiatorial show, in which no quarter was offered. There have been few more brutally savage assaults in academic journals than that in which H. R. Trevor-Roper demonstrated the exaggerations and inaccuracies in my first article about the decline of the Elizabethan aristocracy. 'An erring colleague is not an Amalekite to be smitten hip and thigh,' protested R. H. Tawney as he nursed his own wounds. Perhaps; but the debate was conducted with a ferocity which not only appealed to the sadism in us all but also gave it a sharp cutting edge.

There were, however, more important grounds for public interest. Many of the younger generation of historians, in France, in England and in the United States, believe that the future of history lies in a selective cross-fertilization with the methods and theories of the social sciences, particularly politics, economics, sociology, social anthropology and social psychology. The problems that arise from any such attempt were brought sharply into focus by the gentry controversy. In the first place it raised, in an acute form, some fundamental problems of methodology. Today every historian, whatever his political persuasion, lays great stress on social forces as operative factors in history. We all talk glibly about social mobility, the rise of the middle classes and so on. This being so, the problem arises of how we are to demonstrate social change in a way that will carry conviction. Social historians of an earlier generation, such as G. M. Trevelyan, constructed their hypotheses on the basis of readily accessible personal documents – the Paston Letters, Pepys's Diary, and so on – bolstered by a certain amount of contemporary comment and by quotations from the imaginative literature of the day from Chaucer to Dickens.[1] These methods were applied, by all parties, to the debate about the gentry. Individual examples of rising peers, decaying peers, rising courtiers, decaying courtiers, rising gentry, decaying gentry were batted triumphantly to and fro. The stream of contemporary comment was quoted extensively, or dismissed as biased and misguided, as the occasion suited. The poets

[1] G. M. Trevelyan, *The Social History of England*.

and playwrights were conscripted into the lines of battle. In the hands of dextrous polemicists the result was a bewildering variety of contradictory evidence which to an outside observer above the smoke and noise of conflict seemed to prove precisely nothing at all.

This was a superficial judgement; but what the controversy did bring out more clearly than has ever been apparent before was the shoddy basis of much traditional historical methodology. Plausible rational grounds were found for quite contradictory hypotheses; since the proponent of each theory was free to choose his own evidence, and since there were too many individual facts pointing in too many different ways, this theorizing could not – and here demonstrably was not – being controlled by facts. This criticism was extended by philosophers to historical methodology as a whole, not without some signs of quiet satisfaction at the humiliation of a sister profession.[1]

It was to meet this objection of the futility of quoting individual examples to demonstrate a sociological proposition that R. H. Tawney attempted to give some scientific basis to his theories by applying the methods of the social sciences: quantitative measurements, systematic sampling and statistical testing. And it is on the reliability or otherwise of the statistical method employed – the counting of manors – that a good deal of the controversy has focused. As a result, a second conclusion of some general significance has emerged: namely that the use of such methods enormously improves the quality of the evidence, but that in the last resort it is human judgement which determines its reliability: judgement about the meaning of the data, judgement about the way it is handled, judgement about the degree of error involved, judgement about the significance of the conclusions. Though hideous errors have been exposed, though disagreement continues, the whole level of the debate has been raised to a higher plane by the introduction of new, and potentially more empirical, evidence. This part of the debate has pointed the way to a fresh approach to the problems of establishing the direction and measuring the speed of social change in the past; it has also high-lighted the danger of embarking upon statistical calculation without statistical training or advice.

Analogous methodological argument has arisen from the attempts of D. Brunton and D. H. Pennington and of G. Yule to use the mass biographical technique to analyse the composition of the various political groupings in the 1640s. What has become all too clear is that

[1] P. Gardiner, *The Nature of Historical Explanation*, Oxford, 1952. W. H. Walsh, *An Introduction to the Philosophy of History*, New York, 1960.

in inexpert or timid hands this tool can become either useless or positively misleading. J. E. C. Hill's criticism of the methods of Brunton and Pennington, and D. Underdown's of that of Yule prove once again that it is necessary to ask the right questions and to employ the right categories if the new techniques of the social sciences are to contribute to the historical discipline more than jargon, obfuscation and a false sense of certainty.

H. Eckstein has observed that: 'The corpus of any field of study is in the first instance an accumulation of issues, resolved or unresolved'. The charge that can be levelled against the protagonists in the debate over the gentry is not so much that they were premature in formulating hypotheses, but that they gave inadequate thought to problems of classification, and that they were unwilling to recognize the large number of questions which had yet to be answered satisfactorily. Like the standard of living of the English worker in the early nineteenth century, or the quality of education in late seventeenth-century Massachusetts, the dispute has thrown up a vast mass of contradictory evidence and disputed statistics. Of the latter controversy Professor Bailyn has written: 'We seem to be dealing here with one of those "questions mal posées" that need restatement before they can be answered.' This is equally true of the gentry controversy, and the search for new definitions of terms and new categories has been in progress for fifteen years or more.[1]

If the historian is to reduce his evidence to intelligible order he is obliged to use abstract concepts and collective nouns. In discussing society he deals in groups labelled peasants, yeomen, gentry and aristocracy; or tenants and landlords, wage-labourers and capitalists; or lower class, middle class and upper class; or court and country; or bourgeois and feudal. Some of these categories, like titular aristocracy, are status groups; some, like capitalists, are economic classes with similar incomes derived from similar sources; some, like 'court', describe groups whose income, interests and geographical location are all temporarily based on a single institution. The problem of how to choose the most meaningful categories is particularly difficult when dealing with mobile societies like that of seventeenth-century England. In 1640 do the divisions between titular status groups bear any statistically significant relation to divisions between classes based on differences of wealth, prestige and sources of wealth; has the category of gentlemen been expanded to such a degree as to be valueless for

[1] H. Eckstein, *Internal War*, New York, 1964, p. 26.

analytical purposes; if so, what is to be put in its place, how is the gentry to be subdivided? It was failure to clarify these issues in the first place which led to so much misunderstanding and recrimination as the debate proceeded. There is, moreover, the danger of treating these abstractions as personalized entities. In assessing the motives of the single individual, the precise admixture of calculation and emotion, the effects of heredity and environment, are difficult enough to determine even when the evidence is available in unusual quantities. How much more complicated it all becomes when it is a question of handling these abstract nouns, of dissecting them and of perceiving the precise relevance of the various threads which make up the pattern not of individual but of collective behaviour.

This is not exclusively a problem that besets the social historian, since it applies equally to the handling of religious or political history in this revolutionary age, for terms like Royalist or Parliamentarian, Presbyterian or Independent, have been shown to be applicable to individuals only with respect to certain issues at certain specific times. To very few men active in public affairs can a single political or religious label be attached which remains valid from, say, 1638 to 1662. This is because the English revolution, like all others we know of, had the habit of devouring its children. The alignment of forces of 1640 was quite different from that of 1642, by which time a large block of former Parliamentarians had moved over to reluctant royalism; it was different again in 1648, when the conservative element among the Parliamentarians, misleadingly known as the Presbyterians, swung back to the side of the King. In 1640 or 1642 virtually no one was republican; in 1649 England was a republic. In 1640 or 1642 virtually no one favoured religious toleration; by 1649 wide toleration for protestants was achieved. One of the major causes of the muddled thinking about the causes of the English revolution has arisen from the failure to establish precisely which stage of the revolution is being discussed. Since each stage was triggered off by different immediate issues, since each was made possible by different long-term movements of society and ideology, and since each was directed by a different section of society, these distinctions are vitally important. It is a measure of the insularity of English historians that they failed to profit from the lessons to be drawn from studies on the French Revolution, where the need for strict periodization when advancing theories of social causation has been obvious for over a century.

Another methodological difficulty arises from the lamentable fact that a single individual may be classed as gentry, bourgeois, country, capitalist and puritan, each valid for certain analytical purposes, none adequate as a single all-embracing characterization. Under each label, moreover, the individual will find himself lumped together with others, only some of whom will be his companions under other labels, and only a few under all of them. It is this multiple variability of categorization which makes the task of the social historian so extremely difficult.

J. H. Hexter has been particularly active in demonstrating the dangers and confusions which may arise from the use as opposing categories of concepts like middle class and feudal class, gentry and aristocracy, court and country, Presbyterian and Independent. His demolition work is invaluable, but the historian must perforce work with some such collective vocabulary; other words, other concepts have therefore to be invented in their place, or the old ones have to be used with greater sophistication and a greater awareness of their artificiality. As R. H. Tawney observed: 'Categories so general are not useless and cannot be discarded. Apart from their serviceableness as missiles in the mutual bombardment of historians, they have the virtue of suggesting problems, if at times they increase the difficulty of solving them.'

Political ideas are equally liable to misinterpretation, and J. Schklar has brilliantly demonstrated how Harrington has been refashioned generation after generation to suit the preconceptions and pre-occupations of the commentators. A more striking example of the subjectivity of scholarship could hardly be found. Similarly, it is necessary to be particularly careful when handling the evidence of contemporaries. For example, Royalist propaganda, repeated subsequently by Clarendon, was concerned to cast doubts on both the purity of the motives and the social standing of their opponents. They therefore put it about that the Parliamentarians were activated by selfish ambitions for profit and office, and that they were men of inferior status, many of whom gained a living from disreputable trades. It is noticeable that both these ideas (which were part of the stock official line on any group of rebels, from the Pilgrimage of Grace to the Essex Rebellion) are reflected in the Trevor-Roper thesis of a declining 'mere gentry' driven on by a desire to become the 'Ins' rather than the 'Outs'. This hypothesis has striking similarities to the modern assumption of a decaying petit-bourgeois base to Nazism, Fascism and such later manifestations as Poujadism.

Lastly, there is the question of objectivity. It seems clear that in history, as in the social sciences, the hypothesis of the rigid segregation of facts and values is quite unrealistic. E. H. Carr believes that the first question a student must ask is what are the political and religious beliefs and the social background of the historian he is reading. The validity of this hypothesis is raised obliquely by the widely differing interpretations of the social origins of the Civil War and of the aspirations of the rebel leaders advanced by a conservative like H. R. Trevor-Roper, by a socialist like R. H. Tawney, by an American liberal like J. H. Hexter and by an English liberal (which is not quite the same thing) like myself. How far has the way we look at the seventeenth century been affected by our political attitudes towards the twentieth?

As well as these questions of methodology, the controversy has also raised important issues of substance, which are of general application over a wide field of historical studies. In one way or another they are all tied up with the question of what causes revolutions. And since it looks as if the twentieth century above all others is going to be the age of revolutions, this is a matter of some interest to politicians and planners as well as to historians. In the first place, is it possible to construct a 'model' of a revolutionary situation, or is P. Zagorin correct in arguing that 'there is not, in fact, any model pattern of a bourgeois revolution, and while the investigation of analogies can be most illuminating, there are far more differences between the English and the French Revolutions than analogies'.

One of the first in the field of model-building was Crane Brinton, who as long ago as 1938 put forward a series of uniformities common to the four great western revolutions, English, French, American and Russian. These included an economically advancing society, growing class antagonisms, an alienated intelligentsia, a psychologically insecure and politically inept ruling class and a governmental financial crisis.

More recently both historians and social scientists have tried to put these uniformities into a more ordered framework. The preconditions of revolution are seen to fall into three broad categories: first, the preconditions, arising from a structural disharmony between the political system, on the one hand, and the social system, on the other, as a result of which certain important groups and interests find that the former fails to satisfy their aspirations (this formula embraces the Marxist theory of conflict between the social conditions generated by the means of production and the laws, institutions and ideas of the existing owners of property, as well as non-Marxist theories of conflicts between different interest groups); secondly, the organizational forms, administrative and military, and the degree of ideological alienation of the dissidents; and thirdly, the obstinate intransigence of the government attacked, which is likely to be weakened by military or diplomatic defeat, disunity, loss of self-confidence, corruption, treachery or financial bankruptcy.

Most of the factors involved are socio-economic in character, and there is some reason to think that a revolutionary mood is often the product of frustrated expectations, most likely due to a setback after a period of improvement. This improvement and setback seem to be more a question of relative position within a society than of absolute well-being. Moreover, there are signs that in this respect status may be more important than wealth. It is possible for a group to increase in material prosperity, but remain stationary or decline in terms of status, as did the English working classes in the nineteenth century; or conversely, at any rate for a generation or so, it may decline in income but retain status, as did the Anglican clergy in the first third of the twentieth century. Radical feelings may be engendered more by a relative decline in respect than by a relative or even an absolute decline in income.

If this is correct, how does the seventeenth-century English revolution fit in? Is it a protest movement of socially frustrated and economically stagnant or declining mere gentry? Or of rich and rising gentry temporarily thwarted in their aspirations by the arbitrary taxation, the religious policy and the authoritarian rule of the Eleven Years' Tyranny? On the other side, was there a court group whose ever-increasing size, wealth and arrogance provoked the outsiders to rebellion? Or were crown, court, Church and aristocracy all sinking – either absolutely or relatively – in power, wealth and prestige, and so tempting the outsiders to seize control? Can the two sides of the Civil War really be equated, as the Marxists would have it, with the rising bourgeoisie, on the one hand, and the declining feudal classes, on the other?

A related problem, first posed in this particular form by H. R. Trevor-Roper, is whether or not the English revolution is part of a general European movement. The nation state, with its complex bureaucratic structure, its extensive interference in the private lives of its subjects and its huge financial and military resources, is perhaps the most striking, if not the most admirable, contribution of Western

[1] See item 84 in the Bibliography.

civilization to the world over the past 500 years. It is generally agreed that decisive steps forward in this evolution took place towards the end of the fifteenth century, and that the middle of the seventeenth century saw a major crisis of some sort in most of the great European states: England, France and Spain were all racked by revolutionary movements on a considerable scale. Are these revolutions similar in character and causation; and, if so, what is it they have in common? H. R. Trevor-Roper believes that they *are* similar, and that their basic characteristic is a revolt of the underprivileged and over-taxed 'country' against the expanding, oppressive, corrupt and authoritarian courts and bureaucracies of the age; that it was in fact, the last, futile, attempt to stop the process of national centralization before the age of absolutism set in. What is still in dispute is whether England possessed a bureaucracy and court on a scale at all comparable to those of Brussels, Paris or Madrid, and whether the aspirations of the Parliamentary opposition of 1640–42 were in fact anti-court and decentralizing in character. This raises the question whether England between the mid-sixteenth and mid-twentieth century should be considered as a normal part of the European scene, or as an idiosyncratic sport best studied in isolation.

Not all historians are agreed that great events must necessarily have great causes. There are those who see the breakdown of 1640 and the war of 1642 as the product merely of a series of political blunders by certain individuals in positions of power. Miss C. V. Wedgwood begins her narrative history of the English revolution in 1637, and it is undoubtedly true that her straightforward *post hoc, propter hoc* narrative is less open to objections on philosophical grounds than the more ambitious constructs of the analytical historians. If one takes this view, the whole controversy over the trend of social movement in the previous half-century becomes totally beside the point. The objection to this, however – and to my mind a decisive objection – is that it muddles up two quite different things: the *preconditions*, the long-term social, economic and ideological trends that make revolutions possible, and which are subject to comparative analysis and generalization; and the *precipitants*, the personal decisions and the accidental pattern of events which may or may not trigger off the revolutionary outbreak, and which are unique and unclassifiable.

Finally there are serious differences of opinion about three propositions put forward by Karl Marx (indeed, at one stage the discussion threatened to get mixed up with the battle of Cold War ideologies).

One theory, first advanced by Aristotle, revived by Harrington in the seventeenth century and reformulated by Marx in the nineteenth, is that a constitution is a direct reflection of the distribution of social and economic power; consequently, the two must alter in step together if major upheavals are to be avoided. The main weakness of Harrington's doctrine, and the aspect which distinguishes it most sharply from that of Marx, is his obsessive preoccupation with landed property, to the exclusion of all other forms of wealth. But this was not altogether unrealistic in the seventeenth-century English context, despite the growing resources and political influence of the London mercantile and financial community. This view, moreover, was not merely confined to a handful of members of the Rota Club, as H. R. Trevor-Roper has suggested. The prolonged parliamentary debate on the revival of a second chamber in 1659 shows that there was considerable agreement in the House of Commons on the Harringtonian thesis of the relationship of the constitution to the balance of property, though only the republicans thought – wrongly as it turned out – that the peers had lost most of their property and that the balance had consequently been destroyed, rather than modified. We can see today that this hypothesis needs to be qualified in various ways, and in particular that very much greater weight needs to be given to ideological enthusiasm, military force and traditional habits of obedience, which together or in isolation may often outweigh crude economic pressures. Like Hobbes, Harrington had little understanding of the complex web of social relationships which bind man to man, quite apart from the economic and physical necessity for co-operation and obedience. He failed altogether to recognize the force of passion and prejudice, even though his own political theories and actions were in large measure dictated by an impractical admiration for the Roman Republic. He did realize that in certain cases, such as the Norman Conquest of England or the Spanish Conquest of Central America, violence has been used to distribute wealth and power in a manner appropriate to the new – and extremely tenacious – political establishment. More frequently, political power has been manipulated to channel wealth into the hands of the ruling *élite*, thus keeping the social structure and the political constitution in line by adjusting the former to the latter, rather than vice versa. It was Sir Thomas More who produced the disillusioned judgement that 'when I consider and weigh in my mind all these commonwealths, which nowadays anywhere do flourish, so God help me, I can perceive nothing but a certain conspiracy of rich men procuring their own commodities under the name and title of the commonwealth. They invent and devise all means and crafts, first how to keep safely, without fear of losing, that they have unjustly gathered together, and next how to hire and abuse the work and labour of the poor for as little money as may be. These devices, when the rich men have decreed to be kept and observed under colour of the commonality, that is to say, also of the poor people, then they be made laws.'[1]

With these important qualifications – with some of which Harrington is not altogether in disagreement – the view that there must be a direct relationship between social structure and political institutions and that the former tends to dictate the latter, is widely accepted today, even by historians and politicians of a strongly anti-Marxist cast of mind. It is generally agreed, for example, that land reform is a necessary preliminary to the introduction of democratic institutions and ideals in Latin America.

The notion that constitutional or administrative history can be studied in a social vacuum, as an isolated story of the growth of liberty or bureaucracy or whatever, is one that few historians are now prepared to countenance. The problems of power and its distribution are seen to be entangled with the whole complex of nurture, education and the family system, social norms and ethical values, religious beliefs and ecclesiastical organization, the land law, status hierarchy and economic structure of the society as a whole. The major problem is to explain how, and to what extent, the various parts all fit together.

The second of Marx's theories is that the first major shift in European society was from the feudal to the bourgeois phase, which occurred in the seventeenth century in England and in the late eighteenth century in France. This lies at the back of Tawney's definition of the rising gentry as progressive-minded and capitalist and of the Royalist supporters as old-fashioned and feudal. It is this equation of the gentry with the bourgeoisie which has been, in my view rightly, severely criticized by J. H. Hexter and P. Zagorin.

The third proposition of Marx which is involved in the controversy concerns the relationship of social and economic forces, on the one hand, and ideology, on the other. Marx saw the latter as a sociologically motivated superstructure, and H. R. Trevor-Roper similarly regards religion as economically determined. Tawney took a far more sophisticated view of the relationship between ideas and interests, but his interpretation also laid great stress on material motives. It is doubtful

[1] T. More, *Utopia* (Everyman ed., Dent), p. 112.

whether he was prepared to give much weight to the ostensible issues of political liberty and religious reform in assessing the causes of the upheavals of the 1640s. So complex is the human personality that materialism and idealism, reason and emotion, interests and morals, are constantly confused, first one and then the other rising to the surface. There is no final solution to this problem, and every historian must work according to his private judgement. At bottom it seems to come down to whether he takes an optimistic or a pessimistic view of human nature: optimists stress ideals, pessimists material interests.

Looking back on the controversy today, it seems clear that all parties in the early stages were taking an indefensibly narrow view of the causes of revolution. They paid too much attention to changes in the distribution of wealth, and too little to less tangible factors, such as changing ideals, aspirations and habits of obedience. They confused two different things: a material and moral weakening of the ruling *élite*, and a strengthening of the size and intensity of the dissident elements. They failed to see that revolutions have extremely complicated origins: partly intellectual – a matter of conflicting ideologies, revolutionary philosophies, loss of self-confidence by the *élite*; partly economic – a short-term setback after a long-term boom period, an impoverished government machine; partly political – failures of foreign policy, governmental disunity, inefficiency, dishonesty, lack of skill and tact in meeting or heading off demands for reform; partly social – shifts in the distribution of wealth, power and influence, a sense of rootlessness arising from excessive mobility, or of frustration caused by a blockage of the channels of advancement into the *élite*. What can be said in defence of the protagonists, however, is that it is in part because of their pioneer efforts and blunders that a more sophisticated view of the causes of revolution is beginning to emerge.

The selections in this book are predominantly taken from the writings of contemporary historians, and a relatively small amount of space is devoted to first-hand materials. This is because so much of the evidence used is, as has been said, either ambiguous or contradictory in character. The bulk of it has consisted of individual examples, the multiplication of which would merely be wearisome and confusing. The original sources are extracts from the principal theorists, contemporary comment on the prewar social scene and the social line-up in the Civil War, and some family histories and memoranda which illustrate the confusing complexity of the forces at work in individual cases. In studying the secondary authorities the reader should bear in mind that the exigencies of space have enforced rigid compression. Not merely is much of the illustrative material omitted but also many of the qualifications. The various theories are here set out in a balder and more uncompromising manner than in the fuller version. It will help the reader to follow the argument if he remembers that several different problems are being discussed simultaneously, and recur again and again. What were the principal changes in the social structure and the distribution of wealth in the century 1540–1640; what categories are the most useful for analysing these changes; what evidence can be used to demonstrate these changes, particularly what statistical evidence; how do these changes relate to the religious differences in early Stuart England; how far do they prepare the way for the political revolution of the 1640s; who led the Long Parliament against the King in 1640; who was prepared to fight the King in 1642; who were the Independents who seized power in 1648, and what were their objectives?

Part One
PROBLEMS OF HISTORIOGRAPHY

I
Social Change

1 The Bourgeois Revolution
F. ENGELS

... The long fight of the bourgeoisie against feudalism culminated in three great, decisive battles.

The first was what is called the Protestant Reformation in Germany. The war cry raised against the Church by Luther was responded to by two insurrections of a political nature: first, that of the lower nobility under Franz von Sickingen (1523), then the great Peasants' War, 1525. Both were defeated, chiefly in consequence of the indecision of the parties most interested, the burghers of the towns – an indecision into the causes of which we cannot here enter. From that moment the struggle degenerated into a fight between the local princes and the central power, and ended by blotting out Germany, for two hundred years, from the politically active nations of Europe. The Lutheran reformation produced a new creed indeed, a religion adapted to absolute monarchy. No sooner were the peasants of northeast Germany converted to Lutheranism than they were from free men reduced to serfs.

But where Luther failed, Calvin won the day. Calvin's creed was one fit for the boldest of the bourgeoisie of his time. His predestination doctrine was the religious expression of the fact that in the commercial world of competition success or failure does not depend upon a man's action or cleverness, but upon circumstances uncontrollable by him. It is not of him that willeth or of him that runneth, but of the mercy of unknown superior economic powers; and this was especially true at a period of economic revolution, when all old commercial routes and centres were replaced by new ones, when India and America were opened to the world, and when even the most sacred economic articles of faith – the value of gold and silver – began to totter and to break down. Calvin's church constitution was thoroughly democratic

3

and republican, and where the kingdom of God was republicanized could the kingdoms of this world remain subject to monarchs, bishops and lords? While German Lutheranism became a willing tool in the hands of princes, Calvinism founded a republic in Holland, and active republican parties in England and, above all, Scotland.

In Calvinism the second great bourgeois upheaval found its doctrine ready cut and dried. This upheaval took place in England. The middle class of the towns brought it on, and the yeomanry of the country districts fought it out. Curiously enough, in all the three great bourgeois risings, the peasantry furnishes the army that has to do the fighting, and the peasantry is just the class that, the victory once gained, is most surely ruined by the economic consequences of that victory. A hundred years after Cromwell the yeomanry of England had almost disappeared. Anyhow, had it not been for that yeomanry and for the plebeian element in the towns, the bourgeoisie alone would never have fought the matter out to the bitter end, and would never have brought Charles I to the scaffold. In order to secure even those conquests of the bourgeoisie that were ripe for gathering at the time, the revolution had to be carried considerably further – exactly as in 1793 in France and 1848 in Germany. This seems, in fact, to be one of the laws of evolution of bourgeois society.

Well, upon this excess of revolutionary activity there necessarily followed the inevitable reaction, which in its turn went beyond the point where it might have maintained itself. After a series of oscillations the new centre of gravity was at last attained, and became a new starting point. The grand period of English history, known to respectability under the name of 'the Great Rebellion', and the struggles succeeding it, were brought to a close by the comparatively puny event entitled by Liberal historians 'the Glorious Revolution'.

The new starting point was a compromise between the rising middle class and the ex-feudal landowners. The latter, though called, as now, the aristocracy, had been long since on the way which led them to become what Louis Philippe in France became at a much later period, 'the first bourgeois of the kingdom'. Fortunately for England, the old feudal barons had killed one another during the Wars of the Roses. Their successors, though mostly scions of the old families, had been so much out of the direct line of descent that they constituted quite a new body, with habits and tendencies far more bourgeois than feudal. They fully understood the value of money, and at once began to increase their rents by turning hundreds of small farmers out and

4

replacing them by sheep. Henry VIII, while squandering the Church lands, created fresh bourgeois landlords wholesale; the innumerable confiscations of estates, regranted to absolute or relative upstarts, and continued during the whole of the seventeenth century, had the same result. Consequently, ever since Henry VII, the English 'aristocracy', far from counteracting the development of industrial production, had, on the contrary, sought to indirectly profit thereby; and there had always been a section of the great landowners willing, from economic or political reasons, to co-operate with the leading men of the financial and industrial bourgeoisie. The compromise of 1689 was, therefore, easily accomplished. The political spoils of 'pelf and place' were left to the great landowning families, provided the economic interests of the financial, manufacturing and commercial middle class were sufficiently attended to. And these economic interests were at that time powerful enough to determine the general policy of the nation. There might be squabbles about matters of detail, but, on the whole, the aristocratic oligarchy knew too well that its own economic prosperity was irretrievably bound up with that of the industrial and commercial middle class.

From that time, the bourgeoisie was a humble but still a recognized component of the ruling classes of England. With the rest of them it had a common interest in keeping in subjection the great working mass of the nation. The merchant or manufacturer himself stood in the position of master, or, as it was until lately called, of 'natural superior' to his clerks, his workpeople, his domestic servants. His interest was to get as much and as good work out of them as he could; for this end they had to be trained to proper submission. He was himself religious; his religion had supplied the standard under which he had fought the king and the lords; he was not long in discovering the opportunities this same religion offered him for working upon the minds of his natural inferiors and making them submissive to the behests of the masters it had pleased God to place over them. In short, the English bourgeoisie now had to take a part in keeping down the 'lower orders', the great producing mass of the nation, and one of the means employed for that purpose was the influence of religion.

There was another fact that contributed to strengthen the religious leanings of the bourgeoisie. That was the rise of materialism in England. This new doctrine not only shocked the pious feelings of the middle class; it announced itself as a philosophy fit only for scholars and cultivated men of the world, in contrast to religion, which was good enough for the uneducated masses, including the bourgeoisie. With Hobbes it stepped on the stage as a defender of royal prerogative and omnipotence; it called upon absolute monarchy to keep down that *puer robustus sed malitiosus* [robust but malicious boy], to wit, the people. Similarly, with the successors of Hobbes, with Bolingbroke, Shaftesbury, etc., the new deistic form of materialism remained an aristocratic, esoteric doctrine, and, therefore, hateful to the middle class both for its religious heresy and for its anti-bourgeois political connections. Accordingly, in opposition to the materialism and deism of the aristocracy, those Protestant sects which had furnished the flag and the fighting contingent against the Stuarts continued to furnish the main strength of the progressive middle class, and form even today the backbone of 'the Great Liberal Party'.

[Introduction to the English edition of *Socialism: Utopian and Scientific*, 1892, from Marx and Engels: *Basic Writings on Politics and Philosophy*, ed. L. S. Feuer, Doubleday: Anchor, 1959.]

2 The Rise of the Gentry

R. H. TAWNEY

... To M. Coste, in 1695, the triumphant ascent of the English gentry – neither a *noblesse*, nor a bureaucracy, but mere *bons bourgeois* – seemed proof of an insular dynamic of which France, with the aid of his translation, would do well to learn the secret.[1] ... Ten English counties had been blessed in 1640 with some sixty-two leading landowners, masters of six or more manors apiece. Of those in the whole ten one-half, of those in five just under two-thirds, had descendants or kin who owned 3,000 acres or upwards in 1874.[2]

I

The political role of this tenacious class has not lacked its eulogists. It has itself, however, a history, which is not only political but also economic; and the decisive period of that history is the two generations before the Civil War.... Observers became conscious, in the later years of Elizabeth, of an alteration in the balance of social forces, and a stream of comment began which continued to swell, until, towards the close of the next century, a new equilibrium was seen to have been reached. Its theme was the changing composition, at once erosion and reconstruction, of the upper strata of the social pyramid. It was, in particular, since their preponderance was not yet axiomatic, the increase in the wealth and influence of certain intermediate groups, compared with the nobility, the Crown and the mass of small landholders. . . . Barred themselves by no rule as to *dérogeance* from supplementing their incomes from whatever source they pleased, yet never, as in Holland, wholly severed from their rural roots, the English gentry combined the local and popular attachments essential for a representative role with the aristocratic aroma of *nobiles minores*, and played each card in turn with tactful, but remorseless, realism. . . . Sir Thomas Smith had said that a gentleman is a man who spends his money like a gentleman.[3] Of the theorists rash enough to attempt a definition, few succeeded in improving on that wise tautology. In spite, nevertheless, of ambiguities, the group concerned was not difficult to identify. Its members varied widely in wealth;[4] but, though ragged at its edges, it had a solid core. That core consisted of the landed proprietors, above the yeomanry, and below the peerage, together with a growing body of well-to-do farmers, sometimes tenants of their relatives, who had succeeded the humble peasants of the past as lessees of demesne farms; professional men, also rapidly increasing in number, such as the more eminent lawyers, divines and an occasional medical practitioner; and the wealthier merchants, who, if not, as many were, themselves sons of landed families, had received a similar education, moved in the same circles, and in England, unlike France, were commonly recognized to be socially indistinguishable from them. It was this upper layer of commoners, heterogeneous, but compact, whose rapid rise in wealth and power most impressed contemporaries. . . .

The facts were plain enough. The ruin of famous families by personal extravagance and political ineptitude; the decline in the position of the yeomanry towards the turn of the century, when long leases fell in; the loss, not only of revenue but of authority, by the monarchy, as Crown lands melted; the mounting fortunes of the residuary legatee, a gentry whose aggregate income was put even in 1600 at some three times that of peers, bishops, deans and chapters, and richer yeomen together, and who steadily gathered into their hands estates slipping from the grasp of peasant, nobility, Church and Crown alike – such movements and their consequences were visible to all. . . .

7

II

The movement passed through the three familiar stages of breakdown, reconstruction and stabilization. If one aspect of the first phase consisted in the political and legal reforms[5] by which the Tudor State consolidated its power, another aspect was economic. Jolted sharply by the great depreciation; then squeezed by its masters to find the means for new styles in fashion and display; then pulled by expanding markets, when expedients adopted to stave off catastrophe were discovered, once systematized, to pay dividends beyond hope, agrarian society was under strain. . . . The wave of rising prices struck the dyke of customary obligations, static burdens, customary dues; rebounded; struck again; and then either broke it or carved new channels which turned its flank. . . .

Some groups can adapt themselves to the new tensions and opportunities; others cannot. The former rise; the latter sink. Examples of both are to be found in every stratum of society. There are grounds, nevertheless, for thinking that what Professor Bloch has called *la crise des fortunes seigneuriales*[6] was felt more acutely, and surmounted with greater difficulty, by the heirs of ancient wealth, with its complex and dispersed interests, and large public responsibilities, than by the men of humbler position or more recent eminence. . . .

'What by reason,' wrote a close observer, 'of their magnificence and waste in expense, and what by reason of a desire to advance and make great their own families',[7] the life of a considerable part of the aristocracy was apt to offer an example of what a modern economist has called 'conspicuous waste'. Other regalities might have gone; what remained, and, indeed, increased, was a regal ostentation. The overheads of the noble landowner – a great establishment, and often more than one; troops of servants and retainers; stables fit for a regiment of cavalry; endless hospitality to neighbours and national notabilities; visits to court, at once ruinous and unavoidable; litigation descending, like an heirloom, from generation to generation – had always been enormous. Now, on the top of these traditional liabilities, came the demands of a new world of luxury and fashion. With the fortunes resulting from inflation and booming trade all standards are rising. London, rapidly advancing in financial and commercial importance, with a Court that under James is a lottery of unearned fortunes, exercises a stronger pull. Town houses increase in number; visits to the capital are spun out; residential quarters are developed;

to the delight of dressmakers, something like a season begins to emerge. Culture has demands to which homage must be paid. New and more costly styles of building; the maintenance of a troop of needy scholars and poets; collections of pictures; here and there – an extreme case – the avenues of posturing nudities which Bacon saluted at Arundel with ironical dismay – 'the resurrection of the dead!'[8] – all have their votaries. Public duties, in some cases, complete what private prodigality has begun. They yielded some pickings; but, under Elizabeth and her two successors, more than one bearer of a famous name was brought near to ruin by the crowning catastrophe of a useful career.

So towering a superstructure required broad foundations. Too often they were lacking. The wealth of some of the nobility, and especially of the older families, was not infrequently more spectacular than substantial. It was locked up in frozen assets – immobilized in sumptuous appurtenances, at once splendid and unrealizable. More important, the whole structure and organization of their estates was often of a kind, which, once a pillar of the social system, was now obsolescent. Side by side with more lucrative possessions, their properties included majestic, but unremunerative, franchises – hundreds, boroughs, fairs and markets; a multitude of knight's fees, all honour and no profit; freeholds created in an age when falling, not rising, prices had been the great landowners' problem, and fixed rents were an insurance; hundreds of prickly copyholds, whose occupants pocketed an unearned increment while the real income of their landlord fell.... The administrative machine which controlled a great estate had some of the vices of a miniature state department. It was cumbrous, conservative, difficult to divert from its traditional routine to new and speculative enterprises. The very magnitude and wide dispersion of the interests concerned – property, of a dozen different kinds in a dozen different counties – made drastic reconstruction a formidable business, which it needed an exceptional personality to force through. It is not surprising that inherited opulence should sometimes have lacked the initiative to launch it.

Such difficulties confronted all conservative landowners, both peers and commoners, in proportion to the magnitude of their commitments and the rigidity of their incomes. The most that can be said is that the former usually carried more sail than the latter, and found it, when the wind changed, more difficult to tack....

The materials for generalization have hardly yet been put together; but to say that many noble families – though not they alone –

encountered, in the two generations before the Civil War, a financial crisis is probably not an overstatement. . . .

Whether their embarrassments were increasing it is impossible to say; some debts, it is fair to remember, represented reproductive expenditure on development and improvements. But soundings, wherever taken, show much water in the hold. The correspondence of Burleigh,[9] in the last decade of Elizabeth, reads like the report of a receiver in bankruptcy to the nobility and gentry. A few years later, when, with the opening of the great boom which began in 1606, things should have been better, Cranfield, no financial leviathan, had a score of them in his books, while, to judge by stray references, Hicks the silk-man and banker – later Lord Campden – and Herriott, the goldsmith, may well have had more. . . . Of the commercial magnates who, a few years later, scrambled for confiscated estates, not a few, as Dr Chesney[10] has shown, were creditors entering on properties long mortgaged to them. It was discovered, not for the last time, that as a method of foreclosure war was cheaper than litigation.

III

For, if the new world had its victims, it had also its conquerors. . . . 'The age was one,' writes Miss Wake in her account of Northampton-shire under James, 'which had recently seen the rise of the solid middle class of lesser landowning gentry on the ruins of the ancient aristocracy. The families were few which . . . managed to survive the turbulent end of the middle ages. . . . Many of the knights and squires belonging to families of local and extraneous origin who had made money early in the previous century by the law, trade, or sheepfarming.'[11] That picture is true of more counties than one. The conditions which depressed some incomes inflated others; and, while one group of landowners bumped heavily along the bottom, another, which was quicker to catch the tide when it turned, was floated to fortune. The process of readjustment was complex; but two broad movements can be observed, affecting respectively the technique of land-management and the ownership of landed property. . . .

Several lines of attack were possible, but the most characteristic were four. First, customary payments dwindling, the landlord could revise the terms on which his property was held, get rid of the un-profitable copyholders when lives ran out, buy out small freeholders and throw the land so secured into larger farms to be let on lease.

Rent at this period is an ambiguous category; but leasehold rents were certainly rising – on the view of Thorold Rogers[12] six-fold in half a century, on the estimate of a contemporary[13] five-fold in rather less, on the evidence of some estate documents about three- to four-fold. Second, instead of, or in addition to, letting, he could expand his own business activities, run his home-farm, not to supply his household, but as a commercial concern, enlarge his demesnes, and enclose for the purpose of carrying more stock or increasing his output of grain. Third, if he had the means he could invest capital in bringing new land into cultivation, clearing woodlands, breaking up waste, draining marshes. Finally, he could supplement his agricultural income by other types of enterprise, going into the timber trade, exploiting coal, iron and lead, speculating in urban ground-rents. Naturally, none of these departures was without abundant precedents. Naturally, again, the particular policy, or combination of policies, adopted depended both on local circumstances and on individual resources. But the tendency of all was the same. In each case, whatever the particular expedient used, the emphasis of the up-to-date landowner is increasingly thrown on the business side of land-management. He relies for his income on the rents or profits derived from it. . . .

Then, as now, therefore, what appeared at first sight a mere pedestrian improvement in methods of administration set in motion, as it developed, subtle social changes. It was to be expected that men with the resources and ambition to play the part of pioneers should gain at the expense of groups, whether below them or above, less qualified by means and traditions to adapt themselves to a new climate. The well-to-do yeoman, the *kulak* of the day, might maintain, or even improve, his position; but the extension of demesne farms, the upward movement of rents and fines, and encroachments on commons, combined in parts of the country to tilt the scales against the humbler peasants. To that chapter of the story, whose local diversities still remain to be worked out, but of which the outlines are known, must be added another, of which historians have said less, but by which contemporaries were impressed. There was a struggle for survival, not only between large landowners and small, but between different categories among the former.

It was primarily a struggle between economies of different types, which corresponded more closely with regional peculiarities than with social divisions. There are plenty of gentry who stagnate or go down hill. It would be easy to find noble landowners who move with the times, and make the most of their properties; the sheep-farming of Lord Spencer; the enclosures of Lords Brudenell, Huntingdon and Saye and Sele; the coal-mines of the Earl of Northumberland and the Earl of Wemyss; above all the grandiose reconstruction carried through by the Russells, are cases in point. The smaller the part, nevertheless, played by passive property, as compared with active enterprise, the larger the opportunities of rising; and the increased rewards to be reaped by the improving landlord favoured classes still ascending the ladder compared with those already at the summit. The charms of established wealth might be represented by an Earl of Newcastle, with a rent-roll of £22,000, or an Earl of Pembroke, with the ninety-three manors, four boroughs and estates scattered over ten counties from Middlesex to Yorkshire, which gave him, at his death in 1630, the reputation of one of the richest peers in England.[14] But, when experiment and innovation were the order of the day, the cards were in other hands. They were all on the side of the enterprising country gentleman. . . .

It was agricultural capitalists . . . who were making the pace, and to whom the future belonged. Nor, if land supplied the base from which they started, were their interests confined to it. The lament that 'it is impossible for the mere country gentleman ever to grow rich or raise his house, he must have some other profession',[15] was uttered at a moment when pessimism was pardonable, and was too pessimistic. It is true, however, that many of the class, whether of necessity or by choice, were up to the eyes in other branches of business. Naturally, they turned first to the industries native to their own districts – iron in Sussex and the Forest of Dean; tin in Cornwall; lead in Derbyshire and North Wales; coal in Nottinghamshire, Durham and Northumberland; textiles in a dozen counties. But their business connections were not merely local. The habit of investment was spreading rapidly among the upper classes, and the starry host of notabilities, who lent lustre to the Virginia and East India Companies, contributed less to its development than did the web woven by the humbler ventures of hundreds of obscure squires. Some of them, too, held shares in those much advertised undertakings. More had relations in the City, and sent their sons into business. An increasing number – for the current did not run only one way – had been in business themselves.

'See,' wrote Cobden to Bright, 'how every successful trader buys an estate!'[16] The remark might have been made with equal truth under James I. . . . The movement from trade into land had long been an old story. By the middle years of James, if not indeed, earlier, it is difficult to find a prominent London capitalist who is not also a substantial landowner; even such dubious cosmopolitans as Van Lore and Burlamachi, like Pallavicino before them, feel obliged to astonish the natives by setting up as country gentlemen. Fortunes made in law went the same way.... In the 'twenties the inroads of the London plutocracy on the home counties gave rise to complaints; and what was true of the neighbourhood of London was hardly less true of the environs of other growing cities, for example, Bristol.[17] In such conditions the social categories used to distinguish the landed and trading classes, which in France and Germany remained terms with a legal significance, lost in England any claim to precision which they may once have possessed. The landowner living on the profits and rents of commercial farming, and the merchant or banker who was also a landowner, represented, not two classes, but one. Patrician and *parvenu* both owed their ascent to causes of the same order. Judged by the source of their incomes, both were equally *bourgeois*.

IV

The advance of the classes representing a more business-like agriculture was accompanied by a second movement, which at once reflected its influence and consolidated its results. That movement was the heightened rapidity with which land was changing hands.... In the age of Elizabeth and her two successors, economic and political conditions combined to mobilise real property, while the hostility of the courts to entails gave both forces free play.[18] The former, apart from occasional severe depressions, acted continuously, and with increasing force, to augment the demand for it. The latter, by periodically bringing fresh blocks of land into the market, supplied recurrent opportunities for profitable speculation....

The statistical evidence of the dimensions of the movement has not yet been put together, nor is it often in the form most instructive to posterity. Contemporaries commonly thought in terms, not of acreage, but of manors; they spoke of a man owning manors, or selling them, much as today he might be said to hold, or to dispose of, large investments, in order to convey an impression, not to record precise facts. The category, needless to say, is a highly ambiguous one, embracing estates varying widely in magnitude, value and organisation. At best, it covers only one species of real property, and that not the most marketable. In the two generations before the Long Parliament such property seems, nevertheless, for what the fact is worth, to have changed hands with fair rapidity. Of 2,500 odd manors in seven counties, whose owners can be traced, just under one in three were sold once in the forty years between 1561 and 1600, and rather more than one in three between 1601 and 1640. In the case of the six hundred odd in Hertfordshire and Surrey, which felt the wash of the London whirlpool, the figure in the second period was over 40 per cent. . . .[19] But in England the results of an accelerated economic tempo were heightened by adventitious causes. The State threw its weight into the scales, and permanently depressed them. Intending to buttress its own foundations, it released currents which, in the end, carried them and it away. . . .

There were two immense confiscations, the result of revolution and civil war, and a steady alienation, under financial duress, of estates formerly used to provide a revenue for public purposes. The opening act of the drama is not here in place. But the story which had begun with the Dissolution had not ended with it. Like taxation, the fruits of confiscation do not always rest where they first light. . . .

V

What, if any, were the social consequences of these portentous land-slides? . . . As to the tendency of private transactions, little can at present be said. Some great estates can be seen disintegrating, and others being formed. A comparison of the distribution at different dates of certain categories of property reveals the results. But the threads in the intricate skein leading from the first stage to the last can rarely be unravelled. The dealings in monastic and Crown lands left a trail which is easier to follow. Much is still obscure; but enough is known to suggest certain provisional conclusions. . . .

The settlement of monastic estates into the hands of the most progressive element in rural society may be illustrated by the course of events in one small corner of the country. In Gloucestershire, Northamptonshire and Warwickshire about 317 manors, together with a mass of miscellaneous property – tithes, rectories and land in different places – appear to have changed hands at the Dissolution.[20] Of the manors, which are more easily traced than the smaller acquisitions, between 250 and 260 passed into the ownership of individuals, the remainder being obtained by bishops, deans and chapters, colleges and other corporations. . . . The general result in these counties, in spite of the reputation of Northamptonshire as the Dukeries of the age, was that, of the forty odd manors which had gone to peers at the Reformation, those remaining to them two generations later numbered only six, while the remainder swelled the fortunes of rising middle-class families. Something between two-thirds and three-quarters of the manors secured by private persons had gone originally to the squirearchy. By the early years of the next century, the proportion in their hands was over nine-tenths. Thus, the ultimate consequences of the Dissolution, if similar in kind to its immediate effects, were different in degree. In this part of England, at any rate, it did not so much endow an existing nobility, as lay the foundations of a new nobility to arise in the next century. . . .

VI

What significance, if any, it may be asked, is to be attached to the movement of which the dull transactions described above are specimens? Its financial consequences are obvious; they were those which led Hobbes to make his comment on the futility of attempting to support a State by endowing it with property subject to alienation.[21] The effect on the peasants of recurrent orgies of land speculation, if less conspicuous, is equally certain. . . . Such figures as we possess suggest that the tendency of an active land-market was, on the whole, to increase the number of medium-sized properties, while diminishing that of the largest.[22] Mr Habakkuk has shown in a striking article[23] that 'the general drift of property in the sixty years after 1690 was in favour of the large estate and the great lord', and has explained the causes of that movement. During the preceding century and a half the current, as he points out, appears to have flowed in the opposite direction, with the result that, as the number of great properties was levelled down, and that of properties of moderate size levelled up, the upper ranges of English society came to resemble less a chain of high peaks than an undulating table-land. Is it too incautious . . . to regard as one symptom of the change in the distribution of wealth the acquisition of new dignities by members of the class which gained most from it? Of 135 peers in the House of Lords in 1642, over half had obtained their titles since 1603. They included some lawyers and merchants, but the majority of them were well-to-do country gentlemen. . . .

Nor, finally, were political attitudes unaffected by the same influences. . . . The freezing reception given by the Long Parliament to petitions from the peasants for the redress of agrarian grievances is hardly surprising, when it is remembered that one in every two of the members returned, up to the end of 1640, for the five Midland Counties which were the disturbed area of the day, either themselves had been recently fined for depopulation or belonging to families which had been. . . .[24] Most of the attitudes and measures, in fact, which were to triumph at the Restoration can be seen taking shape between the death of Elizabeth and the opening of the Civil War. . . .

The thesis as to the political repercussion of changes in the distribution of landed property is the central doctrine of Harrington's *Oceana*. . . . Had he shared the modern taste for figures, he would have found little difficulty in supporting his doctrine by some casual scraps of statistical evidence.[25] He would have observed, for example, had he taken as a sample some 3,300 manors in ten counties, that out of 730 held by the Crown and the peerage in 1561, some 430 had left them (if new creations are ignored) by 1640, while an additional 400 had been acquired by the gentry. He would have discovered that, as a consequence, the Crown, which in 1561 owned just one-tenth (9 per cent) of the total, owned in 1640 one-fiftieth (2 per cent); that the peers held one-eighth (12·6 per cent) at the first date, and (ignoring new creations) one-sixteenth (6·7 per cent) at the second; and that the share of the gentry had risen from two-thirds (67 per cent), when the period began, to four-fifths (80 per cent) at the end of it. . . . [Harrington's] argument took its point from his belief that in his own day the balance had been altered. To the sceptic who questioned its historical foundations, he would probably have replied – for he was an obstinate person – by inviting him either to submit rebutting evidence, or to agree that there was some prima facie reason, at least, for supposing that, in the counties in question, the landed property of the Crown had diminished under Parthenia, Morpheus and his successor by three-quarters (76 per cent) and that of the older nobility by approximately half (47·1 per cent), while that of the gentry had increased by not much less than one-fifth (17·8 per cent).[26]

In reality, however, as far as this side of his doctrines were concerned, there were few sceptics to challenge him. To regard Harrington as an isolated doctrinaire is an error. In spite of its thin dress of fancy, his work was not a Utopia, but partly a social history, partly a programme based upon it. Contemporaries who abhorred the second were not indisposed to agree with the first, for it accorded with their own experience. The political effect of the transference of property appeared as obvious to authors on the right, like Sir Edward Walker, whose book appeared three years before the *Oceana*, as to Ludlow, to that formidable bluestocking, Mrs Hutchison and to Neville, on the left. . . .[27]

['The Rise of the Gentry, 1558–1640', *Economic History Review*, XI, 1941.]

Notes

1. Pierre Coste, *De l'éducation des enfants* (1695).

2. The counties concerned are Hertfordshire, Bedfordshire, Buckinghamshire, Surrey, Hampshire, North Riding of Yorkshire, Worcestershire, Gloucestershire, Warwickshire, Northamptonshire. The facts for the first seven in 1640 are taken from the lists of manors and their owners given in the *V.C.H.*, and for the last three from Sir R. Atkyns, *The Ancient and Present State of Gloucestershire;* Dugdale, *Antiquities of Warwickshire;* J. Bridges, *History and Antiquities of Northamptonshire.* Those for 1874 are taken from John Bateman, *The Acreocracy of England, a list of all owners of three thousand acres and upwards . . . from the Modern Domesday Book.*

3. *De Republica Anglorum* (ed. L. Alston, 1906), pp. 39–40.

4. Thomas Wilson, *The State of England Anno. Dom. 1600* (ed. F. J. Fisher, Camden Miscellanea, XVI, 1936), pp. 23–4.

5. See the admirable article by Miss Helen M. Cam, 'The Decline and Fall of English Feudalism' in *History*, XXV (December 1940), and *Transactions of the Royal Historical Society*, n.s., XX, R. R. Reid, 'The Rebellion in the North, 1569'.

6. M. Bloch, *Les Caractères Originaux de l'histoire rurale française*, pp. 117, 127 *et seq.*

7. Bacon, 'Of the True Greatness of the Kingdom of Britain', in *Works* (Bohn edn.), I, p. 507.

8. L. Aikin, *Memoirs of Court of King James I*, p. 300.

9. See *Hist. MSS. Comm., MSS. of the Marquis of Salisbury, passim.* Some references to the indebtedness of the nobility will be found in Thomas Wilson, *A Discourse Upon Usury*, Introduction, pp. 31–42.

10. H. E. Chesney, 'The Transference of Lands in England, 1640–1660' in *Transactions of the Royal Historical Society*, 4th ser., XV, pp. 181–210.

11. *The Montague Musters Book, 1602–1623*, ed. by Joan Wake (VII of the Publications of the Northamptonshire Record Soc.), Introduction, pp. xiv–xv.

12. Thorold Rogers, *A History of Agriculture and Prices*, V, p. 812.

13. *Harleian Miscellany*, III, pp. 552 *et seq.*, 'The Present State of England', by Walter Carey, 1627.

14. Marg. Duchess of Newcastle, *Life of the Duke of Newcastle* (Everyman edn.), pp. 98–100; *Abstract of Wilts Inquis. p/m.*, pp. 97–101; Clarendon, *History of the Rebellion*, I, pp. 120–6.

15. *A Royalist's Note-book, the Commonplace Book of Sir John Oglander of Nun-well, 1622–1652,* ed. Francis Bamford, p. 75.

16. Quoted by O. F. Christie, *The Transition to Democracy,* pp. 147–8.

17. S.P.D., James I, XXII, no. 63, contains complaints of the purchase of Suffolk manors by Londoners. For Bristol, see S.P.D., Charles I, XXXV, no. 43 (8 September 1626), and W. B. Willcox, *Gloucestershire, 1590–1640,* p. 105.

18. The attitude of the Courts is well summarized in Mr H. J. Habakkuk's article, 'English Landownership 1680–1740' in *The Economic History Review,* X, no. 1 (February 1940).

19. The counties concerned are Surrey, Hertfordshire, Bedfordshire, Buckinghamshire, Hampshire, Worcestershire and North Riding of Yorkshire. The figures, which I owe to the kindness of Mr F. J. Fisher, are taken from the lists of manors and their owners given in the *V.C.H.* They exclude transfers of leases, and transfers due to marriage, gift, inheritance, forfeiture, or other non-commercial transactions.

20. The following account of the fate of monastic property in three counties does not pretend to complete accuracy. It is based mainly on Sir Robert Atkyns, *The Ancient and Present State of Gloucestershire,* and *Men and Armour in Gloucestershire in 1608* (London, 1902, no editor stated), a list compiled by John Smythe from the Musters roll of 1608; J. Bridges, *History and Antiquities of Northamptonshire;* and Dugdale, *Antiquities of Warwickshire.*

21. *Leviathan,* chap. xxiv.

22. See *infra,* p. 42.

23. H. J. Habakkuk, 'English Landownership, 1680–1740' in *The Economic History Review,* X, no. 1 (February 1940), 2.

24. *Chancery Petty Bag, Miscellaneous Rolls,* no. 20, gives the names of persons fined for depopulation 1635–38. The five counties in question are Leicestershire, Northamptonshire, Nottinghamshire, Huntingdonshire and Lincolnshire, which accounted for 560 out of 589 individuals fined and for £44,054 collected. The names of M.P.s are taken from the *Official Returns of Members of the House of Commons* (1878).

25. See *infra,* p. 42.

26. The figures in this paragraph relate to the counties of Hertfordshire, Bedfordshire, Buckinghamshire, Surrey, Hampshire, Worcestershire, North Riding of Yorkshire, Gloucestershire, Warwickshire, Northamptonshire. For those of the first seven counties I am indebted, as before, to Mr F. J. Fisher.

27. Sir Edward Walker, *Observations upon the Inconveniences,* etc. (1653), especially his remarks on the effect of granting monastic lands to 'mean families'; E. Ludlow (1750 edn.), pp. 311–13; *Somers Tracts,* XIII, 679, Richard Harley, 'Faults on Both Sides'; C. Davenant, *A Discourse upon Grants and Resumptions.* See also P. Larkin, *Property in the Eighteenth Century* (1930), pp. 33–57.

3 The Decline of the Mere Gentry

H. R. TREVOR-ROPER

I

... I believe that Professor Tawney's interpretation is evidentially weak in two important respects which, advanced by him as a hypothesis, are now in danger of becoming an orthodoxy. I refer to his hypothesis of 'the rise of the gentry', based, as he suggests, on new agricultural techniques, and his parallel hypothesis of the contemporaneous decline of the aristocracy, caused as he maintains, by a combination of economic conservatism with fashionable extravagance. I believe both these hypotheses to be not indeed incorrect, but wrongly formulated, and I believe that the faulty formulation of them seriously affects our understanding of political as well as of economic history.... I believe it will appear, first, that the distinction between aristocracy and gentry, as if they were separate social classes, is an arbitrary distinction; and, secondly, that even if such a distinction be allowed, the conclusion that 'the aristocracy' was being replaced by 'the gentry' in the manner suggested is not only unsupported by such evidence as has been adduced, but is positively repugnant to it. ...

II

Let us take Professor Tawney's statistics first. These at least are hard and factual.... My reasons for doubt ... are, first, that the whole method of counting manors as units of wealth is, at the least, unhelpful; secondly, that, even if such a method of calculation were permissible, the distinction between 'aristocracy' and 'gentry' is so entirely arbitrary that no useful conclusions can be based upon it. For what is a manor? It is not a unit of wealth but a definition of rights. The number of tenants holding of it, the payments and services due from them, the value and extent of the demesne land – all these are subject to the widest variations. This point is so obvious that it needs no emphasis. The second point is more important. For who are the aristocracy, who are the gentry, whose landed property Professor Tawney has chosen to distinguish and contrast? ... While his aristocracy consists of a diminishing group of those families who happened to be noble at the beginning and still noble at the end of the period, his gentry consists both of the gentry who remained gentry throughout the period, and

19

of those men who began as gentry and ended as peers, and of those who began as merchants, yeomen or anything else, and ended as gentry. No wonder the gentry, thus calculated, appear to 'rise' at the expense of the peerage.

If we thus think it permissible to doubt Professor Tawney's statistics, what are we to say of his 'stream of comment'? . . . Is the evidence of economic difficulty (which may or may not be evidence of economic decline) inseparable from the nobility, and is the evidence of economic advance inseparable from the gentry? In my opinion the answer is clearly, No. It seems to me that in using the evidence of individual cases the advocates of these theories have looked for the evidence which they wanted only in the field in which, if found, it would fit those theories. . . . Peers and gentry had, on their different levels, the same problems, the same ambitions, the same conventions, the same tastes. Both were landlords; both had large families; both accepted the rule of primogeniture and the custom of entail; both had to find portions for daughters and younger sons. They built – according to their capacity – similar houses; they were buried in similar tombs. It was an aristocratic age, and the gentry accepted – in general – the standards of value and conduct of the aristocracy. . . . The history of the Elizabethan and Jacobean gentry is strewn with their casualties, although Professor Tawney's searchlight, seeking to illuminate only prosperity among the gentry and aristocratic decline, has seldom lit upon them. If it has, he dismisses them as 'exceptions'. In this essay I shall hope to shed upon them a less flickering light.

If economic problems and expensive tastes thus threatened many of the Elizabethan and Jacobean gentry as well as of the peerage, it is equally true that 'good husbandry' was practised by many of the peerage as well as of the gentry. . . . To this it is sometimes answered that we must distinguish between the 'old' aristocracy of Elizabeth and 'the new Jacobean aristocracy' who, being 'risen gentry', are not admissible as evidence of 'aristocratic' husbandry. But this distinction between 'old' and 'new' peers seems to me just as arbitrary as the distinction between peers and gentry. . . . To call the Elizabethan peerage 'old' as if it represented a different type of landlord from the 'new' Jacobean peerage – an antique caste clinging to obsolete ideas – is absurd. . . .

Thus if we examine the evidence fairly, unprejudiced by the artificial distinction between peers and commoners, we find that the same sort of evidence which shows extravagant habits and economic difficulties among the nobility shows also similar habits and similar difficulties among the gentry, and the same sort of evidence which shows improvement and good husbandry among the gentry shows similar achievements among the nobility. It is not proper to write off improving peers and decaying gentry as exceptions to the rule until some evidence has been produced to prove the rule. The whole distinction between the peerage and gentry, upon which so much has been built, becomes again what it has always been in England, a distinction of nomenclature and legal rights, not a difference of either habits of mind or economic practice; and the theory that, because of such differences, one class – the peerage – declined while the other – the gentry – 'rose' is by definition untenable.

III

I thus conclude that Professor Tawney's theory of the rise of the gentry at the expense of a declining peerage is a mistaken formulation. . . . But there nevertheless is a phenomenon, which may still be called 'the rise of the gentry', and this phenomenon, even if it needs to be differently stated, still needs to be explained. The rising class may not have been 'the gentry' as distinct from 'the peerage'; but certain families within the landlord class – whether peers or gentry – undoubtedly did prosper and acquired, through their political machine the Houses of Parliament, political power at the expense of the Crown. The question is, who were these families, and to what did they owe their prosperity? . . .

How shall we begin to isolate the 'rising' families? One obvious group at once presents itself. The new peers created by James I and Charles I are admitted by Professor Tawney to have been 'risen' gentry, and I readily accept this definition. . . . Almost without exception they were office-holders. Cecils and Howards, Herberts and Villiers and their numerous kindred – there is no need to pry closely into the origins of those new windfalls. They were the great court-fortunes; beneath them came the lesser, but still considerable, fortunes that could be derived from offices in the household, the army, and – particularly – the law. To divide the new Stuart peers exactly into these categories is impossible, for many were pluralists; but between these categories at least 90 per cent of them can be easily and obviously accounted for. . . .

Do none of the new peers then represent the landed fortunes of agriculturally minded squires? We cannot exclude some possibilities.

The Spencers of Althorp were certainly great sheep farmers (though mercantile and legal wealth was also infused by marriage into the family); and it may well be that land was to them not only the expression and evidence of their great wealth but also its principal source. But apart from this one family is there a single instance, among the new peers created by the early Stuarts, of a fortune based solely or even mainly on the profits of land? As far as positive evidence is concerned, I can find none. . . .

Thus in an analysis of the 'new' peerage I find no adequate support for Professor Tawney's theory. Rather I conclude that whereas many families indubitably increased the yield of their lands, the great new fortunes were almost invariably made either by offices or in trade. Indeed, I would go further and say that between 1540 and 1640 land alone, without the help of offices or trade, even if it were improved, was hardly capable of causing the significant rise of any but a most exceptional family. For against the increased rents shown on estate accounts in this period must be placed the decline in the value of money. . . . It would therefore seem logical to assume that land was at best a long-term investment, yielding only a marginal profit. Indeed, in the reign of Elizabeth, when the fall in the value of money continued steep and the great rise in rents had not yet begun, the whole position of the landowning classes must sometimes have seemed perilous; and although, after 1590, rentals seem generally to have risen, the general economic depression of the following decade must have postponed recovery, for many families, into the next reign. In these circumstances to doubt whether the mere management of land could raise a family from one social class into another would seem not a 'paradox' but common sense. . . . In almost every case where evidence is attainable that evidence shows that the rise of these families was accompanied by the tenure of offices or the profits of trade; and, further, that when these advantages were withdrawn, and the families concerned were driven back into absolute dependence upon land, they at once apprehended and often experienced not a rise but a decline. . . .

IV

I have already suggested that office rather than land was the basis of many undoubtedly 'rising' families. I would now go further. Instead of the distinction between 'old' and 'new' landlords, between peers and gentry, I would suggest as the significant distinction of Tudor and

Stuart landed society, the distinction between 'court' and 'country', between the office-holders and the mere landlords. And by the words 'court' and 'office' I do not mean only the immediate members of the royal circle or the holders of political office: I use the words in the widest sense to cover all offices of profit under the crown – offices in the household, the administration and, above all – for it was most lucrative of all – the law; local office as well as central office, county lawyers as well as London lawyers, deputy-sheriffs as well as ministers, 'an auditor or a vice-admiral in his county' as well as a Teller of the Exchequer or a Warden of the Cinque Ports. These were the sheet anchors on which precarious landlords depended in a storm.

Admittedly the supply of offices was increasing. So was their value. In England, as throughout western Europe in that period, the new centralized monarchies, with their new councils and new apparatus of administration, required an ever-increasing bureaucracy; and since this bureaucracy was in part created to carry out great social and economic changes, and since the members of it were not, and could not be, strictly supervised, their opportunities, both for direct self-enrichment and for patronage, were, of course, enormous. What fortunes were made by the officials of Henry VIII who carried out the nationalization of monastic property! Naturally the best bargains went to them and to their local agents, the office-holding gentry in the counties. But what of the gentry who remained outside this charmed circle? They saw the opportunities which their more fortunate neighbours exploited, saw them growing rich on fees and perquisites, on grants and leases, as stewards of under-rented Crown or Church lands, as paymasters, commissioners, auditors, receivers, surveyors, feodaries; saw the gradual elevation of their style of living; and finding that they themselves not only lacked these advantages but also, as taxpayers, paid the cost of this ever-increasing apparatus, they naturally longed to exchange conditions with those happier men. But how could they do it? The first necessity was to qualify by education. Educate your children! That was the advice which the gentry pressed upon their relatives: 'make them but scholars and they are fitted for any employment'.[1] So the upper classes, who seemed hitherto to have neglected learning, now pressed into the schools previously reserved for the poor or the clergy and crowded into the Universities and the Inns of Court.[2] Even so, they might be disappointed, for just as in Spain, where the passion for offices – *empleomania* – and the glut of unemployable graduates was deplored by every economist, or in France, where the same phenomena were the despair of Richelieu,[3] so in England the demand for offices far exceeded the supply. To compete for this limited supply, the gentry attached themselves to patrons who, by their patronage or position at court, might determine its direction. Thus, there grew up that system of aristocratic *clientèles* which for so long formed the pattern of English politics.

But this was not the end of the matter. There is an iron law of supply and demand, and the competition had its economic side. Offices acquired a price, and that price was increased by the competition. Offices had long been sold in France, where a regular market machinery – the *Bureau des Parties Casuelles* – had been developed to handle the business. In England the machinery was less developed but the result was the same. By the time of James I almost every office was bought, either from the Crown, or from the favourites who made a market of the Crown's patronage, or from the previous holder; and the price, in that era of boom and scramble, was continually rising. . . .

But what of the mere gentry who had no such positions? As each prize became more valuable it moved farther away from their reach. Education was expensive: the mere gentry of the north and west could not always afford to send their sons to Oxford and Cambridge; and prices in London, that ever-growing all-absorbent metropolis, were high and rising. Offices themselves became too costly for their purses, and reversions were often barred to them by the dynastic solidarity of the possessing families. What, then, were they to do? . . . Perhaps they would plunge into debt and become ultimately desperate – such were the men who in the end staked all on the ventures of the Earl of Essex; perhaps they would follow Sir John Oglander's advice, to 'get a ship and judiciously manage her' – in time of war there were always the hopes of great windfalls from privateering, and it was no coincidence that the Earl of Essex's party, the party of the excluded, was also the war-party, while the party of the Cecils, the party of office, was also the party of peace; or perhaps, weary of the struggle, they would contract out of it altogether, spurn the Court and its offices, its competition and corruption, echo the words of their ultimate hero Sir Walter Raleigh

> *Say to the Court it glows*
> *And shines like rotten wood,*

and compose, in their manor houses – at least while the mood lasted – poems in praise of rural solitude and the simple life. Withdrawing from the Court, these men withdrew also from the ideology of the Court. Some of them withdrew entirely and finally, into recusancy, from which – except through reconversion – there was no way back into public life: it was in the manor houses of the disgruntled country gentry that the missionary priests of the 1580s and 1590s found their converts and their secret refuges. Others withdrew less absolutely, into an opposite ideology, the ideology of puritanism, and organized their opposition more hopefully in other country houses. But in either case the new ideology accepted by these repudiators of the court was an ideology of economy, of retrenchment. . . .

Such, as it seems to me, was the position of many of the English gentry at the end of the sixteenth century. Of course, it was not the position of the whole class, for there were unambitious men just as there were 'good husbands' among the gentry; also the position in some counties (like Warwickshire) seems to have been more stable than in others. Nevertheless, the declining 'mere gentry', for whom Sir John Oglander spoke, were sufficiently numerous to form a significant element in society, and a recognition of this fact seems to me necessary if we are to understand certain important historical problems which Professor Tawney's method, as it seems to me, has rather obscured. First, it will enable us to convert into valid terms the untenable antithesis between aristocracy and gentry; secondly, it will explain, as Professor Tawney has never sought to explain, the rise of Independency in the Great Rebellion; thirdly, it will put a different complexion on that 'stream of comment' by seventeenth-century observers which Professor Tawney (mistakenly, as I submit) has interpreted as evidence for his thesis of the decline of the aristocracy and the 'rise of the gentry'. . . . The Great Rebellion is the central event of the seventeenth century in England, and any interpretation of English society which leaves unexplained that great convulsion is obviously unsatisfying. Now Professor Tawney's thesis, in my opinion, leaves it unexplained, or rather, his explanation explains only his own thesis, not the facts. For what is his explanation? According to him, the Great Rebellion was the logical, though violent, culmination of the process which he imagines, a form of emphatic foreclosure by the creditor class of rising 'entrepreneur' gentry, City merchants and lawyers, upon the mortgaged estates of a half-bankrupt peerage, Church and Crown: 'It was discovered, not for the last time, that as a method of foreclosure war was cheaper than litigation.'

But this explanation, while consistent with his theory, seems to me quite inadequate when we come to examine more closely the actual course of the Rebellion. For apart from the fact that the English peerage, on the eve of the Rebellion, was at least as rich as at any time in the preceding century,[4] this explanation entirely leaves out of account the men who, more than any other, made the Great Rebellion – the men whose radicalism converted it from a series of political manoeuvres into civil war and social revolution: the Independents. . . . They were not 'rising' gentry; they were not a creditor class; nor were they a sudden phenomenon of the 1640s. An examination of their claims, which were loud, and of their previous history, which is long, seems to me to show that the Independents, the men whose spectacular actions have given a revolutionary quality to a whole century, represent a class which Professor Tawney, in his interpretation of that period, has somehow overlooked, or at least has dismissed as insignificant temporary exceptions: the declining gentry.

This identification of the Independents with the declining gentry is not part of conventional historical interpretation, but I believe that it is necessary to historical understanding. I cannot, within the compass of an essay, seek to prove it in detail; but a brief digression into political history may at least demonstrate its plausibility.

V

The long reign of Elizabeth was in effect, and increasingly, the reign of the Cecil dynasty. The first attempt to overthrow that dynasty was made by a group of excluded aristocrats in 1569–72, and the failure of that attempt only confirmed it in power. By 1590, when death had removed the rival dynasty of the Dudleys, all patronage seemed monopolized as never before by the Cecils and their followers. At the same time a general economic depression accentuated the difference in fortune between the fortunate office-holders and the unfortunate 'mere landlords' who, not belonging to the Cecil clientele, had so long and, as they felt, so unjustly been excluded. . . . In the meteoric career of the Earl of Essex, already the most probable minister of the most probable new king, they saw their champion, and he in them saw the instruments of his ambition. The excluded peers, the excluded gentry, recusant and puritan alike, gathered around him. . . . Supported by these classes, and by decayed adventurers from his own armies, Essex sought to force his way into power. He failed, as his predecessors had failed a generation before; and Sir Robert Cecil, by superior political skill, brought in King James to continue, not to break, the Cecilian monopoly. Such was the result of the first 'revolt of the squires'. . . .

The decline of the mere gentry was not reversed by the accession of King James: it was aggravated. For King James was interested in the Court, not the country. Extravagant where Elizabeth had been parsimonious, he was prepared to enrich his courtiers – at the cost of the country. He remembered that the Essexian peers had been his party, and advanced them, but he easily abandoned their inconspicuous gentry followers whom he had not directly known. Therefore, while the Essexian peers joined the Cecilian peers and the Scots peers and the new peers as office-holders in that 'lottery of unearned fortunes', the swollen Jacobean court, the gentry, who had hoped so much from his accession, and who now found themselves saddled instead with a double burden, lamented their 'betrayal'. . . .

For what were the burdens which James I redoubled on the backs of the mere gentry? The literature of the time is full of them. In particular, they were two: wardships and purveyance. Now both these burdens fell with particular severity on the 'mere' gentry: the court gentry and court peers (and under James I almost all peers were court peers) were but lightly hit. For courtiers, if they paid some of the cost, also touched some of the profits of both these taxes. . . .

But James I did not merely continue and increase and concentrate upon the gentry burdens which they had borne, though less heavily and less restively, under Elizabeth. He also added new burdens – or at least withdrew old alleviations. . . . No longer, as in the reign of Elizabeth, could they, through royal favour, detach useful morsels from vacant bishoprics: the Act of 1559, under which that had been possible, was now, in 1604, repealed, and the financial needs of the State, which Elizabeth had so often met at the expense of the Church, were now charged exclusively to the laity. . . . Finally, by his peace with Spain, also in 1604, King James closed, as it seemed, the last safety-valve of the embarrassed gentry. Thereafter it was no longer possible for a mere gentleman, in default of other opportunity, to 'get a ship and judiciously manage her' as a privateer, at least under English letters of marque. King James's peace with Spain was welcome to the Court, to which it brought substantial pensions; it was welcome to the City, which prospered by the resumption of trade; it was hated by the gentry. 'Peace and law hath beggared us all,' declared one of them;[5] increasingly, through joint-stock companies which were at least half privateering ventures, they sought to circumvent it; and along with the new worship of Queen Elizabeth there grew up, among them, a new cult of Sir Francis Drake and their martyr, Sir Walter Raleigh, the types of gentleman-privateer. . . .

Deserted by the king from whom they had once hoped so much; deserted by their aristocratic patrons; kept from lucrative employment by the rising price and growing heredity of the offices they coveted; crushed beneath increased burdens of feudal taxation to sustain a lavish and enlarged court from which they were themselves excluded; threatened by the revival of economic claims by the Church; debarred, by the outbreak of peace, from other opportunities of investment to which they had become accustomed; no wonder if the mere gentry felt themselves betrayed under James I. Naturally they became radical in their politics. . . . Hence those spasmodic risings of the Midland gentry which followed the accession of James I – the Bye Plot of 1603 and the Gunpowder Plot of 1605. . . . Essex revolts without an Essex, desperate ventures by an idiot fringe, too little and too late, they were not dangers but symptoms: symptoms which the Crown failed to heed, to its cost, and which the historians of the 'rise of the gentry' have failed to heed, to their error. . . .

If the mere gentry could find no cure for their difficulties, no relief from government, no hope in rebellion, what were they to do? They would exploit their estates, enclose the open fields, raise their rents; and if their tenants protested, they would break, by force or law, what Sir Thomas Tresham called 'their peevish and paltry proceedings'. . . .[6] At the beginning of the reign of James I the gentry had been powerless against the apparently solid alliance of Crown, Court and City; later in the same reign that alliance had begun to crumble, as internal factions split the Court and the projects of alderman Cokayne dismayed the City. Thus, the dissident gentry saw some of their old allies returning to lead them and to exploit their grievances. Besides, unlike the recusant gentry, the puritan gentry had an institution for the capture of power. They had Parliament, if only they knew how to use it. From 1621 to 1629 a succession of uncontrollable Parliaments warned the Court of its danger. Thereafter, for eleven years, there were no Parliaments. But it was only the voice, not the hand, of Opposition that was thus stilled. Silently, in country-houses and caucus-meetings, the new course of 'Thorough' gradually cemented together a far more formidable opposition. . . . In 1640, with discontented peers to lead them and City money behind them, the gentry were again prepared to challenge the court, and this time the court, incompetent and divided, was unprepared for the struggle.

Of course their interests were different. The City, the peers, the disgruntled officials only wanted a return to the old alliance: the gentry, who had been the victims of that alliance were determined to destroy it. . . . At the crucial moment the timid peers heard from behind them the authentic voice of gentry radicalism: the voice of the Independents, the armed gentry, refusing to heed the aristocratic flags of truce. The New Model Army was a warning to the old court-opposition that they had mobilized forces beyond their power to control or stop.

Where were the Independents heading? They did not know. 'None climbs so high,' said Cromwell, 'as he who knows not whither he is going.'[7] They had no direct understanding of politics – what a hash they made of politics when they found themselves in power! But they knew what they hated, what they wanted to destroy. . . . They executed the King, abolished the House of Lords, purged and re-purged the City, abolished wardships and purveyance, abolished the centralized Church and preserved from Church and peasantry alike their cherished tithes. Further, as the 'country party', haters of the all-absorbent Court and City, they preached decentralization: decentralization of government (they trebled the county seats and slashed the borough seats in Parliament); decentralization of religion (what else in 'Independency'?); decentralization of trade ('I thought,' protested a gentleman of Dorset, 'that long ere this we should have the trade dispersed all the nation over; and this City, it seems, must have all the trade');[8] decentralization of law – 'county registers' of land and local courts; decentralization of education: no longer must the 'mere gentry' of the north and west, by their distance from Oxford and Cambridge, be debarred from qualifying themselves for office: there must be a university in Durham, a university in Wales.[9] Finally, they must have a foreign policy. And what should that foreign policy be? What but a privateering war with Spain as in the days of 'Queen Elizabeth of famous memory', in which a gentleman could 'get a ship and judiciously manage her'? In 1655 the tradition of Drake and Raleigh was revived, and war was reopened in the West Indies. The fanatical hatreds, the impossible demands, the futile foreign policy of the Independents were the culmination of a century of protests: the protests of the declining gentry.

It was a vain dream. The gentry-republic failed. All that they gained by revolution was, in the end, another court, other office-holders, other great financiers, heavier taxes. After 1660 many of the once radical gentry drew out of radical politics. . . . They became the royalist 'young squires' of the Convention and Cavalier Parliaments, the squires of the October Club, the high-flying, non-resisting tories. And in so far as they were still 'mere gentry', whom neither trade nor offices had raised, they remained relatively poor. . . .

VI

Professor Tawney appeals to a commentary of contemporary philosophy. . . . In the late 1650s James Harrington in his *Oceana*, Henry Neville in Parliament (as afterwards in his *Plato Redivivus*), other intellectuals like Thomas Chaloner, Republican Army officers like Captain Baynes and Lieutenant-General Ludlow, all in turn expressed or referred to a consistent doctrine. That doctrine is, first, that in society, as a universal law of nature, power always follows property; and secondly, that, in politics, government – if it is to be natural, not 'perverted' – must always reside in that social class which has the 'balance' – i.e. the preponderance – of property. . . . Applying these doctrines to contemporary English society, their advocates further declared that such a shift in the 'balance' had in fact now taken place, since the Crown and the nobility had lost their property and 'the gentry have all the lands'. . . .

Paradoxically, the Harringtonians . . . were poor illustrations of their own thesis. Like Harrington, they were, in general, lesser gentry. . . . But . . . this is not enough to explain their politics. Within the body of the Independents they formed a smaller group. Politically, they were all Republicans: not necessarily Rumpers – the Rump, to most of them, had not been a 'Commonwealth' but an 'oligarchy'[10] – but republicans in the negative sense: radical backbenchers, a country-party within the old country party, opponents of that new court, and its new office-holders, which the problems of government were creating even in that centrifugal commonwealth, the republic of the gentry. . . .

Thus, the doctrines of their champion, James Harrington, became, for a brief time, the slogan of the 'mere gentry' in their last losing struggle against the Court. The fact that they lost in that struggle is evidence of the falsity of the doctrine: for if power always follows property, and the gentry had all the property, the gentry should clearly have prevailed against the successive 'oligarchical' courts by which in fact they were ruled. But in fact power does not necessarily follow property: property – as the economic rise of the office-holder shows –

often follows power; and 'the gentry' had not acquired 'all the lands' (which anyway is not synonymous with the balance of property) – although it is true that some gentry, through mercantile or official activities, had increased their share of them. The statement that 'the gentry have all the lands' was in truth not an objective observation of fact, but – like the statements that 'the saints shall rule the earth', or 'all power is from the people' – a political dogma whereby a class seeking power sought to sanctify its claims. . . .

VII

Thus, if my analysis is correct Professor Tawney's thesis must be revised: the gentry did not rise as a class, nor at the expense of the aristocracy, nor on the profits of agriculture. . . . And if, in the nineteenth century, the solid conservative structure of English rural society seemed to foreigners so eccentric and remarkable, that solidity (I suspect) was due to developments after, not before, the Great Rebellion. The Tory squires of Victorian England were indeed prosperous and educated men, and when they read Macaulay's famous but merciless description of their ancestors, the clownish tory squireens of 1680, they were as outraged as contemporary parsons when they were assured by Darwin that their ancestors had been apes. They protested, loudly and desperately, that Macaulay was wrong, actuated by mere Whig spite. But is it not equally possible that squires had changed since 1680 – indeed, that the great change in their status had occurred since then? Remembering the mutinous squires of the reign of Queen Anne, Addison's foxhunters[11] and Fielding's Squire Western, I am ready to end this essay by hazarding a hypothesis: that while the sixteenth century, with its offices for the few, may have elevated an *élite* of official county families – an elastic, changing *élite*, like the English peerage, but still an *élite* – it was the eighteenth century, whose agricultural revolution and tax-relief brought benefits to every landlord, that witnessed that more general phenomenon, the Rise of the Gentry.

[*The Economic History Supplement*, I, 1953.]

Notes

1. *A Royalist's Notebook, The Commonplace Book of Sir John Oglander of Nunwell 1622–1652*, ed. Francis Bamford (1936), p. 249.

2. On this subject see Mr J. H. Hexter's admirable essay, 'The Education of the Aristocracy in the Renaissance' (*Journal of Modern History*, 1950).

3. See his *Testament Politique*, I, ii, 10, 'Des Lettres'.

4. Mr L. Stone indeed ('The Elizabethan Aristocracy, A Restatement', *Econ. Hist. Rev.* (1952), 2nd ser., IV, 311) states that, according to his own calculations, based on Professor Tawney's method of counting manors, the English peerage, on the eve of the Civil War, was poorer than ever: it 'had more than doubled its numbers, but its landed property had failed to increase'. Now this firm statement can be tested by a more reliable method than counting manors. Mr Stone himself, in the same article (p. 304), insists that the average landed income of a late Elizabethan peer was '£2000 to £3000 p.a.' – i.e. that the total landed income of the peerage in 1600 was about £170,000 p.a. It therefore follows, if he is right, that in 1642 the total landed income of the 128 Caroline peers (if the measure of property is value) was still only about £170,000 p.a. But in fact we possess evidence of the landed income of several Caroline peers, which, thanks to the courtesy of Mr J. P. Cooper (to whom I am indebted for much other assistance in preparing this article), I am able to publish . . .; and this evidence shows that . . . such peers – less than one-fifth of the Caroline peerage – had an annual income from land of at least £194,000 – more than Mr Stone's argument assigns to their whole order. Even we accept acreage, not value, as the measure of property, and so allow for appreciation, it would be difficult to squeeze the remaining 104 peers (some of them princely landlords) into the narrow margin left for them by Mr Stone.

Apart from land in England, many of the Caroline peers also had land in Ireland, e.g. the Earl of Essex, whose Irish lands (Mr Cooper tells me) were worth some £3,000 p.a. in 1638; and many of them, of course, enjoyed huge incomes from offices and pensions: e.g. Lord Goring, whose landed estate was valued at only £3,300 capital value, but who, in 1641, was credited with an income from offices and monopolies of £26,000 p.a. (Cal. Committee for Compounding, p. 2051; Cal. S.P. Dom. (1663–64), p. 6.)

5. *A Royalist's Notebook*, p. 14.

6. H.M.C. Var. Coll. III, 127.

7. Quoted in S. R. Gardiner, *Great Civil War*, III (1891), p. 143.

8. Burton, *Parliamentary Diary*, I, 177.

9. The gentry of County Durham petitioned for a college at Durham in 1650 (*Commons Journals*, VI, 410; cf. Carlyle, *Letters and Speeches of Oliver Cromwell*, letter clxix). Durham College was founded in 1657. A college for Wales was advocated by a Welsh gentleman, John Lewis of Glasgrug, in two pamphlets, *Contemplations upon these Times* (1646) and εὐαγγελιόγραφα . . . (1656), the latter of which was dedicated to Oliver Cromwell. The project also interested Richard Baxter and others (see article by J. H. Davies in *Wales* (1896), p. 121, and T. Richards, *The Puritan Movement in Wales* (1920), p. 233). Hugh

Peters, in his *Good Work for a Good Magistrate* (1651), advocates, as an ultimate ideal, colleges in Yorkshire, Cornwall and Wales.

10. Burton, *Parliamentary Diary*, III, 134; Harrington, *Oceana* (1700), p. 76.

11. 'For the honour of His Majesty and the safety of his government, we cannot but observe that those who have appeared the greatest enemies to both are of that rank of men who are commonly distinguished by the title of fox-hunters' (Addison, *The Freeholder* (1716), no. 22).

4 The Military Decline of the Aristocracy

J. H. HEXTER

... We may tentatively venture an examination of the evidence offered by Professor Tawney and by Professor Trevor-Roper in support of their respective theses.

The evidence is of several different kinds. First, Tawney presents a good deal of comment from seventeenth-century writers, Trevor-Roper a little, intended to show that contemporary witnesses were conscious of the very social transformations which their mutually contradictory contentions allege to have been in process. Second, Tawney and Stone on one side, Trevor-Roper on the other, offer a number of specific instances, observations on the careers and fortunes of sixteenth- and seventeenth-century individuals and families, to illustrate their conflicting general theses. Here the similarity in kinds of evidence ceases. For Tawney and Stone support their arguments with a considerable mass of statistical data on the fortunes of whole social classes, while Trevor-Roper, though challenging the validity of his opponents' statistics, provides few of his own. On the other hand, Trevor-Roper offers a broad reinterpretation of the political history of England from the rebellion of the Earl of Essex to the Restoration, and Tawney, while ignoring his opponent's interpretation of that history, offers none of his own.

Let us now examine these different kinds of evidence.

First, as to general statements by the men of the times, alleged by Tawney and Trevor-Roper in support of their divergent conceptions. A little caution suggests itself in dealing even with ostensibly pertinent contemporary remarks about the condition of this or that class. The human propensity to make a poor mouth knows no bounds of time or space.... To this chronic human proclivity to conceive of oneself as in

33

disgrace with fortune, there are sometimes added motives for pleas of poverty more immediately and materially pertinent to the private interests of the persons who advance them. . . . Moreover, the notion that one's own time is a brazen time, an epoch of decay, a mess, in contrast to some good old golden age is common enough in every era. . . .

We may quickly dispose of the evidence that consists of individual instances, tales of the fortunes of families, told by Tawney, Stone, and Trevor-Roper to illustrate the destinies of the classes to which those families belonged. In gross they constitute a magnificent but, I fear, misplaced deployment of erudition. . . . If the individual instances sufficed to prove the general process, both Tawney and Trevor-Roper would have the better of the argument, and the conclusions of both as to the nature of the general trend of social change in seventeenth-century England would be validated. Since their conclusions are diametrically opposed, however, this is impossible. . . . In such circumstances the significance of the individual instance for both theories depends on the validity of the general argument, not the other way about. So we 'will have grounds more relative than this'.

Tawney provides such grounds in the form of statistics. His statistics are of two kinds: (1) casual statistics off-handedly dropped to lend artistic verisimilitude to large and bald assertions; (2) systematic statistics intended to provide a quantitative foundation for the general hypothesis that he is propounding. . . .

The second kind of statistics, the systematic ones which Tawney uses to support his general hypothesis concerning the rise of the gentry, are provided by the counting of manors, 2,547 manors in six and one-third counties. . . .[1]

But the statistics will not bear analysis. For: (1) they have imbedded in them a number of serious biases; (2) manors – the units of counting – are anything but homogeneous; and (3) the contrast between aristocracy and gentry that the statistics are supposed to reveal involves an arbitrary and largely false taxonomic assumption.

First let us look at the statistical evidence that is supposed to demonstrate the superior economic strategy of the small gentry. The basis of this evidence is a count of the manors held by men owning no more than four manors in six and one-third counties. If all such men held no manors at all anywhere else, the inference drawn from this evidence might be of some interest. But seventeenth-century English landlords did not conform their holdings to the statistical convenience of twentieth-century economic historians. A very considerable number of gentlemen with no more than four manors in the six and one-third sample counties owned manors in the remaining thirty-three and two-third counties in England, in Wales and in Ireland. Some of them, far from being small landowners, were very large landowners indeed. And of course any assertion about the total number of manors held by small landowners becomes meaningless when we actually have no notion how many of the landowners so classified really were small.

Tawney's estimate of a very heavy loss of manors by large landlords is open to a somewhat different criticism. The trouble in this instance is that one of the aristocratic large holders included in Tawney's statistics was too aristocratic and too large. He was the King. Between 1561 and 1640 the Crown divested itself of vast chunks of land; this is one fact that Tawney has established beyond all doubt. In his sample of six and one-third counties the Crown holding of nearly 250 manors in 1561 dwindled to about fifty manors in 1640. *This whole loss Tawney appears to have debited to the holders of ten or more manors.* When we remove the Crown lands from consideration, the loss of the large holders, men who owned ten or more manors in the sample counties, drops from the lordly 33 per cent that led Tawney to consign them to bankruptcy, to a somewhat less lordly one-half of one per cent, hardly a presage of impending economic catastrophe. With respect both to the rise of the small holder and the decline of the large, 'Professor Tawney's table maximizes errors in the direction of the trend that it is supposed to reveal.'[2]

What, then, does account for the losses of the nobility and the gains of the gentry, which Tawney's other set of statistics seems to reveal? For one thing the 'nobility' held fewer manors in 1640 than in 1561, because there were fewer 'nobles' in 1640 than in 1561. For in his first computations Tawney classified as noble only men who held peerages in 1560 and the inheritors of those peerages. But by 1640 one-third of such peerages were extinct, and extinct peers hold no manors at all. So some part of the loss of manors by the nobility, which Tawney ascribed to economic causes, was due to normal demographic attrition. . . .

A hypothetical biography of a grandson of a peer of 1561 may make clearer how Tawney's statistics worked. In this case our subject is a younger son, and his father generously settles five manors on him. Then the king ennobles him; he is now a peer. He marries the rich sole survivor of another noble family of 1561, who brings him twenty-five manors held in 1561 by the head of her family. In Professor Tawney's statistics all the thirty manors our man now holds will appear as a *debit* against the nobility, a *credit* to the gentry. Then gradually our man buys up twenty manors of needy squires. In Professor Tawney's table – where our man is classified as gentry – *these purchases do not register at all*, since they are transfers within the gentry. So in 1640 this descendant of a noble family of 1561, himself a noble, holds fifty manors, twenty of which he bought from poor gentlemen; and Professor Tawney's table will score the effect of such a career on the balance of property as follows: *noble losses – 30 manors; gentry losses – 0 manors; noble gains – 0 manors; gentry gains – 30 manors.*[3]

At this point our confidence in Professor Tawney's method of counting manors may have shrunk somewhat. It may shrink further if we consider what a manor is. Economically manors are not equivalent units like dollars or pounds or even bushels of wheat. They are in-commensurate units of ownership like 'blocks' of stocks or the 'pro-perties' of present-day real-estate parlance. . . .

Nor are we quite at the end of our difficulties. In quest of a new rising rural middle class and an old declining aristocratic class to con-trast with one another, Tawney hit upon the gentry for the former role, the lay peerage for the latter. Tawney's scheme of classification, his identification of the peerage with the aristocracy and the gentry with the middle class, renders *all* his statistical findings irrelevant to the theory that they are intended to support. For, whether rising or not, the gentry did not stand to the peerage in the relation of a middle class to an aristocracy. . . . Collectively, but not individually, the peers were the first gentlemen of England in honor and wealth, clearly distinct from the rest neither in source of livelihood nor in way of life. So Professor Tawney's numerical evidence is erected on an error in classification – a statistical mirage reared on a taxonomic illusion. . . .

I can suggest no more fitting farewell to the peculiar terrain we have just traversed than that composed by Mr Cooper, whose guidance I have relied on almost all the way. 'The counting of manors seems to have effects dangerously similar to the counting of sheep. It introduces us to a dream world in which, as in our own dreams, reality may not be entirely absent, but appearances are often deceptive.'[4]

Instead of statistics Trevor-Roper offers us a brief but brilliant sketch of his conception of the role of the 'mere' or declining gentry in the politics and society of England from the age of Elizabeth to the Restoration. Now Trevor-Roper's declining gentry are no figment of his imagination. . . . That this perdurable and undistinguished group was at large in England between 1540 and 1660 is evident. That its numbers may have been somewhat augmented and its collective temper somewhat exacerbated by the combined operations of adverse economic circumstances and Stuart indifference to its plight is quite probable. That various mere gentlemen had a hand in every attempted *coup d'état* from the rebellion of the Earl of Essex to the march of the New Model Army on London, Trevor-Roper has demonstrated beyond doubt. . . .[5] So far what Trevor-Roper has to say seems plausible. But rather often he goes beyond these plausibilities to broad though somewhat vague assertions. Politically, he seems to indicate, there are really only two kinds of gentry – the fat court gentry and the depressed country gentry.[6] The Great Rebellion thus becomes 'the rising of the poor country gentry against the office holders'. . . .[7] Dividing the English landlords of the century before the Great Rebellion between rising court and declining mere gentry is a little like dividing the participants in the French Revolution between aristocrats and *enragés*: it leaves out a lot of important people and makes it unduly hard to explain what actually happened.

This omission, neglect, or minimization of the role of one segment – the same segment – of the landed class is one of the few elements that the hypotheses of our two historians have in common. The hypnotic fascination that the rising lesser landholders have for Professor Tawney, the declining lesser landholders and the court folk for Professor Trevor-Roper, has prevented both writers from paying much attention to that third group of English landlords. Unlike Tawney's owners of small-to-middling estates, these men of the third group have large holdings. Unlike Trevor-Roper's rising court gentry, they draw a very great part of their incomes from land; and while – one, two or three generations back – the fortunes some of them enjoy were built up through court favor, by 1640 the current possessors of those fortunes are under no present obligation to the current Court and receive little of its patronage. The logic of the arguments of both Tawney and Trevor-Roper puts this group of landlords in a bad way by 1640. Tawney appears to believe that the conservatism of such landlords in the turbulence created by the Price Revolution doomed them to disaster both economic and political. Trevor-Roper suggests that at the very least they faced creeping economic malnutrition consequent on inadequate access to royal bounty and courtly graft.[8] Denying themselves the bonanza of demesne farming, denied by the Crown the sustenance of court favor, these country magnates seem to have got themselves the worst of both worlds – Tawney's and Trevor-Roper's. As we shall see later, this shared depressing picture well comports with the divergent general conceptions of the historical process into which each of our twentieth-century historians seeks to fit the realities of the seventeenth century. How well does the picture comport with the realities themselves?

The evidence available for answering this question is not all that one might wish.[9] There are, however, some clues. Recent investigation seems to show that, without the benefit of either demesne farming or court favor, from the 1580s on, the large landlords may have been doing very well for themselves indeed. Around the 1580s the land market began to boom, and it seems to have continued to boom for the next half century. In those roaring days the annual rental on some estates climbed to a third of what those estates had sold for a few decades earlier. . . . But on the whole a general increase in land values is likely to be most profitable in gross to the men who have the most land to profit from, that is, to the very segment of the landed class which both Tawney and Trevor-Roper have consigned to economic debility. The neglect or misplacement of this segment by both writers leaves an unfortunate gap in their respective reconstructions of the socio-economic configuration of the English countryside between 1561 and 1660.

It leaves a political gap even more unfortunate. For the large landholders provided the realm with the more important part of that 'self-government at the king's command' which is the most significant trait of the English polity. They were the deputy lieutenants. They were the sheriffs. They were the justices of the peace. They were the commissioners in the counties to look into the myriad of things that the Tudors and early Stuarts thought needed looking into, and the commissioners to do in the counties the enormous number of things that the Tudors and early Stuarts thought needed to be done. . . .[10] And from before the accession of Elizabeth I it was these same men who came to Parliament from the counties and the boroughs to make up the larger part of the membership of the House of Commons. This majority of local magnates seem to have increased right up to 1640, so that in the House of Commons of the Long Parliament all other groups appear as auxiliaries – mere Balearic slingers and Nubian cavalry – to the close-packed legions of the rich much-landed country gentry. . . .[11]

Not only does the personnel of the early Stuart House of Commons fall outside the orbit in which Tawney and Trevor-Roper ordinarily move; its political behavior does not reflect what they – and, I fear, a great many others – believe the purposes and aims of a powerful politico-social group must be. In short, from the accession of Elizabeth I to the summoning of the Long Parliament the rich country gentlemen who fill the House of Commons make no consistent or concerted effort to win permanent control and direction of the government. . . . They neither talked nor acted like would-be rulers of the realm.[12] Trevor-Roper's presentation of the House as the politically befuddled and obtuse head of a rout of angry hard-pressed yokels is not very convincing either. For the leaders of the early Stuart Parliaments were an unusually well-educated group of men; and it is hard to believe that the members who so neatly, quickly, and effectively won the initiative in Parliament from the Stuarts were an inept gang of political Calibans. . . .[13]

From the Apology of the Commons in 1604 to the Declaration of Rights in 1688 their line of action is consistent, clear, and effective. And the latter document is not an assertion of the social supremacy of the middle-class gentry or of the political supremacy of the House of Commons; it is precisely what on the face of it it appears to be: a charter of liberties of free Englishmen in the right line of Magna Carta, the Confirmatio Cartarum and the Petition of Right. . . .

We have hitherto been more concerned to criticize what appear to be errors than to render due praise to merit. Yet in Trevor-Roper's studies there is substantial merit to praise.

(1) A very considerable part of Trevor-Roper's contribution to the controversy has taken the form of an all-out assault on the interpretive structures reared by Professor Tawney and Mr Stone. Up to now we have paid little of the tribute due to his magnificent if terrifying work of destruction. . . .

(2) In insisting on the Court-against-country element in the crisis of the seventeenth century and in giving substantial content to the otherwise evanescent conception of 'Court', Trevor-Roper has performed a service of inestimable benefit to historians of the period. For in the crisis of the seventeenth century the Court in conflict with the country was certainly one of the vital spots, and of all the vital spots the one whose morphology and physiology has been least studied and least understood. . . .

(3) For the rest of Trevor-Roper's interpretation of the crisis of the

seventeenth century we may take our stand on the grounds afforded by our previous criticism of his argument. He has provided us with a study of a social group, the declining gentry, that historians of the period from 1540 to 1660 have hitherto neglected. . . . A trifle exalted perhaps by his discovery, he has claimed for the declining gentry of the seventeenth century a somewhat larger historical role than a calmer and fuller analysis is likely to attribute to them – a sin, possibly, but a venial one. . . .

It is otherwise with the theory espoused by Tawney and Mr Stone. . . . What can be said for it? Only that it is an interesting theory, that the evidence thus far adduced in its support is unconvincing, that the data underlying that evidence is in large part misleading, ambiguous, irrelevant or merely erroneous. It is not wholly certain that the transformation of Professor Tawney's thesis into a commonplace will prove an immeasurable boon to the cause of historical enlightenment.

When historians as able as Professor Tawney and Professor Trevor-Roper pile on their evidence a burden of hypothesis heavier than that evidence can sustain, we may suspect that their judgment has been clouded by over-addiction to some general conception of the historical process. Professor Tawney is sufficiently explicit about the incentive for his fascinating redrafting of the historical picture of the gentry and for his singular view of their social orientation. . . .

The English gentry . . . must be transfigured into a *bourgeoisie* to maintain the view that the rise of the *bourgeoisie* is the indispensable framework for almost a millennium of history. The necessity becomes the more pressing if one is committed to the belief that socially the Reformation was a bourgeois revolution. For then between the bourgeois revolution of the sixteenth century and the bourgeois revolution that broke out at the end of the eighteenth century in France, the English revolution of the seventeenth century is egregiously out of line unless it, too, is bourgeois. . . . Those who recall the magnificent and ambivalent sketch that Marx draws of his hero-villains, the *bourgeoisie*, in the *Communist Manifesto* will hardly fail to recognize the lineaments of his old acquaintances in Tawney's description of 'the agricultural capitalists . . . who were making the pace, and to whom the future belonged', the rising gentry revolutionizing the relations of production in the countryside in their ruthless single-minded drive to appropriate the surplus value of England's largest industry. . . .

The general conception that dominates Trevor-Roper's studies also

finds the source of human action in the circumambient economic configuration. But for him the motor of history is not the great impersonal
secular movements of economic change; it is simpler than that. Groups
of men in similar market situations are driven to common action and
a common outlook by the similar way in which the same events
impinge on their identical economic interests. The motor of history
for Trevor-Roper is a sort of behavioristic reflex system of stimulus
and response triggered by twinges in the pocketbook nerve. . . .

We are still left with the problem that started Tawney on his quest.
The problem may be defined in the following fashion. . . . Why at
this particular historical juncture did the 'country' find its leadership
in social strata beneath the top? Why among the gentry rather than
among the nobility? . . . In the sense set forth in the preceding paragraph the rise of the gentry is not a hypothesis to be verified; it is a
simple fact, a fact that requires exaplanation. . . .

Among the quotations from contemporaries on which he [Tawney]
relies – quotations which, it seems to me, do little to support his
argument – there are several that point clearly to a line of inquiry that
he disregards. . . . All these men [Raleigh, Bacon and Selden] seem to
be saying much the same thing about the noble magnates; but what
they are saying is not that the nobles are bankrupt, or even much
poorer than they used to be. They are saying very emphatically that
*the magnates do not directly control arms and men as they once did, that the
old relation between high status or great landed wealth and a great
military* following no longer subsists. On the face of it, then, all the
observations set out above direct our attention not to the economy but
to the organization of armed forces. And if we follow their leading,
we discover that in the century and a half between Henry VI and the
death of Elizabeth there was indeed a radical transformation in the
structure of England's military reserve. In the middle of the fifteenth
century the larger part of the battle-ready military reserve was made
up of the retinues of the magnates. Besides the magnates' tenantry,
lesser landlords bound themselves to the great men of the realm by
'writing, oath, or promise';[14] in return they often received from their
lord a sort of uniform, his livery, which they wore as a sign of their
clientage. They also usually received a money fee which conjoined them
to the lord's band of retained men, his retinue. . . .[15]

At the end of the sixteenth century the bare form of the retaining
system survived; but it was a shell, a feeble shadow of its former self.
The squirearchy no longer rose in arms at the behest of the great lords,

although for show they might ride about the country in some personage's train. . . .

Fully to account for the shift in English society that crippled the retaining system lies beyond the scope of this essay and transcends the capacities of its author. Certainly one major element in the process was the institution of the Lord-Lieutenants and the formation of the county trainbands. When county militia under the command of Crown officers replaced private retinues under the command of territorial magnates as the reserve of its armed forces, England advanced with giant strides toward domestic tranquillity and military incompetence. With its cement of retaining fatally weakened the whole framework of goodlordship, from which the fifteenth-century magnate derived his power, loosened up. . . . Elizabeth further reduced the capacity of noble magnates to function as centers of 'country' discontent by keep-

Professor Tawney's Statistics (see n. 1)

Economic History Review, 2nd ser., VII, 94.

The Ownership of 2,547 Manors in Seven Counties in 1561 and 1640.

	Crown	Peers	Gentry	Other
1561	242	335	1,709	261
	9·5%	13·1%	67·1%	10·2%
1640 (Assigning to gentry manors owned by families ennobled 1561–1640)	53	157	2,051	286
	2%	6·1%	80·5%	11·2%
1640 (Assigning to peers manors owned by families ennobled 1561–1640)	53	343	1,865	286
	2%	13·4%	73·3%	11·2%

Economic History Review, XI, 33

	Manors belonging to owners who held four manors or less		Manors belonging to owners who held five to nine manors		Manors belonging to owners who held ten or more manors	
	Number	%	Number	%	Number	%
1561	1,445	56·7	490	19·2	612	24·0
1601	1,457	57·2	544	21·3	648	21·4
1640	1,638	64·3	488	19·1	421	16·5
1680	1,684	66·1	556	21·8	347	13·6

ing most of the magnates who were of any account enmeshed in the transaction of her own and the realm's affairs. . . .

The result was a power vacuum in England during the very years when a concurrence of fiscal, constitutional, political and religious grievances evoked widespread opposition to the Crown and made it necessary for that opposition to achieve some measure of co-ordinated action. Into that vacuum created by the temporary incapacity of the magnates poured the country gentry – not the brisk hard-bitten small gentry of Professor Tawney, nor yet the mouldy flea-bitten mere gentry of Professor Trevor-Roper – but the rich, well-educated knights and squires who sat in the Parliaments of James I and Charles I. . . .

['Storm over the Gentry', *Encounter*, x, 1958, reprinted in *Reappraisals in History*, 1961.]

Notes

1. The statistics that Tawney derives from the counting of manors are tabulated opposite. The counties in which the count was made are Bedfordshire, Hampshire, Hertfordshire, Surrey, Worcestershire, and the North Riding of Yorkshire (R. H. Tawney, 'The Rise of the Gentry, 1558–1640', *Economic History Review*, XI (1941), p. 22, n. 1).

2. J. P. Cooper, 'The Counting of Manors', *Economic History Review*, 2nd ser., VIII (1956), p. 385.

3. . . . When Tawney recomputed his figures for noble holdings to include all families ennobled between 1561 and 1640, his statistics lost their oddity, but the peerage regained its manors (see opposite). What seems striking to me is the difference in the statistical result which would have followed from the death without successors of a half-dozen rich peers, on the one hand, and a dozen well-chosen ennoblements, on the other.

4. Cooper, *op. cit.*, p. 388.

5. H. R. Trevor-Roper, *The Gentry*, pp. 38–9, 42–4.

6. Trevor-Roper is actually a little ambivalent on this point. See n. 8 below.

7. *Op. cit.*, p. 22.

8. After an elaborate portrayal in the grimmest hues of the economic horrors suffered by men who relied for their income on land rather than the Court (Trevor-Roper, *op. cit., passim*, esp. pp. 26–44), Trevor-Roper rather grudgingly acknowledges that 'the improving gentry survived, . . . weathered the economic storm', and by the seventeenth century 'were once again prosperous as before. Sometimes they were perhaps even more prosperous' (*ibid.*, p. 51). Yet these improving landlords play not even a minor role in Trevor-Roper's account of the revolution of the seventeenth century and of the events that precipitated

that revolution. Having belatedly spared them from economic damnation he promptly consigns them to political oblivion. 'They were the solid substance of rural society, its soundest members, and, because sound, generally unobtrusive' (ibid.). Trevor-Roper produces no proof to validate his equation between economic vigor and political passivity in the countryside; and it is not the sort of equation whose face value is so evident as to impose acquiescence. It does not coincide with what Sir John Neale has to say throughout his work and in a special chapter on the subject about 'The Quality of the House' of Commons in Elizabeth's day: J. E. Neale, *The Elizabethan House of Commons* (New Haven, 1950), esp. pp. 301–20. And it fits no better with what, thanks to Mrs Keeler, we now know about the members of the Long Parliament: Mary F. Keeler, *The Long Parliament 1640–1641: A Biographical Study of its Members*, Memoirs of the American Philosophical Society XXXVI (1954), I, 20–1, 22–7. Mrs Keeler's meticulous and painstaking studies of the individual biographies of all members of the Long Parliament in 1640–41 reveal two most widely shared traits. (1) The members were overwhelmingly local men. Eight out of nine members had local ties – mainly in the form of estates – in the region whence they came to Parliament (ibid., p. 20). (2) The members were extraordinarily rich. Of the four-fifths of the members on whom she has data 60 per cent had annual incomes of above £1,000; only 10 per cent *may* have had incomes below £500.

9. The conclusions arrived at in the following paragraph are based primarily on E. Kerridge, 'The Movement of Rent, 1540–1640', *Economic History Review*, 2nd ser., VI (1953); G. R. Batho, 'The Finances of an Elizabethan Nobleman: Henry Percy, 9th Earl of Northumberland', *Economic History Review*, 2nd ser., IX (1957); M. E. Finch, *The Wealth of Five Northamptonshire Families, 1540–1640*, Northamptonshire Record Soc. Publications, XIX.

10. According to Mrs Keeler, among the members of the House in 1640–41 there were over seventy men who were or had been deputy-lieutenants, 122 sheriffs, 219 justices of the peace and probably more, and 250 members of various local commissions. Keeler, op. cit., p. 18, Table 3.

11. See Neale, op. cit., p. 162, and Keeler, op. cit., p. 20, n. 99.

12. By far the best account of political attitudes of the 'good Parliament men' under the early Stuarts is that of Margaret Judson, *The Crisis of the Constitution* (New Brunswick, N.J., 1949), pp. 44–106.

13. For the education of the members of the House of Commons in the reign of Elizabeth I, see Neale, op. cit., pp. 302–6; for the education of the Commoners in the Long Parliament, Keeler, op. cit., pp. 27–8, and D. Brunton and D. H. Pennington, *Members of the Long Parliament* (Cambridge, Mass., 1954), pp. 6–7, 27. On the general question of upper-class education and service to the 'commonwealth', [J. H. Hexter] 'Education of the Aristocracy in the Renaissance', [*Reappraisals in History*, pp. 45–70].

14. *Statutes of the Realm*, 8 Edward IV, c. 2.

15. The term retainer has survived in the legal profession to describe a payment giving one a claim on the services of a lawyer.

5 Critique of the Trevor-Roper Thesis

P. ZAGORIN

I

... There are, it appears, two issues around which the current controversy turns:

1. Did the gentry rise, as Tawney maintains; that is to say, was there becoming preponderant in the century before 1640 a class of landed proprietors mostly occupying medium-size estates who, enriching themselves at the expense of the Crown, the older aristocracy, the church, and small tenants, managed their acres with a steady view to profit accumulation and were alert for favorable investment opportunities in industrial, commercial, and colonial enterprise?

2. What was the connection between the social and economic evolution of the gentry before 1640 (whatever that may have been) and the origin and course of the English revolution?

Now those who have followed the current controversy closely will probably have singled out various grounds for dissatisfaction with its results thus far. As Tawney's views have received far the widest attention and criticism, I shall, owing to limitations of space, say little respecting them at present. I shall only observe that besides Trevor-Roper's strictures, J. P. Cooper has recently shown his statistical data to contain deficiencies so serious as to make untenable the conclusions founded upon them. It may still be the case (I personally believe it is) that Tawney is in general correct or at any rate nearer the truth than his critics. But it is clear from Cooper's comments that in the form in which he has advanced his thesis, it has yet to be proved, and that some of its details must certainly be rejected.

What now of Trevor-Roper's counter-thesis that the condition of the gentry worsened during this period, except for a minority possessed of wealth from trade or court office, and that the English revolution was the act of this declining 'mere' gentry, whom exclusion from court favor and other sources of enrichment had maddened, led by their political vanguard, the Independents? Of this interpretation as a whole, it must be said that it is very inadequately supported; the account of the Independents, in particular, is scarcely more than a speculation, for the evidence offered in its behalf is too slight to entitle it to the name of a theory.

Trevor-Roper holds that only very exceptionally could agriculture enable a family to rise; office or trade, he declares, were essential to this result. While it may turn out that he is right, the weight of evidence at present strongly suggests the contrary. It is difficult to believe that the gentry as a whole – an order numbering thousands of landed proprietors – was in distress in the buoyant circumstances of the later sixteenth century, and the handful of instances he cites are quite incapable of demonstrating that such was the case. It is admitted by all, including Trevor-Roper, that during this period the yeomanry prospered and that numbers of them were entering the ranks of the gentry.[1] I can see no good reason why the factors that favoured this process should not have operated with equal or greater benefit to the gentry themselves; for if the gentry had a more expensive style of life to maintain and indulged more in noneconomic expenditure, they also had greater resources to deploy in the quest for agricultural profit. Moreover, there is no ground for believing, as Trevor-Roper would have us do, that the methods of careful saving and watchful estate management that enabled a Robert Loder to thrive did not extend to men with gentry tastes and a gentry status to keep up in the world. The Northamptonshire families recently studied by M. E. Finch employed just these methods. . . .[2]

In fact, if any one thing has been coming clear in recent research, it is that landed incomes, whether derived from rents or from direct farming, rose markedly towards the end of the sixteenth and in the earlier seventeenth centuries. . . .[3] The conclusion appears probable that land at this period might be an excellent investment and that prevailing economic tendencies favoured landlords, especially those capable of good estate management. There is nothing known at present about these tendencies that permits us to speak of the decline of the gentry as a whole.

I have not the space at my disposal to pursue and expose as illusory all the political metamorphoses through which the unfortunate gentry of the seventeenth century are made to pass under the wand of Trevor-Roper's conjectures.[4] I shall confine myself, therefore, to pointing out some of the reasons which make very questionable his interpretation of the revolution as the act of the declining gentry and their supposed leaders, the Independents.

There is, to begin with, the fact that the revolution began in 1640, with the meeting of the Long Parliament, not in 1645, the earliest time at which the Independents, in any of the meanings that may be ascribed to that term, became influential. It is, indeed, a curious explanation, which omits to account for the Long Parliament's fundamental and lasting legislation of 1640–41 and for the outbreak of the Civil War in 1642, as if these things were no part of the English revolution. And it is difficult to see how any claim to sufficiency can be made for a view that, in order to stress the role of the Independents, pays no attention to the important part taken at the outset by Presbyterians – by Denzil Holles, for example, who had done his best, says Gardiner, 'to reduce Royal authority to a cipher', or by Sir Thomas Barrington and some of his relatives and connections in the Commons, many of whom were men of considerable wealth.[5]

Besides this, the various correspondences that this interpretation sets up between party alignments and social groups can all be shown to have little or no foundation. Having first divided the gentry into a declining majority and an advancing minority enjoying, besides its landed income, the profits of office or trade, Trevor-Roper then identifies the former with the Independents, whom he calls the 'country' party of excluded 'mere' gentry; the latter furnish the basis both of Royalism and, later, of opposition to the domination the Independents gained.[6] On this showing, the 'mere' gentry ought mainly to be found opposing the King; the Independent leaders ought to have consisted mainly of 'mere' gentry; and Crown officials ought to have been mainly Royalists. Each of these equations, however, admits of too many and too important exceptions to be acceptable.

If, for instance, we look for specimens of lesser gentry having nothing but an income from land, and that income small – in the neighbourhood of perhaps £200 per annum – we shall find many score in the Welsh counties and in Devon. Yet the Welsh gentry were predominantly Royalists.[7] As for the gentry of Devon, Trevor-Roper has himself, when controverting Tawney's thesis, pointed to their considerable indebtedness on the eve of the Civil War. He has failed to notice, however, that the evidence for this fact works also against his own interpretation of the revolution. For if the latter is right, these encumbered landlords of Devon ought to have opposed the King and looked to help themselves from the spoils of a Parliamentarian victory. But they did not. They were Royalists; and the very source which informs us of their mortgage debt consists of Royalist composition papers – documents relating to the estates of men fined for taking the King's side in the Civil War.[8]

Let us see, next, whether the leading Independents consisted of 'mere' gentry, taking the Independents in the House of Commons as a case in point. . . . We shall adopt the usage of historians of Parliament and consider as Independents – and, indeed, as their leading body, regarded as a political force – the 209 members who retained their seats in the purged remnant of the Long Parliament, the Rump. . . .[9]

In most respects, the Rump was a cross section of the Commons as originally elected in 1640, when the majority was composed of substantial landed gentlemen, many from families with a Parliamentary record. 'There was as little sign of class division' in the Rump, we are told, 'as at the outbreak of war'. Its 'main characteristic . . . was its lack of characteristics'. . . .[10]

An examination of the Rump's policies, would, I think, provide additional matter by which the incorrectness of Trevor-Roper's conception of the Commonwealth could be demonstrated. But such a task is too long to be undertaken here. One particular point, however, may be noticed. Trevor-Roper has fancied that the essence of the political outlook of the excluded 'mere' gentry and its Independent leaders was decentralization. Yet the Independents, as a little reflection upon the facts makes plain, stood in certain fundamental ways for just the opposite policy. Though they had rebelled against the despotism of Charles I, they themselves created a powerful central authority under the Commonwealth – one far more effective than that of their Stuart predecessors. A Council of State possessed of extensive powers and whose wide-ranging and multifarious activities are easily perceived from a perusal of its records; extraordinary courts of justice set up to try political offenders; elaborate tax and other financial ordinances whose execution was supervised from the capital by committees responsible to Parliament; toleration itself possible only when the government's strong hand was extended to secure peaceable men in the profession of their religious beliefs – these do not suggest a decentralized or a weak authority. Indeed, the position of the Independents in this respect can be seen from the very beginning of their influence when they succeeded in 1645, under the spur of political and military necessity, in carrying the ordinance that established the New Model Army. For what was the significance of that measure? It meant the installment of a central and unified military command in place of the former fragmented control of fighting forces and the absorption of county and regional soldiery into a national army. It represented, in short, the triumph of a national viewpoint over a county viewpoint, and was a decisive victory for the center.[11]

Finally, let us inquire whether the royal officials in the Long Parliament – those fortunate insiders in the distribution of court benefits from which the 'mere' gentry had been excluded – were Royalists, as most of them should have been if Trevor-Roper's interpretation is correct. According to the recent account of M. F. Keeler, twenty-seven royal officials were among the original members of the Commons in 1640–41; about half of these, she says, 'supported the King, two managed to straddle, and ten were Parliamentarians'.[12] Ten is a respectable figure; but by another count which makes no pretence at being exhaustive, though it probably includes as officials some whom Keeler did not, the number of royal opponents is increased to fifteen. ...

We have now noticed some of the reasons that make it necessary to reject Trevor-Roper's interpretation of the revolution. His thesis, it must be said in conclusion, suffers not only from the specific deficiencies that have been indicated, but is quite implausible when taken as a whole. The resentment at exclusion from court office and financial benefits which he alleges to be the basis of the revolutionary course pursued by the 'mere' gentry and the Independents seems to me incapable of accounting for events of the magnitude of the Civil War and its consequences. The demand for the gains of office and for admission to the inner circles of influence may result in a Fronde; but it could not sow the dragon's teeth of a New Model Army and bring a king to the block in the name of the sovereign people. A declining order such as he paints the gentry does not beget leaders of the granite mold of Oliver Cromwell; it produces Catilines, sterile conspirators and exiles from an irretrievable past ready to venture all in a single desperate gamble. If the revolution were the profitless anarchy Trevor-Roper has imagined it to be it could not have achieved the wonderful ferment of thought that made these two decades a heroic age of the English intellect. If it were the compounded failure he has pronounced it, it could not have laid the foundation of the liberal and parliamentary order in which its significance largely consists. ...[13]

II

First, then, it seems likely that English social structure was being broadly reshaped during the sixteenth and seventeenth centuries. On this general point, Tawney is probably right, despite the criticisms that are justifiably directed against his statistics and the dubious character of several of his formulations. Certainly, the evidence economic historians have assembled to demonstrate that such a process was occurring is massive. Its basis lay in various economic changes that functioned as a single interacting complex to achieve a common result. The price revolution; the greatly increasing scale of capital investment; the development of colonial enterprise; the rapid growth of those sectors of the economy in which investment for profit accumulation was taking place; the introduction of new industries, particularly in mineral extraction and metals, and the application of new technical methods to older industries, all on a scale so great as to have been described by J. U. Nef as an 'industrial revolution';[14] the immense development of London; the further elaboration of the division of labor in the crafts and the growing decrepitude of gild regulation in the textile industry – such were some of the factors which were helping to stratify English society in a fresh pattern.

To formulate their effects on the social structure in generalizations sufficiently precise and careful of nuances to do full justice to the complexity of the subject is extremely difficult. But their tendency, none the less, seems clear. It was to give to the men whose activity they reflected – men in a position to deploy capital in agriculture, trade, and industry – the command of social life. By the end of the seventeenth century, these changes had stamped upon the aristocracy of titled and armigerous landlords who continued to form the apex of the social and political hierarchy a new character that set them apart from their contemporaries in every other European monarchy. This is what struck Tocqueville when he reflected in his profound work, *L'Ancien Régime*, on the divergent natures of the English and French dominant classes. He says of England:[15]

> ... you will find from the seventeenth century, the feudal system substantially abolished, classes which overlap, nobility of birth set on one side, aristocracy thrown open, wealth as the source of power. ... Seventeenth-century England was already a quite modern nation which had merely preserved in its heart, and as it were embalmed, some relics of the Middle Ages.

There does not seem to be anything in these changes, however, that necessarily requires that their character should be expressed in the terms in which the disputants over the gentry have conducted some of their argument. We need not, for example, suppose that the economic decline of the Elizabethan peerage was an indispensable condition of the formation of this new dominant class. Nor is it profitable in this connection to distinguish peers from gentry, gentry from wealthy merchants, or gentry engaged exclusively in agriculture from those occupied also in commercial or industrial enterprise. Neither is it very material that the rise or progress of landed families should often have been made possible by the gains derived from trade or office. Such distinctions, though illuminating and even indispensable in other contexts, are not particularly relevant in this one. The class whose formation is the present focus of interest was being continuously recruited, and it naturally comprised diverse elements as to status, wealth, and source of income. But despite these and other differences, its members were species of the same genus. They constituted a single economic class, for what they had in common was the possession of capital that they employed for the end of profit and further accumulation.

What was the connection between these changes and the genesis of the English revolution? According to some historians, the Civil War was a struggle for state power between the newly forming class and semifeudal landlords and monarchy ruling an obsolete order whose overthrow was necessary for the consolidation of a higher mode of production.[16] I do not think this analysis is correct, however, and it seems doubtful even that it would have been put forward had not the French Revolution come to be mistakenly accepted, under Marx's influence, as a classic model to which the interpretation of other revolutions described as 'bourgeois' must necessarily conform.[17] But there is not, in fact, any model pattern of a bourgeois revolution, and while the investigation of analogies can be most illuminating, there are far more differences between the English and French revolutions than similarities. A study of the upper layers of the Parliamentarian and Royalist parties leads to a different view of the conflict. While it is very likely true, as David Mathew has written, that 'the King had all the archaic forces . . . the adventurers and younger sons, and all those who, like the Elizabethans, felt branded by the accusation of disloyalty',[18] there were on his side as well as on Parliament's numerous representatives of the most advanced economic developments of the age. Among the gentry, for instance, could be found plenty of Royalists of prosperous and thriving families. Clarendon remarked that 'the revenue of too many of the court consisted principally in enclosures and improvements of that nature'; and he noted that the troop of noblemen and gentlemen who formed the King's guard at the battle of Edgehill possessed estates and revenues equal to those of all the members who remained in both houses of Parliament.[19] Indeed, the majority of the gentry was probably for the King.[20]

The great trading centres, too, on whose seditious spirit Clarendon and Hobbes commented,[21] were by no means unanimously for Parliament.[22] In London though the largest part of the city was Parliamentarian, the Lord Mayor and most of the aldermen at the end of 1641 were for the King.[23] Newcastle, whose great coal owners and merchants were themselves frequently of important gentry families, seems to have been predominantly Royalist.[24] At Bristol, which was held for Parliament, there were wealthy Royalists who had occupied the highest offices in the city and the Society of Merchant Venturers. . . .[25] It may well be that the structure of commerce and the relation of its various sections, whether beneficial or detrimental, to the action of the Crown and council had much to do with determining the political stand that men such as these took up. But the fact remains that a number of important capitalists were Royalists, even if they became so because they enjoyed financial privileges and profits as customs farmers or recipients of royal grants and licenses.

Such considerations show that the genesis of the English revolution is not to be sought in a class struggle – for the leading sections of both sides in the Civil War included many who were drawn from the same economic class, whose development had been steadily proceeding during the preceding century. It is to be found, rather, in a conflict within this class among England's governing groups. Thus, the explanation of the revolution's origin turns on an analysis of this conflict.

During the reigns of James I and Charles I to the eve of the Civil War the nation's ruling groups were increasingly divided into what may be called, in the good old language of the seventeenth century, the Court and the Country, and their sharpening antagonism determined the political strife of nearly forty years.[26] The material is not yet at hand to depict fully the nature of these parties and the combinations and permutations within them at various stages to 1640. We may say, however, that, on the one hand, was the Court with its network of ministers, courtiers, officials and their clients and connections throughout the land; and on the other, the Country composed of landed proprietors, both peers and gentry, and merchants outside the range of Court benefit or antagonized by its policies. While it is a conspicuous merit of Trevor-Roper's interpretation to have restored the Court–Country relation to the place of central importance it deserves in the treatment of the seventeenth century, the position of the two parties is far from adequately represented, as his own view implies, as one of 'insiders' versus 'outsiders'. Nor did the Country consist, as he would suggest, of lesser gentry and declining men whose maimed fortunes could be mended only by access to office and favour or by the seizure of power. Its leadership centred, rather, in important peers and gentlemen. It included at different times such noblemen as the third Earl of Southampton, the first Earl of Clare, the second Earl of Warwick, the fourth Earl of Lincoln and the second Earl of Hertford. It numbered, as during the opposition to the forced loan of 1626–27, many wealthy and influential landlords.[27]

The elements forming these parties were by no means wholly fixed, of course. Within each, shifting groupings existed, and men also passed from the Court to the Country, as did Sir John Eliot in 1625–26, and from the Country to the Court, as did Sir Thomas Wentworth in 1628. . . .[28] Only in the later 1630s, as the affairs of Charles I moved to a crisis, would an unprecedented political stirring appear, and then Puritanism was one of the means through which this broadening political consciousness was linked largely to the Country.

No definite social basis for the Court–Country division is discernible. Among the Country, it is true, could be found some who opposed the regulatory and protective measures that the Crown attempted to impose on economic activity; and with Nef, we may, if we like, describe the opposition to these measures as 'an economic conflict between the Stuart kings and some of their most powerful subjects, the leading town merchants and the improving landlords'.[29] But I do not think we can connect it with some advanced form of enterprise that necessitated those engaged therein to demand on principle a freedom from state control. The error of such an opinion is shown by the support the Crown itself extended, with fiscal ends in view, to progressive undertakings like the draining of the fens or the enclosure of royal forests.[30] There was, indeed, little consistency in the economic policies pursued by the Stuart monarchy, and the resistance to them rose chiefly from the threat to the security of vested property that substantial landed and corporate interests perceived in royal administrative activity, whether in the form of enclosure commissions or in grants of monopoly to rings of projectors. Criticism of the Government on this point was but one of several grievances that set the various sections of the Country apart from the court. Resentment at the sway of a favourite and exclusion from office; Puritan dislike of the Established Church, whose ceremonies and liturgy were thought to retain the mark of the Roman anti-Christ and whose rule under the masterful primateship of Laud aroused the bitterest anti-clerical feeling; condemnation of an ineffectual foreign policy suspected of inclining secretly towards Spain and popery; the conviction that the King was using his prerogative to subvert the law and destroy the liberty of the subject – such were some of the other differences that drove the Country to opposition. While the Court formed the executive and controlled the central government, the Country's influence was paramount in local government and the House of Commons. Through its dominance in that body, the Country made Parliament not only a forum in which to demand the redress of national grievances, but also an instrument of disaffection in the state.

In the later 1630s, with the Court pulling one way and the Country another, the process of government verged on paralysis. Central government and local government were deadlocked, as everywhere sheriffs, lieutenants, deputy-lieutenants, and justices increasingly dragged their feet or showed active insubordination in the execution of the measures with which the King's Council charged them. Then the outbreak of the Scottish rebellion created the emergency that broke the deadlock. At this perilous juncture, the King found no way left but to summon the Long Parliament.

With its convening, the Country triumphed, and the demoralized Court groupings began to disintegrate. It is striking with what unity the representatives of England's dominant class in Parliament went to work in 1640-42 to repudiate all that the King had done. Amidst wide agreement, men who not two years later were to take opposite sides in the Civil War abolished some of the highest prerogative powers of the Crown and struck down forever the system of paternal rule, with its infringement on vested property interests: ship money, conciliar courts, patents of monopoly, forest laws, and enclosure commissions that Archbishop Laud, says Clarendon, 'did a little too much countenance'....[31] Thenceforth, no king could retain rule in England except by governing in conformity with the wishes of Parliament and those for whom it spoke.

All this the members achieved in near unanimity. But already deep differences such as the church question were dividing the victorious Country, and now a fresh and unforeseen issue arose that led to civil war. For when the great Irish insurrection broke out in October 1641, it became necessary to raise an army for its suppression. But who was to control it? The King had given up much, but he steadfastly refused to abandon this crux of his prerogative, his legal right to command his army; while Parliament was naturally unwilling to entrust him with a sword whose edge he might well turn against his political enemies. On this issue, no agreement proved possible. So King and Parliament each started to recruit forces and the Civil War began.[32]

With armed conflict imminent, the Country, its unity already much impaired, fell to pieces and the political alignment of the nation was re-formed, as Royalist and Parliamentarian emerged. These parties of the Civil War did not correspond to the earlier division of Court and Country. In the dominant class, many previous Country opponents of the King became Royalists. Such men thought change had gone far enough, and they dreaded the possible consequences of a military rebellion against the King, the center of the whole hierarchy of rank and privilege that their interests and sentiments were bound up with....

The character of the first stage in the social history of the English revolution was thus determined by the split within the dominant class out of which the conflict took its rise....

In short, while momentous political issues were at stake, no social change was yet in question at this stage. Only with the formation of the New Model Army and the unforeseen complications that followed its victory would a second stage open. Then the spokesmen of classes either excluded from the political nation or having a place only on its margins would strive for the first time to seize the initiative. The Levellers, allied with the army radicalism they had called into being, would attempt to make the constitutional–political revolution of 1640–41 the prologue to the creation of a democratic republic and would seek the destruction of the entire existing system of privilege.

III

This and the following stages in the revolution's social history cannot be discussed within the limits of this paper, but several general points may be noticed by way of conclusion. The greatest single event of the revolutionary decades was the trial and execution of the King. This act demonstrated as nothing else did the mighty insurgent temper that had been conjured up in the heat of civil war, and it gave unforgettable symbolic expression to the revolutionary belief in the sovereignty of the people. But the necessity for such a deed, for which Cromwell and his allies and followers were responsible, showed how far out of control the political situation had gone. Cromwell tried to avoid the terrible step, for the Independent leaders had no material interest in destroying kingship, the institution that guaranteed the regime of property and order of which they were beneficiaries. Socially and economically, they and their chief supporters among the gentry and in the towns seem indistinguishable from the Presbyterians who opposed them. But their inability to agree on a political and religious settlement either with the Presbyterians or with the defeated King finally left them no choice but to proceed alone in safeguarding the ends that they conceived the war had been fought for. It was the increasing fragmentation of the dominant class – the overthrow and exclusion of the Royalists, then the divisions that arose in the leadership of the Parliamentarian cause – that provided the opportunity for the radical rank and file to make its influence felt and led to the politically disastrous move of ending the monarchy.

['The Social Interpretation of the English Revolution', *Journal of Economic History*, XIX, 1959.]

Notes

1. Cf. M. Campbell, *The English Yeoman* (New Haven: Yale University Press, 1942) and J. Thirsk in *Victoria County History, Leicestershire* (3 vols.; London, 1907–55), II, pp. 207–9; Trevor-Roper, *The Gentry*, p. 9.

2. Trevor-Roper, *The Gentry*, pp. 9–10; *Robert Loder's Farm Accounts 1610–1620*, ed. G. E. Fussell, in *Camden Society*, 3rd ser., LIII (1936); Finch, *Five Northamptonshire Families*.

3. Cf. Habakkuk, Preface to Finch, *op. cit.*, p. xiv. Trevor-Roper's description of economic conditions shows a curious inconsistency. On the one hand, 'in the reign of Elizabeth . . . the great rise in rents had not yet begun' and 'the whole position of the landowning class must sometimes have seemed perilous . . . although, after 1590, rentals seem generally to have risen . . .' On the other hand, 'from about 1580 the rents of land show a marked rise which continues till the end of the price revolution in the middle of the seventeenth century'. *The Gentry*, pp. 13, 51. Similarly, on the one hand, there was a 'general economic depression' in the decade after 1600; on the other hand, the peace of 1604 with Spain 'had produced a period of unexampled prosperity . . .' *Ibid.*, pp. 13, 27.

4. Cf. Part V of his essay. First, the non-official gentry are described as resentful and opposed to Elizabeth after 1590. On the strength of a single

reference to Goodman's *Court of James I*, they are next shown greeting King James as their saviour, only to turn against him as the betrayer of their hopes. A reference to Holles's *Memorials* makes possible the statement that the 'mere gentry' now change their attitude towards Elizabeth, who becomes for them the patron saint of a Golden Age. (We are not informed why Gervase Holles, the author of these *Memorials*, should, as a spokesman of the oppressed 'mere gentry', have been a Royalist in the Civil War.) A further feat of prestidigitation enables the 'radical recusant gentry, after their vain risings in *1603–5*', to relapse 'into Roman Catholic quietism and become the most devoted royalists'; while the 'radical puritan gentry' who killed the King and created the republic relapse after 1660 'into gentry quietism' and become 'high-flying, non-resisting tories'.

5. S. R. Gardiner, *History of England, 1603–1642* (10 vols.; London: Longmans, Green, 1887), x, p. 129. On Barrington and Holles, see J. H. Hexter, *The Reign of King Pym* (Cambridge, Mass.: Harvard University Press, 1941), and M. F. Keeler, *The Long Parliament 1640–1641: a Biographical Study of its Members* (Philadelphia: American Philosophical Society, 1954), s.v.

Holles was one of the Presbyterian leaders; cf. S. R. Gardiner, *History of the Great Civil War* (4 vols.; London: Longmans, 1898), III, p. 216, and D. Holles, *Memoirs* (London, 1699).

6. *The Gentry*, pp. 26 ff., 32–4.

7. A. H. Dodd, 'Nerth y Committee', *Studies in Stuart Wales* (Cardiff: University of Wales Press, 1952), pp. 2–4, 111–12.

8. Trevor-Roper, *The Gentry*, p. 41. W. G. Hoskins, 'The Estates of the Caroline Gentry', in W. G. Hoskins and H. P. R. Finberg, *Devonshire Studies* (London: Cape, 1952), p. 353. An equally striking instance is Sir John Oglander, whom Trevor-Roper appears to regard as the very prototype of the 'mere' gentry and whose well-known lament about his economic difficulties he cites (*The Gentry*, p. 26). Yet this classical declining country gentleman, who had neither office, nor trade, nor the law as strings to his bow, was a Royalist.

9. D. Brunton and D. H. Pennington, *Members of the Long Parliament* (London: Allen & Unwin, 1954), p. 41.

10. *Op. cit.*, pp. 52, 182, 45–7.

11. Cf. A. M. Everitt, *The Country Committee of Kent in the Civil War* (Leicester: University College, 1957), pp. 25–30, for a suggestive account of how the triumph of the centre was reflected in the changing composition of the Committee of Kent.

12. *The Long Parliament*, p. 22; cf. also Table 5.

13. For a similar view of the significance of the English revolution, cf., *inter alia*, C. H. McIlwain, *The High Court of Parliament and its Supremacy* (New Haven: Yale University Press, 1910); D. L. Keir, *The Constitutional History of Modern Britain* (London: A. and C. Black, 1938), pp. 230–3; and M. A. Thompson, *A Constitutional History of England 1642–1801* (London: Methuen, 1938), pp. 53–5.

14. J. U. Nef, *Industry and Government in France and England 1540–1640* (Philadelphia: American Philosophical Society, 1940), pp. 1, 145.

15. *L'ancien régime*, trans. M. Patterson (Oxford: Basil Blackwell, 1947), p. 21.

16. C. Hill, *The English Revolution 1640* (3rd rev. edn.; London: Lawrence & Wishart, 1955); and C. Hill and E. Dell, *The Good Old Cause* (London: Lawrence & Wishart, 1950): cf. the conclusions of a conference of British Marxist historians in 1947, cited in Fisher, 'The Sixteenth and Seventeenth Centuries: The Dark Ages in English Economic History?', *Economica*, n.s., XXXIV (1957), pp. 5–6.

17. Hill, *The English Revolution*, p. 6.

18. *The Age of Charles I*, p. 323.

19. *History of the Rebellion*, ed. W. D. Macray (6 vols; Oxford: Clarendon Press, 1888), I, p. 204; VI, p. 74; cf. Sir Philip Warwicke, *Memoires of the Reign of King Charles I* (2nd edn.; London, 1702), pp. 230–1.

20. This is the general impression derived from Clarendon; cf., besides, his remarks about particular counties (thus, *History*, IV, 340; VII, 157), his statement, *ibid.*, VII, 99, that 'most of the gentry ... throughout the Kingdom' was 'engaged against' Parliament. Clarendon was, of course, prejudiced and could have been wrong. Cf. also in support of this impression Warwick, *Memoires*, pp. 216–18; Sir John Oglander, *A Royalist's Notebook*, ed. F. Bamford (London: Constable, 1938), pp. 104, 105–6; Lucy Hutchinson, *Memoirs of the Life of Colonel Hutchinson*, ed. C. H. Firth (2 vols.; London: 1885), I, p. 141; R. Baxter, *Autobiography* (Everyman edn., London: Dent, 1931), p. 34. Many other contemporary testimonies to the same effect might be cited.

21. Clarendon, *History*, V, p. 385; T. Hobbes, *Behemoth*, in F. Maseres, *Select Tracts* (2 parts; London: R. Bickerstaff, 1815), II, pp. 459, 477, 576.

22. Cf. P. Hardacre, *The Royalists during the Puritan Revolution* (The Hague: Martinus Nijhoff, 1956), pp. 5–6.

23. Gardiner, *History of England, 1603–1642*, X, pp. 83, 107–8; but cf. M. Wren, 'The Disputed Elections in London in 1641', *English Historical Review*, LXIV (1949). Clarendon remarks (*History*, IV, 340) on the strength of Royalist attachment among the 'most important citizens of London' in the controversy over the Militia Bill.

24. *Extracts rom the Records of the Company of Hostment at Newcastle-upon-Tyne*, ed. F. W. Dendy (*Surtees Society*, vol. CV [1901]), pp. 80–3. Among the Newcastle Royalists were such important colliery owners and financiers as Sir John Marley, Sir John Mennes, Sir Thomas Riddell, Sir Francis Anderson, the Tempests, the Coles, and the Lidrells (*Records of the Committee for Compounding ... in Durham and Northumberland*, ed. R. Welford (*Surtees Society*, vol. XCI [1905]), s.v.

25. For Royalism in Bristol, see J. Latimer *The Annals of Bristol in the Seventeenth Century* (Bristol: W. George's Sons, 1900), *passim*. Bristol's original

PROBLEMS OF HISTORIOGRAPHY

members in the Long Parliament, Humphrey Hooke and Richard Long, were both Royalists. On their expulsion from the House of Commons the city elected two other Royalists, John Glanville and John Taylor, *ibid.*, p. 157; cf. Brunton and Pennington, *Members of the Long Parliament*, p. 222. Also the biographical accounts of Bristol merchants in *The Deposition Books of Bristol, 1643-1647*, ed. H. E. Nott (Bristol Record Society, vol. VI [1935]), App. I; *Records Relating to the Society of Merchant Venturers of . . . Bristol*, ed. P. McGrath (Bristol Record Society, vol. XVII [1952]), p. xxx; and the remarks of P. McGrath, *Merchants and Merchandise in Seventeenth Century Bristol* (Bristol Record Society, vol. XIX [1955]), pp. xxvi-xxviii. Perhaps the outstanding Bristol Royalist was Humphrey Hooke, a city magnate, owner of much landed property, twice mayor and seven times master of the Society of Merchant Venturers.

26. This distinction was made in the sense indicated above in the 1620s. W. Notestein, 'The Winning of the Initiative by the House of Commons', *Proceedings of the British Academy*, XI (1924-25), p. 152 n. Sir John Eliot employed it (H. Hulme, *The Life of Sir John Eliot* [London: Allen & Unwin, 1957], *passim*), as did Clarendon (e.g. *History*, IV, p. 180). The terms came into general use after the Restoration; cf. O. Airy, ed., *Burnet's History of My Own Time*, Part I: *The Reign of Charles II* (2 vols.; Oxford: Clarendon Press, 1897), I, p. 489; II, p. 82 n.; H. C. Foxcroft, *A Supplement to Burnet's History* (Oxford: Clarendon Press, 1902), pp. 99 n., 151, 258; and T. B. Macaulay, *The History of England from the Accession of James II* (5 vols.; Philadelphia, n.d.), I, p. 190.

27. For the opposition among the peers, cf. C. H. Firth, *The House of Lords during the Civil War* (London: Longmans, 1910), ch. ii. On the resistance of the gentry to the forced loan, see Gardiner, *History of England*, VI, pp. 155-57.

28. For Eliot, see Hulme, *Sir John Eliot*, chs. v-vi, and J. N. Ball, 'Sir John Eliot at the Oxford Parliament, 1625', *Bulletin of the Institute of Historical Research*, XXVIII (1955); for Wentworth, Gardiner, *History of England, 1604-1642*, VI, pp. 126-7; VII, pp. 25-7.

29. Nef, *Industry and Government*, p. 149.

30. Cf. H. C. Darby, *The Draining of the Fens* (Cambridge: University Press, 1940), pp. 38-64. The attempt in pursuance of the King's commands to enclose royal forests in Dorset, Wiltshire and Gloucestershire led to considerable resistance; cf. D. G. C. Allan, 'The Rising in the West, 1628-1631', *Economic History Review*, 2nd ser., V (1952).

31. *History*, I, p. 204.

32. Cf. C. V. Wedgwood, 'The Causes of the English Civil War, a New Analysis', *History Today*, V (1955).

6 The Bourgeois Revolution Reconsidered
C. HILL

... For the landowning classes – at all levels, from peers down to free-holders – this century marks the watershed, when their fate was decided: thrift, skill and luck could bring quick riches; extravagance and bad luck could be fatal. Many factors were involved: a fortunate geographic location, in a sheep-farming or clothing area, access to markets or to cheap water transport; the discovery of minerals on an estate.... Gaining a lucrative office at Court, as Professor Trevor-Roper has conclusively shown, could count as luck; but it is also certain that as many were ruined drawing blanks in the lottery of an expensive Court as made their fortunes there. To have a successful lawyer or merchant in the family, or to make a judicious marriage into either of these forms of wealth, may be counted either as luck or as skill. Skill consisted in keeping a careful watch on profits and losses, in good book-keeping, in checking and shortening the duration of leases, in exacting exorbitant entry fines, in watching the markets. Professor Tawney has maintained, not implausibly, that such qualities were more likely to be found among lesser landowning families than in the great noble households with their feudal traditions of lavish hospitality....

It seems clear that families with habits of conspicuous consumption would take longer to adjust to modern business methods than the lesser landowners. But Professor Trevor-Roper is right in maintaining that the greater landowners (particularly the peers) had enormous reserves to draw on. Once they took in hand the reorganization of their estates, they soon left behind the lesser men, whose rate of growth was more gradual. The recently published family papers of the Herberts and the Percys suggest that a drastic financial overhaul took place in both these families, between 1590 and 1610, and 1611 and 1615 respectively.[1]

Given the lack of entirely convincing statistical proof (on both sides), the most solid argument in favour of Professor Tawney's thesis is the fact that contemporaries believed that a substantial part of the gentry was rising economically. Professor Tawney quotes the Venetian ambassadors, Bacon, Raleigh, Goodman, Selden and Wilson; one might add Sir Henry Spelman, Francis Quarles, Henry Parker, Henry Ireton and Gerard Winstanley. In his *Oceana* (1656) Harrington was merely summing up and systematizing ideas which had been current for a long time; even his conclusion that the acquisition of land by the gentry and yeomanry inevitably led to a shift in political power had been anticipated by the peer who said in 1628 that the House of Commons could buy out the Lords thrice over. . . .[2]

The Parliamentary areas were the South and the East, both economically advanced, while the strength of the royalists lay in the still half-feudal North and West. All the big towns were parliamentarian; though often (as in London) their ruling oligarchies were for the King and had to be ousted before the will of the majority of citizens could prevail. Only one or two cathedral towns, such as Oxford and Chester, were royalist. The ports were all for Parliament. The King's advance on London in 1643 was checked by the resistance of Plymouth, Gloucester and Hull. The Navy went over solidly to Parliament. The firm support which the mass of Londoners always gave Parliament was decisive, because of the economic pre-eminence of the capital. After he had taken Bristol, Charles I tried to build it up as a rival export centre, but failed completely. The clothiers of the South-West continued to send their cloth across the battle lines to London.

The same pattern is repeated in the counties. In Sussex, Lancashire and Yorkshire the industrial areas were for Parliament, the agricultural areas for the King. In Yorkshire, the clothing town of Bradford rallied the surrounding countryside, forcing the reluctant Fairfax to lead them into action against the King. In Staffordshire, a group known as the Moorlanders, 'led by a person of low quality', bore the brunt of the early fighting.[3] It was the London trained bands who checked the royalist advance at Turnham Green in 1642, and later marched across England to raise the siege of Gloucester in 1643. The yeoman cavalry volunteer was as typical of the Parliamentarian party as were Newcastle's Whitecoats (his tenants and dependants) of the Royalists.

At first troops raised in the more lawless frontier regions and led by their own gentry provided better soldiers than the units levied by Parliament. Oliver Cromwell made his mark by appointing officers solely for their military efficiency, regardless of social status or political or religious convictions (so long as a man had 'the root of the matter in him'). . . . Cromwell's recruitment policy was the chief reason for his first military successes. But most of the Parliamentarian army leaders had been appointed for social reasons and lacked enthusiasm for the war. Before it could be won, Cromwell and his supporters had to secure the 'Self-denying ordinance' which dismissed all members of

Parliament from their military appointments. Peers and others who owed their commands to social status had to retire. The New Model Army of the career open to the talents was created.

Cromwell's victory in the Commons was made possible by the support for his policy which the logic of war imposed at the local level. We still know too little about local administration during the Civil War. But in two widely separated counties which have been studied in depth we find the same picture.[4] At first the County Committee was controlled by the old ruling families, mainly concerned to use the local militia to protect their own property, and not at all anxious to wage all-out war on the King. But gradually a nucleus was formed among those engaged in actual fighting who, in the interests of military efficiency, could not afford to take account of social considerations. New blood appeared among the county leaders, drawn from the lesser gentry and even the common people. The win-the-war party looked to London for leadership, to lower social groups in the counties for support. As in the French Revolution, the driving force came from the 'middling sort' of the capital, forcing the Parliamentary leaders to adopt ever more radical courses.

At Westminster the picture is the same. It used to be thought that the conflict between 'Presbyterians' and 'Independents' was purely religious, but this view is wrong. The 'Presbyterians' were the compromise-peace party, the 'Independents' the win-the-war party; the latter supported Cromwell's demand for an army of volunteers chosen regardless of political or religious views, and for freedom of discussion and organization ('religious toleration'), not only in the Army, but also outside it. . . .

Cromwell's victory introduced a new power into politics: the New Model Army, nationally recruited, nationally controlled and financed, which replaced the county levies commanded by their own local gentry. The Presbyterian establishment, which was designed by Parliament to replace episcopacy, never really worked. For a few years there was effective toleration and no censorship: those were years of intoxicating discussion, of bold political speculation, in the course of which, almost for the first time, we hear the authentic voice of ordinary men and women in politics.[5]

However, the 'Presbyterians' were right: the new forces proved difficult for the 'Independents' to control. From 1646 a democratic party, the Levellers, appeared in London, who advocated manhood suffrage, redistribution of the franchise, the abolition of monarchy and

House of Lords, abolition of tithes (and hence of an established church), law reform, the ending of the privileges of the great trading companies and of corporate towns, and radical economic reforms. They found support from the artisans and apprentices of London and from the Army, and were beginning to extend their propaganda activity to the rest of the country when they were ruthlessly suppressed by Cromwell and his generals in 1649. . . . After the suppression of the Levellers the Government rested on the narrow base of a military dictatorship, and all later attempts to extend this base were towards the right.

['*La Révolution anglaise du XVIIe siècle (Essai d'Interprétation)*', *Revue Historique*, CCXXI, 1959 (retranslated).]

Notes

1. E. Kerridge, ed., 'Surveys of the Manors of Philip, 1st Earl of Pembroke', *Wiltshire Archaeological Society*, 1953; 'The Movement of Rent', *Economic History Review*, 2nd ser., VII, pp. 25, 30; M. E. James, ed., *Estate Accounts of the Earls of Northumberland, 1562–1637*, Surtees Soc., 1955; G. R. Batho, 'The Finances of an Elizabethan Nobleman', *Economic History Review*, 2nd ser., IX (1957); M. E. Finch, *The Wealth of Five Northamptonshire Families, 1540–1640*, Northants. Rec. Soc., 1956. See also H. Percy, 9th Earl of Northumberland, *Advice to His Son* (ed. G. B. Harrison, 1930), pp. 80–4.

2. T. Birch, ed., *The Court and Times of Charles I*, I, p. 331.

3. See B. S. Manning's remarks in the course of a discussion on 'Revolutions in the Seventeenth Century' reported on in *Past and Present*, 13, p. 70, and D. H. Pennington and I. A. Roots, *The Committee at Stafford, 1643–1645*, 1957, p. lxii.

4. *Op. cit.*; A. M. Everitt, *The County Committee of Kent in the Civil War*, 1957; see also A. C. Wood, *Nottinghamshire in the Civil War*, 1937, and A. H. Dodd, *Studies in Stuart Wales*, 1952.

5. D. M. Wolfe, *Milton in the Puritan Revolution*, 1941; K. V. Thomas, 'Women and the Civil War Sects', *Past and Present*, 13.

7 The Crisis of the Aristocracy

L. STONE

The socio-political breakdown of 1640–42 had three main causes. The first was a long-term decline in respect for and obedience to the Monarchy, caused partly by the personal ineptitude of kings, partly by growing financial impoverishment, partly by structural defects in the Court system, and partly by the widening gap between the moral standards, aspirations, and way of life of the Court and those of the Country. This movement began in the latter years of Elizabeth, gathered impetus under James, became an avalanche under Buckingham and could not be arrested by Charles after 1629. The second was the failure of the Established Church to comprehend within itself all but the Roman Catholics. Elizabeth's wilful refusal to reform scandalous clerical abuses and her encouragement of Whitgift's persecution of the Puritans was followed first by the successful sabotage by the bishops of any chance of compromise at the Hampton Court conference, and then by the seizure of power within the Church by a strongly High Church party. Between them, Elizabeth, Whitgift and Laud managed to alienate from the Anglican Church an ever-increasing body of influential opinion. The policy of Laud in the 1630s – at least as much in matters of ritual and church organization as in social and economic affairs – was the final instrument which brought the whole edifice to the ground in 1640.

These two factors could not alone have caused the prolonged upheaval of the 1640s if it had not been for a third, the crisis in the affairs of the hereditary *élite*, the aristocracy. For a time this group lost its hold upon the nation, and thus allowed political and social initiative to fall into the hands of the squirearchy. It surrendered its powers or physical coercion to an increasingly powerful state; it permanently alienated much of its capital resources in land; for a period, admittedly not a very long one, its purchasing power declined absolutely; its subsequent decision to jack up rents and fines did much to break down old ties of personal allegiance; it was obliged to share more and more of the commanding heights of administrative and political authority with a confident and well-educated gentry; and, partly because of guilt by association with a corrupt, licentious and in the end tyrannical Court, partly because so many of its members belonged to a feared and hated religious minority, partly because of the workings of the puritan conscience, it temporarily forfeited much of its influence and prestige. The rise of the gentry is to some extent – though certainly not entirely – an optical illusion, resulting from this temporary weakness of the aristocracy. . . .

The early Tudors had striven, not without success, to undermine the strength of the nobility, which they had regarded as a menace to quasi-absolute monarchy. In the reign of Elizabeth it was thought that the balance of society was just about right, with the aristocracy filling a useful role as 'brave halfe paces between a Throne and a People', to use Fulke Greville's famous phrase. By the early seventeenth century things had gone too far, and the Early Stuarts began anxiously trying to shore up the tottering edifice. 'Though their Dependences and Power are gone, yet we cannot be without them,' wrote the republican Henry Neville in the middle of the century. This many-sided crisis in the affairs of the aristocracy did not itself *cause* the Civil War, but it created the conditions which made it possible. As James Harrington said at the time: 'A Monarchy devested of its Nobility has no refuge under Heaven but an Army. Wherefore the dissolution of this Government caus'd the War, not the War the dissolution of this Government.' . . . [1]

The titular peerage was a status group defined by special privileges of its own, and the major component of a power *élite*. But was it any more than that? Was it a class in the narrow sense of the word, a body of men with similar economic interests, enjoying similar incomes derived from similar sources? . . . There were 121 peerage families in 1641 and there were probably another thirty to forty upper-gentry families who were as rich as the middling barons and richer than the poor ones. . . . It would be foolish to claim that in 1558 and 1641 all titular peers were men of similar wealth or even of identical interests. . . . But for all that, they still represented – at any rate up to about 1620 – an *élite* with distinct legal and political privileges, a common outlook upon their social duties, and a common motivation arising from a common source of income in the land. . . . The titular peerage should be seen, therefore, as the majority component, and the only common factor, in a whole series of over-lapping ranking variables in a hierarchical social structure. . . . It comprised the most important element in a status group, a power *élite*, a Court, a class of very rich landlords, an association of the well-born. . . .

The Inflation of Honours

Knighthood was the first dignity which the Crown openly allowed to be sold, not by the King himself but by deserving courtiers and servants. . . . In the forty-four and a half years of her reign Queen Elizabeth and her generals and lords deputy created 878 knights, a fair proportion of whom were adventurers in Ireland. In the thirty-nine years from 1603 to 1641 the first two Stuarts created 3,281, all but a tiny fraction of whom were English. . . . If Elizabeth was frugal in her distribution of knighthoods she was even more conservative in the creation of new peerages. . . . James came south in 1603 with a reputation for generosity over the granting of titles, and as soon as he arrived he was faced with a demand for new creations that had been dammed up for nearly twenty years. . . . The increase of numbers by about 40 per cent over 1603 (and 1558) was certainly substantial, but not unreasonable in view of the number of respectable gentry families newly risen to outstanding wealth and position.

In 1615, however, there occurred a radical change of policy, to a system of direct cash sale of titles by the Crown, and the granting of nominations as rewards for courtiers. . . . In the thirteen years from 31 December 1615 to 31 December 1628 the numbers of the English peerage rose from 81 to 126, and at the same time the number of earls increased still faster, from 27 to 65. . . .

During the long years of the Interregnum a number of royalists looked back over the history of the previous half-century to try to discover how it was that the institution of monarchy had fallen into such disrepute. Without exception they all agreed in laying great emphasis upon the sale of honours. . . . There is a good deal of evidence that respect for the titular peerage was declining in the early seventeenth century. An important cause of this development was the partial divorce of titular rank from both wealth and status, caused by the fact that titles could be bought for money; that mere merchants or merchants' sons like Hicks, Craven or Bayning could acquire them; that a few of the new peers, particularly Villiers' relatives and hangers-on, lacked the financial resources to maintain the position their titles demanded; and that they had become so numerous that familiarity bred contempt. . . . The peers under Charles I were a more upstart group than at any time in the previous 200 years – far more so than at the present day, when the pattern more closely resembles that of 1558. ∴.[2]

It was argued by both Walker and Newcastle that an important factor in creating the opposition group in the Lords was the lack of sufficient public offices to satisfy the ambitions of so numerous a nobility. . . . The inflation of honours not only provoked divisions within the peerage, but also inspired fierce jealousies between order and order, rank and rank. . . . The numerical increase in all ranks, the creation of a new order and the glaring injustices of the distribution of titles tended to set the whole governing class at loggerheads. . . . As set out by the royalist commentators of the 1650s, the folly of the inflation of honours by the Early Stuarts seems obvious enough.

There were, however, a number of facts and arguments which they ignored. . . . The inflation of honours was not the sole cause either of the decline in the prestige of the peerage or of the growth of faction in the countryside. The peerage suffered from other disadvantages, among them close identification with the moral turpitude popularly ascribed to the Court, and the fact that in 1640 some 20 per cent were Papists, while the country gentry had been prone to faction long before the struggle for ranks and titles began.

The further objection to the arguments of the royalist commentators is that they were too obsessed with the mechanics of supply to notice the phenomenon of demand. . . . Though clumsy in operation, the inflation was in principle no more than recognition of an established socio-economic fact, that the class pyramid in its upper ranges had become much broader at the base and rather lower at the top than it had been at the accession of Elizabeth. . . . The insatiable demand for status and honour between 1558 and 1641 is proof of the truth of what has been called 'Tawney's Law': that the greater the wealth and more even its distribution in a given society, the emptier become titles of personal distinction, but the more they multiply and are striven for . . .

Economic Change

The most serious objection raised against counting manors is that the range of values they embrace is so vast and so random as to reduce all calculations to futile arithmetical exercises. The crux of the argument is therefore concentrated upon the problem of the dispersion of values. . . . Samples of manorial values have been taken for 1535 and for around 1602. . . . At first sight the range of values disclosed in the two samples appears to confirm the gloomiest forebodings of the critics. In the [first] sample the annual values run from under £2 to over £165, and in the [second] sample the sale values run from under £100 to over £10,000. But an inspection of the frequency distributions shows that in both samples there was a marked concentration of manors towards the lower end of the range of values. . . . Since one manor may be up to 100 times more valuable than another, the use of manorial counts as indicators of real wealth is only possible, if at all, *provided that the comparisons relate to large numbers* of representative manors – representative in the sense that they are statistically random samples. It was failure to appreciate the significance of this proviso that vitiated Professor Tawney's attempts to stratify the gentry according to the number of manors held by individual families. . . .

There is overwhelming evidence that the holdings of the surviving peers of 1558 had fallen by about a quarter by 1602 and by a further fifth by 1641. Since the mean value of manors relative to price index is believed to have declined slightly in the first period, and risen considerably in the second, only the first provides convincing evidence of declining real income. Both, however, are proof of a shrinking in the landownership of the older peers and therefore in their capital resources – exploited or unexploited – and their political authority. Nor was the balance redressed by the new families who had risen into the peerage, for in 1641 the number of really large manorial holders, old and new, was down by over a third, and the average holdings per peer were down by a half as compared with 1558. . . . There was a very high rate of turnover of property throughout these eighty years, the losses almost amounting to the total holdings of 1558. There is reason to believe, however, that these losses were not spread uniformly over the whole period. . . . By far the worst period of sales was from about 1585 to 1606, during which time the net losses were so alarming that one may reasonably talk about a financial crisis of the aristocracy, which was arrested soon after the death of Queen Elizabeth. . . .[3]

Until similar studies have been carried out for other periods, it is difficult to be absolutely certain whether or not this picture of widespread decay in ownership of landed capital among surviving families is a phenomenon particularly confined to the late sixteenth and early seventeenth centuries, or whether it is common to all times. There are, however, some significant pointers. In her unpublished study of the peerage from 1485 to 1547, Miss Helen Miller has noted that rapid rise and fall was the exception to the rule. . . .[4] The contrast between the two periods is so dramatic, particularly in the figures for losses, that one may reasonably conclude that it represents a real change in the trend of aristocratic fortunes.

The same contrast emerges if one compares the 1558–1641 period with the late seventeenth and eighteenth centuries that succeeded it. Professor Habakkuk has argued that the latter period was a time of growth rather than decay in aristocratic landholding and of increasing stability in landownership.[5] It thus looks very much as if both rapid mobility and marked decay were temporary phenomena peculiar to the late sixteenth and early seventeenth centuries.

The more speculative calculations of 'income' tell much the same story. They support the view that a shrinkage of manorial holdings by about a quarter during the reign of Elizabeth meant an equivalent, or almost equivalent, shrinkage in landed income after adjustment for changes in the price index. At the same time the burden of interest rose and the profits of court and office stagnated if they did not decline. Receipts from land rose throughout the reign, especially towards the end, and may almost have caught up with the cost of living. But they could not compensate for these other factors, much less for the decline in the amount of land held. As a result, the financial position of the peerage was substantially weaker in real terms than it had been forty years before, the greater magnates being particularly severely hit. Nor was this all. The amount of land throughout the country at the disposal of the private landlord had been substantially increased by massive sales of crown land, for which private buyers paid over £800,000 during the reign of Elizabeth.[6] Since the number of manors dispersed among the tenantry by sale by landlords was still very small, the property held by the middle and lesser landlord groups, subsumed under the portmanteau heading of gentry, must necessarily have increased. Relative to those of the gentry, the financial resources of the peerage must therefore have shrunk even faster than any of these figures would suggest.

The next forty years present superficially a much more encouraging picture. Though the burden of interest on debt continued to rise, and though the average amount of land held probably fell a little, receipts from land were rising very rapidly in almost all areas, and those who could obtain a niche at the Court were enjoying rewards undreamed of under the parsimonious Elizabeth. Moreover, some fortunately situated magnates were now drawing large revenues from urban rents in the booming west end of London and from their hitherto largely worthless estates in Ireland, while the benefits of draining the fens in East Anglia and Lincolnshire were just beginning to show themselves. In consequence the net income of the peerage in 1641 was on an average at least as great in real terms as it had been in 1558 – and very much greater than it had been in 1602. . . .

The recovery of the peerage in terms of purchasing power does not mean that their financial position relative to other classes in society was back to what it had been in 1558. . . . There is every reason to suppose that between 1558 and 1641 there had been a striking growth of population, trade and industrial and agricultural production, and the gross national income must have greatly increased. Since the real mean income of the peers failed to show comparable buoyancy, it follows that their share of the whole must have declined. Since their share of the total of land in private ownership had also declined, their position among the landowning classes and in society as a whole was much inferior to what it had been. . . .

In any case, to assume that the financial recovery of the aristocracy meant the end of the crisis in their affairs is to fall into a vulgar error. The crisis was not purely economic, it was moral and social as well, and the methods adopted to solve the one merely exacerbated the other. . . . The crisis of the aristocracy passed through two phases, the second being the direct outcome of the first. Under Elizabeth their capital holdings in land and their incomes deteriorated, both relatively and absolutely, as a result of which respect for their titles and their authority was diminished. . . . The cure to their financial crisis was sought in vigorous reorganization and exploitation of the estates which were left, the result of which was to contribute to this second and graver crisis, the crisis of confidence which came to a head in the reign of Charles I.

The late sixteenth and early seventeenth centuries are characterized by an exceptional speed of turnover of land. . . . The two factors causing the speed of transfer were the booming profits of agriculture on a rising market and the exceptional readiness of existing landowners to sell up, and of the two the latter was if anything more important than the former. . . . Internal transfer of land within the propertied classes must have been the prime stimulus to the land market. What needs to be explained is not so much why a lot of small men were finding it hard to make both ends meet, but why so many important established families were obliged to sell their patrimony. . . .

Both the speed of social change in the late sixteenth century and the generally downward trend of aristocratic finances were governed by a complex of deep-seated forces, economic, political, legal, social and intellectual. . . . To the inevitable changes wrought by the eccentricities of human reproductive capacity were added in the late sixteenth century exceptional temptations and compulsions to overspend on conspicuous consumption, royal service, or marriage portions, exceptional need for adaptability in estate management, novel opportunities and exceptional dangers in large-scale borrowing. Compensations were lacking during the reign of Elizabeth, owing to exceptional stinginess in the distribution of royal favours and snobbish objections to marriage with heiresses of lower social status. To make matters worse, legal obstacles to breaking entails and selling land were exceptionally weak, and moral objections to the dismemberment of the family patrimony exceptionally feeble. A landed aristocracy has rarely had it so bad.

On the other side, a few massive fortunes were being piled up in the law, in trade and in certain government offices, the owners of which were all seeking security and status through the purchase of a landed estate; under James some great properties were being carved out of the royal patrimony for the benefit of favourites; and all the time there was the upward thrust of those landed families who could profit from booming farm prices and who were content to save and reinvest their gains instead of consuming them in gracious living.

After reaching a climax in 1610–20 the rate of economic change in the landed classes declined sharply. For one thing the shock of the 1620–21 economic crisis and the temporary fall in land values may have frightened off some buyers, and the subsequent prolonged slump in wool prices must have adversely affected a large number of small-scale sheep-owners. For another the prospects of the great landlord rapidly improved. Even the most incompetent could not fail to profit from the massive rise in average rents in the early seventeenth century, and thereafter the levelling off of prices reduced the importance of in-efficient estate management. New sources of income opened for some with the draining of the fens, the growth of urban housing around London and the demand for iron and steel; a select few grew rich on royal bounty; a more intensive pursuit of heiresses had a snowball effect upon the greater landed fortunes; swingeing taxes on land after 1642 affected the lesser landowner more severely than the greater; the life interest and later the strict settlement made dispersal of land by sale more difficult, cheaper interest rates and the equity of redemption on mortgages made it less necessary; the growing obsession with property influenced the thinking of all but the most irresponsible of wastrels, the system of social stratification hardened. By the late seventeenth century England was ripe for the Venetian oligarchy of the Hanoverian era, presiding over a landed society which was far more stable in its composition than it had been a century earlier.

Power

Many forces converged to remove at last the centuries-old danger of aristocratic violence, but the most important single factor was the shrinkage both in numbers and in scale of the over-mighty subjects of the Crown. This decline in its turn had many causes, partly economic, partly legal, partly psychological, . . . but there can be little doubt that the action of the Crown was of vital significance. By occasional executions and irreversible attainders and by refraining from building up new landed families to replace those which died out, the Tudors succeeded in reducing the numbers of great territorial landlords. . . . Those great families which survived found that their habits of spending were causing a contraction of their territorial possessions, which in time had far-reaching effects on their authority. . . . The decline in the number of families holding some 70 manors or more from 18 out of 62 in 1559 to 6 out of 121 in 1641 is not very significant in terms of real income; in terms of influence, however, it would be difficult to deny its importance.

Secondly, there was a change in men's ideas of loyalty. The influence of the nobles over client gentry and tenantry was being weakened by their increasing absenteeism due to attendance at Court, and by the shift to economic rents, which severely reduced the service element in landlord–tenant relationships. Tudor monarchy and the Price Revolution were both working to the same end. . . . The all-pervading influence of the central government was seeping steadily into the remoter areas, subsuming local loyalties under allegiance to itself, wearing down the recalcitrant by administrative and legal pressure, and cowing the rebellious by the sheer scale of its resources. The growth of religious enthusiasm was leading men to wonder if God was not a better master than an earl. . . .

Thirdly, the nobility themselves were losing the military capacity to challenge their sovereign, and the technical capacity for leadership in war. . . . A military commander had now to be an expert in logistics, in transport and victualling, in engineering and administration. . . . About three-quarters of the peerage – which means virtually every able-bodied adult peer – had seen service in the wars of the 1540s, but by 1576 only one peer in four had had any military experience.[7] In the early seventeenth century only about one peer in five had seen action, and the proportion both fit and experienced in 1642 was even smaller. One of the reasons why King Charles lost the Civil War is that the English aristocracy no longer knew how to fight. If the Earl of Newcastle had had the professional expertise of Sir Ralph Hopton it might have been a very different story.

Fourthly, the nobility were losing their nerve. . . . The advent of the county muster and the trained band destroyed the concept of a military élite, and the nobility and gentry turned instead to royal administration in the shires. As the military power ebbed they began to doubt their capacity and duty to act as self-appointed watchdogs over royal policies. They were slowly discouraged from keeping either armed bodyguards or numerous liveried retainers, their castles fell into ruins, their military equipment rusted in their armouries. Like the rest of the population, they were deeply affected by the heavy barrage of propaganda from pulpit and printing-press on the subject of the necessity of loyalty to the sovereign. . . . By the end of the century rebellion was becoming not merely very chancy but also very disreputable, and it is not surprising to find that in 1601 Southampton had to be fortified by readings from Aristotle's *Politics* to nerve him to revolt. . . .[8]

Fifthly, and lastly, the nobility found themselves increasingly bound to the Crown by ties of fear and hope. The numerous acts of attainder of the fifteenth and sixteenth centuries were intended as much for threats of retribution in case of further disobedience as for punishments for past rebellion. Most families regained part or all of their land, now held on sufferance from the Crown. . . .[9] Moreover, as the Court machine swelled in importance, so did the amount of gifts, offices and honours at its disposal, and those who wished to have a share in these benefits were well advised to display their loyalty and obedience to the Crown. . . .

The crucial victories of the Crown over the nobility were won between 1570 and 1620. It was then that the great territorial empires were at last broken up, then that the massive bands of armed retainers were cut down to size, then that the nobility abandoned their age-old habits of casual violence, which now became the mark of dangerous eccentricity. . . .

Estate Management

On most estates rents at least doubled between about 1590 and 1640. Since agricultural prices only rose by about a third this must have been an exceedingly prosperous period for the English landlord. . . . Why the 1590s should have marked the turning-point on so many estates is not hard to fathom. The most important factor must have been the demographic explosion beginning about twenty years before, the cause of which is still obscure. . . .[10] Landowners must have found themselves besieged by prospective tenants outbidding each other in their desperate search for a holding. Secondly, this was just the time when very many of the aristocracy found themselves in serious financial difficulties, and were therefore particularly anxious to increase their incomes. To this economic incentive on both sides may be added a number of less tangible factors. This decade saw the last of the age-old habit of regarding land not only as a source of money but also as a means of obtaining military aid and outward signs of loyalty and esteem. . . .

It has been suggested by Professor Tawney that the decline in the prosperity of the aristocracy relative to that of the squirearchy was in large measure due to differences in efficiency in estate management. The essential difference is between 'Court' and 'Country'. Men who live on the spot and devote themselves to the humdrum tasks of administration will obtain a higher economic return from their estates than those who are content to leave things to their officials, and devote themselves instead to the affairs of the Court or national politics, to the busy round of London society, to the pursuit of pretty girls or fallow deer. . . . Since a far higher proportion of the peerage than of the squirearchy were at Court, the peerage were on balance at a disadvantage. This was an important but rarely a crucial factor in governing the prosperity and decay of families, which was more commonly determined by other causes. Different expenditure patterns were more influential than different management policies, even in the late Elizabethan period when the premium on innovation was highest.

It was only for a relatively short period that the balance of advantage favoured the medium-size, personally directed estate against the vast rambling accumulation of properties owned by an indolent or preoccupied absentee. New surveying and mapping techniques and the growth of more systematic accounting methods gave great lords the same intimate sense of control of their estates as did the more direct knowledge of his every field possessed by the smaller gentleman; the general shift away from demesne farming lessened the need for personal attention. When the process was complete, when prices had levelled off and the landlord had become a rentier pure and simple, it could safely be said that 'a gentleman's account is a trifle to a merchant's – one hour or two in a week will do it'.[11]

When that day came, the advantages of personal supervision on the spot which had been so significant in the late sixteenth century would substantially diminish, and the disadvantages of size and dispersal disappear altogether. . . .

Office and the Court

In any discussion of office, it must be remembered that there were deep-seated structural reasons why only a small, and indeed a diminishing, number of total applicants could hope to be satisfied. Two out-

standing peculiarities of England in the sixteenth century were its
failure to create a large standing army and its failure to develop a
national bureaucracy covering both central and local government. . . .
If a guess has to be made – and it can be little more – it would be that
the ratio of aspirants to suitable jobs under Elizabeth was about 2 to 1
for the aristocracy, 5 to 1 for the 500 leading county families and
anything up to 30 to 1 for the parochial gentry. Of the 679 gentry of
Yorkshire in 1642 only 22 held salaried offices under the Crown in
London, Ireland or at home, and only a further 10 held stewardship of
Crown lands. . . .[12]

There were those who suspected that the Tudors deliberately set out
to clip the wings of the over-mighty subject by absorbing his surplus
revenues in expenditure on government service. . . . On the other hand,
it was equally clear, particularly under Henry VIII and James, that a
very large number of families owed their rise to the top, at any rate in
part, to royal office and favour. Though the admixture of other factors
in the history of almost every family makes statistical precision impossible, there is one calculation which may perhaps prove illuminating
for the early seventeenth century. The gross landed income of the 121
aristocratic families of 1641 was about £630,000 – let us say £700,000
to be on the safe side. Capitalized at twenty years' purchase, this
amounts at most to about £14 million. In the previous forty years
these families had been given by the Crown over £4 million in money
of 1640, or in other words about 30 per cent of their total capital assets
at the end of the period. In addition to these grants there should be
added the direct profits of office, corruption and the sale of offices – an
unknown and incalculable figure which it would be reasonable to
capitalize at not less than another £2 million. . . . It is reasonable to
conclude that office and favour in the previous forty years had enabled
between a quarter and third of aristocratic families to live opulently –
some even wildly extravagantly – and were responsible for perhaps a
quarter of the total capital assets of the group in 1641.

The successful operation of the Court system depended on the
maintenance of a delicate and extremely complicated political balance.
Since offices suitable to the nobility were restricted in number, the
greatest care had to be exercised in the distribution of these few so as
to prevent a monopoly of tenure by any one faction. When this
occurred, as under Wolsey, Protector Somerset, Sir Robert Cecil and
the Duke of Buckingham, explosive tensions built up among the
excluded. . . .

The unfortunate consequences of a closing of the opportunity for employment, of allowing a monopoly of political patronage to fall into the hands of a single clique, were most clearly displayed at the turn of the century, for both the Essex Rebellion of 1601 and the Main Plot of 1603 are principally to be explained in terms of thwarted ambition. . . .

If the political stability of the system was delicately poised, so also was the financial. The sixteenth-century state had to support its bureaucracy and its Court and pay for its wars with revenues which were never sufficient for its needs. Without the powerful injection of the wealth of the Church in the middle of the century it could not have survived as long as it did, for the political machine depended on a steady flow of gifts and rewards from the monarch. . . . In the 1580s and 1590s the appalling cost of the Anglo-Spanish War, coupled with a natural parsimony which increased with old age, induced Queen Elizabeth severely to reduce her gifts to all except her favourite, the Earl of Essex – and even he was hard put to it to make ends meet. . . . This austerity programme had two important and unfortunate consequences, the impoverishment of the Court aristocracy and the growth of corruption in the public services. . . .

If Elizabeth's way of solving the financial problem of the Court by ruthlessly cutting costs had unforeseen and disastrous consequences, James's alternative was no better. In the first place he indulged in a massive alienation of royal resources and royal authority. Between 1603 and 1628 the peerage was given well over a million pounds' worth of Crown lands and rents, which was perhaps as much as a quarter of all royal estates in 1603. . . . But Crown lands were not the widow's cruse, and to maintain his reputation James allowed and encouraged the growth of a vast ramshackle structure of concealed income and expenditure administered directly by the courtiers, to whom went all the profits. . . . The burden on the country was not merely far greater than appears at first sight, it was also exacted in the most obnoxious and inequitable way. . . .

The last phase in royal treatment of the problem of the Court opened in 1629 with the death of the Duke of Buckingham and Charles's decision to dispense with Parliament. As it turned out, the sequence of events could not have been more unfortunate for the popularity of monarchy. Elizabeth by her parsimony first endangered the Court system and made corruption an essential ingredient of public service, while at the same time Lord Burghley allowed the propertied classes to fall into the habit of evading their tax responsibilities. James and Buckingham then dissipated royal resources in extravagant gifts and absurdly opulent court festivities. The policy enraged the Commons and provided a legitimate excuse for the refusal to make more parliamentary grants. This refusal in turn obliged the King to auction off his powers for economic regulation, appointment to office and the creation of new honours, actions which still further exacerbated the political situation. Now there came a period of radical reform, including a sharp reduction of royal largesse, an attack on increases in official fees, heavy taxation of the nobility and upper gentry through wardship and forest fines, and a highly unpopular religious policy. Not only did these measures still further exasperate the country gentry, they also alarmed the administrators, whose fees and perquisites were threatened, and alienated many of the Court nobility.

An important by-product of these events and policies was the almost complete alienation of Court from Country, an alienation sharply accentuated by Charles's attempts to drive the gentry and superfluous nobility out of London. By the reign of Charles the concept of harmony within the Commonwealth had broken down, the two words 'Court' and 'Country' having come to mean political, psychological and moral opposites. . . .

It might appear from this analysis that the English Court system collapsed in 1640 because it was too swollen, too expensive – a view which was certainly that of the contemporary Country party. Looked at in a European setting, however, it is clear that the real weakness of the English Court and administration was that it attracted all the odium of the vast tentacular institutions of France and Spain without the compensating advantages of size and strength. . . . Since the Court and the administration were relatively so restricted in size, their total cost to the taxpayer, even in the halcyon days of the Duke of Buckingham, was certainly small compared with the burden in France or Spain. . . . The resentments aroused were out of all proportion to the hardships suffered, and were directed more against the arbitrary methods of levy and the supposed purposes to which the money was to be put than against the weight of taxation as such. . . . When it came to the push those on the inside were not sufficiently numerous, or sufficiently powerful, or sufficiently conscious of their personal stake to resist assaults from without. By 1640 the Court had contrived to arouse the same resentments as those of the Continent, but had failed to create a vested interest large enough to protect it against the legion of its enemies. Such were the consequences of half a century of ineptitude, by three very different monarchs, in the handling of the patronage system. . . .

Prestige

Writing in 1632, Sir Henry Spelman concluded: 'Now I labour in observing the particulars, seeing the whole body of the Baronage is since that [1558] fallen so much from their ancient lustre, magnitude, and estimation. . . .' The manifold causes of this slump in prestige have already been spelt out at length. They include the decline in the wealth of the peers relative to that of the gentry; the shrinkage of their territorial possessions, in both absolute and relative terms; the decay of their military power in men, arms, castles and will to resist; the granting of titles of honour for cash not merit, in too great numbers, and to too unworthy persons; the change in their attitude towards the tenantry from suppliers of manpower to suppliers of rent; the undermining of their electoral influence due to the rise of deeply felt political and religious issues; the increasing preference for extravagant living in the city instead of hospitable living in the countryside; the spread throughout the propertied classes of a bookish education, acquired at school and university, and the demand by the State for an administrative *élite* of proved competence, irrespective of the claims of rank; the pervasive influence of the rise of individualism, the Calvinist belief in a spiritual hierarchy of the Elect and the Puritan exaltation of the private conscience, which affected attitudes towards hierarchy and obedience in secular society; and finally, the growing psychological breach between Court and Country in attitudes, real or supposed, towards constitutional theory, methods and scale of taxation, forms of worship, aesthetic tastes, financial probity and sexual morality. . . .

In 1645 Lord Willoughby remarked bitterly, 'I thought it a crime to be a nobleman'; by the winter of 1648 there were only a handful of peers left to 'sit and tell tales by the fireside in their House in hope of more Lords to drive away the time'. A few months later the House of Lords was abolished, and with it the privileges which had hitherto helped to distinguish peers from gentry.[13] This act was not a mere by-product of the dynamics of war; it was the culmination of a crisis of confidence which had been maturing for well over half a century.

[*The Crisis of the Aristocracy*, Oxford, 1965.]

Notes

1. *Works of Fulke Greville*, ed. A. B. Grosart, 1870, IV, p. 189. [H. Neville], *Plato Redivivus*, 1681, p. 133. J. Harrington, *Oceana*, 1737, p. 70.
2. *The Economist*, 21 July 1956, p. 200.
3. Estimates of Manors held by the Peerage:

Date	Type of family	No. of families	Manors held (to nearest 10)	Av. no. of manors per family	No. of families holding	
					40 manors or more	10 manors or less
31 Dec. 1558	Extant on Dec. 1559 + Kent	63	3,390	54	39	2
31 Dec. 1602	Extant on 31 Dec. 1602 + Essex and Southampton	57	2,220	39	c. 19–21	5
31 Dec. 1641	Pre-1602 creations still extant in 1641	48	1,640	34	14	9
	Post-1602 creations still extant in 1641	73	1,440	20	9	29
	Total families extant in 1641	121	3,080	25	23	38

4. H. Miller, The Early Tudor Peerage, 1485–1547 (London, M.A. thesis, 1950), p. 139.

5. H. J. Habakkuk, 'English Landownership, 1680–1740', *Economic History Review*, x, 1940; 'England', in *The European Nobility in the Eighteenth Century*, ed. A. Goodwin, 1953; 'Marriage Settlements in the Eighteenth Century', *Transactions of the Royal Historical Society*, 4th ser., XXXII (1950); 'The English Land Market in the Eighteenth Century', in *Britain and the Netherlands*, ed. J. S. Bromley and E. H. Kossman, 1960. G. E. Mingay, *English Landed Society in the Eighteenth Century*, 1963, ch. iii.

6. F. C. Dietz, *English Public Finance, 1558–1641* (New York, 1932), p. 298, n. 16.

7. *Letters and Papers of Henry VIII*, III, ii, 1454. Miller, *op. cit.*, p. 181. *Calendar of State Papers Domestic, 1619–23*, p. 159; *1623–5*, pp. 281, 381–2. British Museum, Lansdowne MSS. 683.

8. J. K. Lowers, *Mirrors for Rebels* (Berkeley, Cal., 1953), p. 78. Bodleian Library, Oxford, Ashmole MSS. 1729, f. 100.

9. J. R. Lander, 'Attainder and Forfeiture, 1453–1509', *Historical Journal*, IV, 1961.

10. *Victoria County History, Leicestershire*, III, pp. 138–42. W. G. Hoskins, 'The Rebuilding of rural England, 1570–1640', *Past and Present*, IV, 1953.

11. *A Memoir of Peregrine Bertie*, 1838, p. 135.

12. W. T. MacCaffrey, 'Place and Patronage in Elizabethan Politics', *English Government and Society*, 1961, pp. 99–108.

13. J. T. Cliffe, The Yorkshire Gentry on the Eve of the Civil War, (London, Ph.D. thesis, 1960), p. 61.

II

Revolution

8 Office-holding

G. E. AYLMER

By contrast with the early and mid-Tudor period, the years from 1603 to 1640 saw little change in the institutions of English government. Instead there was a Parkinsonian proliferation of subordinate officials at the lower levels of the existing structure. Many of these additional underlings were the private employees of the existing office-holders, and not – even in theory – the King's servants. This is, of course, related to the practice of performing official duties in absence and by deputy. . . .

To dwell upon such phenomena as absenteeism, pluralism, competition for emoluments, the tendency to increase fees and gratuities at the expense of the public, and generally the attempt to exploit the value of offices to the full, may seem to present the system in a somewhat unfavourable light. But they do *not* in my view indicate any peculiar depravity among Jacobean or Caroline officials. Nor are they necessarily evidence that the gentry was becoming polarized between those waxing gross on the spoils of office and those decaying for the lack of its refreshing streams. Rather they suggest to me the uncertain, fumbling responses of men on relatively fixed incomes to the pressures of an inflationary age, to the exigencies of the 'Price Revolution'. This is not to deny that a few men at the top made huge fortunes, or that some lower down were corrupt and extortionate. It is only to suggest that we should keep a sense of proportion concerning the profits of office.

Here, too, some aspects of royal policy in the 1630s must have frightened many of the office-holders, and may have positively alienated some of them – for instance, the campaign for economical reform in the Household and the defence departments, and the royal commissions to investigate the taking of excessive fees. There was also a drive against absentees, and thus against pluralism, though it was virtually limited to the naval and military service.

These attacks, or possible attacks, on the financial interests of office-holders, should of course be thought of in conjunction with the moves against life tenure, with an increasing reluctance to grant reversions, and with Charles's disapproval of people buying and selling offices. In all this the Crown came up against a perennial problem facing any government which attempts administrative reform without changing its political and social basis: how far such reforms can go without alienating the very men whose loyalty and co-operation is essential for the reforms to be successfully implemented, and indeed for government policy as a whole to be properly executed. The problem is endemic, but it is perhaps at its most acute in autocratic and semi-autocratic regimes, where the men at the top stand to lose most by alienating their supporters in the middle and lower ranks of the ruling hierarchy. Various historical and modern parallels suggest themselves.

Mr Hurstfield has suggested that the Crown found it easier to allow office-holders to recoup themselves by fees, etc., than to raise more money in taxation with which to pay them better salaries. . . .[1] The value of this form of taxation, if it is legitimate to think of it as such, was very large indeed, compared with the Crown's visible income. Naturally, it is difficult to suggest even the most tentative and approximate figures, and I do so only to indicate what seems likely to be the right order of magnitude. I estimate that in the 1630s the total received by office-holders in fees and gratuities was between £250,000 and £400,000 per annum, and within this range probably over rather than under £300,000.[2] At this time, apart from the sale of capital assets, the Crown's visible income, even including all the famous fiscal devices – Ship Money and the rest, was between £600,000 and £750,000 per annum. Thus fees and gratuities brought gross royal income to more like £900,000 to £1,000,000, an increase of something between $33\frac{1}{3}$ and 50 per cent. Still, it was the office-holders who got this extra money, and not Charles I.

The significance of some of this becomes clearer when we consider who these people were, in the light of how they had come to enter office and what they expected to get out of it. The great majority of them came from the landed gentry. This is also true of quite a large number of those who entered the King's service via the law, since many lawyers in turn came from gentry families. Self-made men, in the sense of those without advantages of birth, connection or inherited wealth, were few in number, except at the very bottom levels among copying clerks, artificers and menial servants. The number of men even from such indisputably middle-class groups as the yeomanry, and the citizenry of London and other towns was small. Among the gentry, all ranks were represented, and all gradations of wealth. Nor, within the gentry does there seem to have been that preponderance of younger sons among the office-holders which one might have expected from some generalizations about the effects of primogeniture in England.

Incidentally, the peerage was very well represented in Caroline administration, and not only at the very top. But there were absolutely so few peers that even so, they comprised only a fairly small fraction of all the courtiers, legal officers and administrators. Office-holding may perhaps be said to have affected the peerage more than vice versa. . . .

Leaving aside for the moment the question of how far office was *the* touchstone of economic health within the gentry, it did indisputably act as what some sociologists might call a 'built-in status-elevator'. Most office-holders rose by one degree in the social hierarchy, many by two or more. Men who started out with a dubious claim to the title of Gentleman (the lowest armigerous rank) won a safe right to call themselves Esquire. Farther up the ladder Knighthoods proliferated; and at the top Professor Trevor-Roper was certainly correct in pointing out how many of the 'new peers' of 1603-40 had made their way up wholly or partly via office-holding. But it seems unlikely that there was a large enough number of men rising into the gentry, and up through its various ranks, because of holding office, to constitute a major change in social structure. At the very top, where the absolute numbers were small: yes. But in the middle ranks, where the office-holders numbered some hundreds, and the gentry, according to one reckoning, 16,000 families: scarcely so.[3] And at the very bottom, where the intake of self-made men through office was relatively small, it does not begin to account for any large-scale 'rise into the gentry' such as Professors Tawney and Trevor-Roper agree in visualizing. Obviously it was a factor in this particular rise, along with several others.

This is perhaps the point at which to say a little more about the economic, as opposed to the social, significance of office, especially in relation to the armigerous landowners. As well as the £250,000-£300,000 or more received yearly by office-holders in fees and gratuities, their receipts *from the Crown* in all forms (including payments in kind and perquisites, as well as grants and pensions), may be estimated at the money equivalent of about £340,000–£360,000 per annum. So their total income from the Crown and the public, in money and in kind, was at least £590,000 per annum, and probably well over £650,000. A very large amount; and of course for some individuals, and even for some whole families, the wealth gained from office was the decisive factor in their fortunes. But to see this in perspective for a whole class, let alone for the whole country, one has to set it against the probable income of the peerage and gentry from other sources, mainly from land. For the English lay peers Mr J. P. Cooper has recently suggested a minimum figure of £732,000 per annum from landed wealth towards 1642.[4] And if there were 16,000 gentry families, averaging a landed income of only £300 per annum each (which is almost certainly too low a figure), we get a minimum for them of £4,800,000 a year from land; my own preference would be for a figure of more like £6,000,000. This must be set against office-holding, worth at a guess about £80,000 a year for the peers, and perhaps between £450,000 and £500,000 for the gentry. To say that, at any one time in these years, approximately 800 members of the gentry held offices with a gross annual value of £450,000–£500,000 implies that they enjoyed an average income from this source of between £560 and £625 a year each; but without qualification this would be misleading. Not only was a large part of it not paid in cash, but the average is distorted by a relatively small number of highly lucrative offices, worth say £2,000 a year and upwards; if we deduct these, the average drops steeply. These figures then begin to assume a rather more modest significance than if we just go on talking, in isolation or in the abstract, about the inflated incomes of office-holders, and the vast profits of office. Furthermore, living in London, maintaining their foothold on the patronage ladder and generally competing in Veblenesque expenditure meant that office-holders were more likely to live at the limits of their incomes, or beyond them, than their country cousins. Their large incomes *may* have meant that they enjoyed a more opulent standard of living; but did not necessarily mean that they were in a healthier economic position, or had a better chance of founding a great landowning dynasty. (This last seems in any case to have been largely a matter of demographic luck – or, if you like, of biological fitness.) . . .

There seem to be three ways in which the system of office-holding can be thought of as having interacted with politics. Of course this is only a convenient classification, and the same individuals might be involved in any two, or in all three of them. First, the vested interests of office-holders as such (some of which have been outlined earlier in this paper) might be affected by royal policy, and this might lead to lack of enthusiasm, or even to opposition inside the administration. Second, there was the possibility of ideological opposition from within the government, made likelier by life tenure and the absence of any division between politicians and civil servants. Third, arising in part from both these, in part from the clash of rival cliques and factions for control of patronage and in part from the undoubted material and prestige attractions of office-holding: the struggle for power and place as ends in themselves might assume political significance. To over-emphasize the third of these can lead to the whole of history being interpreted in terms of a conflict between the 'Ins' and the 'Outs'. And even within the more modest limits of a study of office-holding we should beware of exaggerating this, at the expense of the other two forms of interaction. The struggle for office was certainly an important, and in some individual cases, a decisive influence. In particular, men who had for different reasons and in various ways been deprived of office, ejected from it or even passed over for advancement tended to be hostile towards the King and were prominent among his opponents in 1640–42. But exceptions can be found even here, among these game-keepers turned poachers.

Any general attempt to represent the Civil War as a struggle between the 'Ins' and the 'Outs', in terms of pre-1642 office-holders, is hard to reconcile with the facts. Among the 'outsiders', masses of lesser gentry of the West and North who had never had a smell of office before 1640–42, stood by their King and their Church through thick and thin. While on the other hand, among the 'insiders', a sub-stantial minority were active parliamentarians, and many more were passive supporters of Parliament, neutrals or trimmers. . . .

As far as I can interpret it, the evidence concerning office-holders does not provide support for classifying royalists and parliamentarians respectively either as rising and declining gentry (or vice versa), or still less as feudal and bourgeois landowners. This is not for a moment to deny that, as with everybody else, material interests affected officials' political and religious attitudes. This was so under the Personal Government, and during the peaceful revolution of 1640–41, as well as at the outbreak of Civil War in 1642 and during its subsequent course. It is only to say that the analysis of these material interests does not seem to support any single generalized explanation of why there was a revolution in 1640, or a Civil War in 1642, and of what these were about.

['Office Holding as a Factor in English History, 1625–42', *History*, XLIV, 1959.]

Notes

1. *The Queen's Wards*, esp. pp. 345–9.
2. G. E. Aylmer, *The King's Servants*, 1961, ch. iv, s.v.
3. Thomas Wilson, in 1600 ('The State of England', ed. F. J. Fisher, *Camden Miscellany*, XVI, 1936).
4. In *Encounter*, XI, 3 (1958), pp. 73–4.

9 The M.P.s of the Long Parliament

D. BRUNTON AND D. H. PENNINGTON

... We tried to find out whether there were striking differences in social position between Royalist and Parliamentarian M.P.s, and what those differences were – whether they enjoyed a different status amongst that extremely large class, the landed gentry; whether in fact merchants and townsmen tended to take, as is often assumed, the side of Parliament rather than of the King. We found that Royalist and Parliamentarian, so far as can be judged from the members of the Long Parliament, were very much the same; that the greater and lesser gentry were not on different sides; that it made no difference whether a member belonged to an 'old' or to a 'new' family; that merchants and lawyers were to be found on both sides, and in such proportions as to make it doubtful whether there was any general hostility to the King amongst provincial merchants and certain that there was none amongst the lawyers. The only significant difference seems to have been that the Royalists were on average ten years younger, and more often belonged to families with a parliamentary history. . . .

Whatever definitions are accepted we are dealing not with a large body of 'secluded' members and a small minority of Rumpers, but with two lists of comparable size. From these we can ask how far, by the tests already applied to Royalists and Parliamentarians, the 'Independents' differed from the 'Presbyterians'. An examination of the geographical distribution of the Independent members produces only one clear result: Wales and the western counties (the 'Celtic' region, for those who like racial theories) had an appreciably lower proportion than the rest of the country. . . . But the north, far from sharing the low proportion of Independents of the west, had more than the average. . . .

A broad belt of counties, extending across the Midlands from Gloucestershire and Wiltshire to Lincolnshire and Norfolk sent 151 members to the original Parliament and 80 to the Rump. Of the other counties only Kent, Somerset, and Sussex come near to the 50 per cent mark. It could be pointed out that this belt, together with the greater part of Yorkshire, forms the region where open-field agriculture predominated in the seventeenth century. It is also true that Independency was strong among members from the clothing counties, old and new. Yorkshire, Norfolk, Somerset, Gloucestershire, and Wiltshire together have about 60 per cent of Rumpers among their members – but few of these members had any direct connection with wool or cloth. The differences in numbers are too small and the evidence of a connection between the party allegiance of the M.P.s and the special economic interests of their areas too uncertain for much importance to be attached to figures of this kind. . . .

When the numerical tests used on the other groups are applied to the Rumpers they produce for the most part the results we should have expected if the 209 members had been picked at random. . . . Did the barristers in the House resist the unconstitutional interference by the Army? There were 70 of them in 1648, and 33 sat in the Rump. Was Independency attractive to the townsmen more than to the countrymen? There were 19 Mayors and Aldermen among the Rumpers, and we shall show later that a considerable number of merchants of the various kinds continued to sit; but the figures are not significantly larger than those on the other side. . . .

The nature of the 'swing to the left' that produced the Commonwealth is not a matter that can be understood by looking only, or even mainly, at the House of Commons. We are concerned here solely with the composition of a House that proved a necessary instrument of the new regime, not so much by making policy as by providing in its Committees the rudiments of a central administrative system. If we expected to find the Rump a collection of upstart colonels, parvenu land-grabbers, and unheard-of townsmen, analysis would soon demolish that illusion. But it does not show the Rump to be in every respect a cross-section of the original Parliament. Each of the two major changes in the membership since 1642 reduced the proportion of old parliamentary families and increased that of the men who seized the opportunity offered by the exceptional conditions. Many who normally would have been too far from the centre of national, county, or town politics now found the way less crowded and obstructed. But, whether for political, economic, or purely personal reasons, few of these established their names on the list of the greater or lesser 'Governing Families of England'....

Even if we leave out the monopolists, who had obvious reason to support the royal government, and the men who were associated in their enterprises with courtiers, the solid allegiance to Parliament of the Londoners is not found everywhere among provincial merchants. It is true that there were considerably more on the Parliamentary than on the Royal side, and that there were proportionately more Independents than in the Parliament as a whole. But a closer examination of the political allegiance of the provincial merchants does not suggest that commercial interests were in themselves enough to bring a member on to the Parliamentary side. In the north and west the majority for the Parliament among the handful of merchant members is too small to be significant. The Eastern Association, as can be seen in a later chapter, had only Parliamentarians among its merchants; but its Royalists were everywhere in a minority – and one of them was returned by Norwich.

[*Members of the Long Parliament*, London, 1954.]

10 Critique of Brunton and Pennington

C. HILL

... [Messrs Brunton and Pennington] analysed the personnel of the Long Parliament, and asked themselves whether this analysis threw light on the causes of the Civil War. Their conclusions were entirely negative. Gentlemen, lawyers and merchants were found among M.P.s on either side. The only significant difference was that the average age of Royalist M.P.s was thirty-six, that of their opponents forty-seven. Therefore, the authors concluded, attempts to explain the Civil War in terms of class divisions are unfounded.

This conclusion may be criticized on two grounds. First, I believe the facts have in certain important respects been incorrectly interpreted; secondly, even if the interpretation were correct, the conclusion would not follow.

(1) Even on Messrs Brunton and Pennington's own analysis, significant differences between the two groups of M.P.s can be seen. Though there were merchants on either side, they were not equally divided. Of the London merchants elected to the House of Commons, the 12 monopolists were expelled; in the Civil War they naturally supported the Court through which their profits had come. Of the remaining 19 London merchants, 18 were Parliamentarians. The one exception, George Lowe, held estates in Wiltshire and was connected by marriage with Edward Hyde. Provincial merchants were more equally divided. But in the Eastern Association merchants were solidly Parliamentarian, and even in the Royalist-occupied areas a small majority among the merchant M.P.s had the courage to declare for Parliament. The authors did not ask how many of the Royalist merchants were members of local governing oligarchies, like the Royalists Hooke and Long, who 'represented actually the merchant oligarchy of Bristol'; or were Royal officials like the customs farmer and duchy of Lancaster official who were returned for the borough of Lancaster, presumably thanks to duchy pressure.

Similarly, to say that the numbers of gentlemen on either side were roughly equal does not get us very far. The authors warn against the dangers of dividing the landed from the mercantile interest, especially in the clothing counties. But should we not attempt to divide *among* the landed interest? The economic life of most gentlemen in Cumberland or Wales was very different from that of gentlemen in Norfolk or Surrey. Messrs Brunton and Pennington brush aside altogether too lightly the distinction between the economically advanced south and east of the country, which was Parliamentarian, and the economically backward north and west, which was Royalist. Mr Pennington admits that 'a study of how the estates of landed members were managed might reveal an economic line of cleavage corresponding to the political one'. Until this question has been investigated it is premature to tell us what the answer to it is. . . .

[The] contrast between local economic activity (whether in industry or agriculture) and the economic parasitism of the Court would be a profitable field of research for those looking for divisions between M.P.s (and among the gentry as a whole). . . . Independency, the authors note, was strong among M.P.s from the clothing counties: it was weakest in the north and west.

Further, to divide members of the House of Commons into two parties, labelled 'Royalist' and 'Parliamentarian', and then to treat all members of the two groups as statistically equivalent, is misleading. Side by side with men prepared to sacrifice property to principle, like Henry Marten or Sir Bevil Grenville, our authors perforce list the marginal turncoat on either side who had no principles at all. They were aware of the dangers here, and they may be right in arguing that no other division was possible. . . .

(2) [This raises] the larger question of the applicability of 'the Namier method' to periods of acute political crisis. The method was originally devised to illuminate English politics at the accession of George III. It would be difficult to find a period in the whole of English history when political issues were less in dispute, either in Parliament or in the country. It was therefore legitimate to apply a technique of analysis which ignored political principles, or treated them as rationalizations of economic or other interests. But if we go even a few years forward – to the Wilkes question – or a few years back – to the Jacobites, to 1688 – principles begin to rear their inconvenient heads. Here the Namier method is of more limited value. Messrs Brunton and Pennington analyse their M.P.s into family groupings, local groupings, economic groupings, patronage groupings, age groupings. (It may reasonably be argued that family and regional groupings were also economic groupings more often than Messrs Brunton and Pennington recognize.) But none of their groups are united by ideas. Yet there was in the House of Commons a group of republicans; perhaps some M.P.s even took their religion seriously enough to work together with men of like convictions?

About the relation of M.P.s to the electorate questions must also be asked which would have been less relevant in 1760. Politics then was what went on at Westminster. But a civil war by definition transcends the limits of the old governmental institutions. . . .

Men did not die and kill one another for four years over issues which can be satisfactorily analysed by a method evolved for the Parliament of 1760. The Civil War was fought about serious issues of principle which roused large numbers of men to heroic activity and sacrifice. . . .

['Recent Interpretations of the Civil War', *History*, XLI (1956), reprinted in *Puritanism and Revolution*, 1958.]

11 The Independents as a Religious Group

G. YULE

... The aim of the Independents was a new form of Church organization, a form of decentralized Calvinism or, as the Presbyterian Bastwick put it, they wanted not Presbyterianism dependent but Presbyterianism independent....[1] But to describe the Independency of the 1640s as simply a doctrine of decentralized Calvinism may be misleading. In Massachusetts toleration was not the essential part of its creed; but in England, in order to make headway against official Presbyterianism, the Independents at first had to claim the right to be tolerated themselves, and their ground was the right of toleration for all Christians. ...

But the majority of the sectaries drew radical social and political inferences from their beliefs which were not acceptable to the Independent gentry. Consequently, the enthusiast Independents limited toleration to what they defined as the truly religious sphere, and joined with the classical Independents in maintaining some Church–State connection and preserving the social cement of the parish system. Classical Independency was the most promising form of Christianity for encouraging religious enthusiasm while preserving the social framework....

Mr Trevor-Roper ... defined the Independents as a social group consisting of the lesser gentry.... Apart from difficulties of definition, other points must be considered. First, Mr Trevor-Roper does not explain why the declining recusant gentry were such ardent Royalists; surely the abolition of the Court of Wards would have been worth a sermon. Finally, it leaves unanswered the question why so many of the early Independents were not lesser gentlemen; why some declining gentry left the party just as it came to power; and why the actual regicides were political and religious radicals almost to a man, while those Independent gentry who were less radical in religion drew back at this point.

It is important to distinguish between the early Independents and members of the party who subsequently supported the Rump. Until 1647 the future success of the Independents was far from obvious. In the list of those who fled to the Army in 1647 there are the names of many lesser gentry, but it also includes a high percentage of the upper gentry.... In addition to those who fled to the Army in 1647, other early Independents were Sir Henry Vane, junior, one of the leading gentlemen of the kingdom; William Heveningham, a very substantial landowner of Suffolk; and Isaac Pennington, the wealthy former Mayor of London. Vane and Pennington were certainly religiously radical, while I think it likely that Heveningham at least favoured Independency.

Possibly 80 per cent, and certainly 70 per cent, of these were sympathetic to Independency. A very substantial percentage were as much 'greater gentry' as were the Presbyterians, and I should be inclined to say that the reasons for their party affiliation were ideological – an attachment to Independency or Republicanism or both. But it is significant that many of the greater gentry of the party dropped out when events took a very radical turn. Sir William Armine, Bamfield, Sir John Evelyn, Nathaniel and John Fiennes and Augustine Skinner took little part in the Rump, while Bingham, Boone, Darley, Haselrig, Jervois, Lemon, Pierpoint, St John, Vane and Weston were absent from Pride's Purge and the King's trial. By that time the leadership had passed from Vane and St John to Cromwell and Ireton.

Some of the 'declining gentry' backed out of affairs just at the very moment of the party's triumph, when they might reasonably have expected the fruits of victory, with lucrative offices and monetary rewards which would have arrested their decline. . . . Sir John Barrington, one of the leading gentry of Essex, with estates in Hertfordshire as well, withdrew almost entirely after the King's death, although he was in debt for £10,000. His family remained financially embarrassed for the next decade. They were strong Puritans. His father had been engaged with Pym in colonizing activity, and he himself was an Independent and a cousin of Cromwell. It was surely these convictions and connexions, and not the fact that he was a 'declining gentleman', which led to his early allegiance to the Independent party. . . .

A third point is somewhat puzzling. If the Independents were a country party, jibbing at the tenacious and increasing sway of London, where Presbyterianism 'had a notorious power', why is it that such leading London citizens as Isaac Pennington, Samuel Moyer, Rowland Wilson, John Foulkes and William Gibbs supported the party even before Pride's Purge? . . .

One might expect the merchants of the country towns to be Independents, being jealous of Presbyterian London. Many were, but . . . there were proportionately about the same number of provincial merchants in each party; but whereas those adhering to the Presbyterians were largely obscure, I think it is true to say that many of the Independent merchants took a more active part in proceedings. . . .

The Independents' programme was not sufficiently uniform, except in the question of religious toleration, to bear out, without important modification, Mr Trevor-Roper's hypothesis that it was the party of decentralization. . . . Under Cromwell, indeed, there is much evidence to support the view that the Independents did want decentralization, and that the regime was not really supported by the City merchants.[2] Yet that pure Independent Republic, the Rump government, adopted a policy of economic imperialism which certainly had much greater support in the City than did any policy of Cromwell, and it was the City alone that petitioned in favour of the Rump at their expulsion.

The last fact is important. Were the Independents the party of decentralization, as has been claimed, and the Presbyterians the party of London and centralization? Undoubtedly many Independents did want decentralization, but would not this desire be shared by the country supporters of the Presbyterians, the many provincial merchants excluded at Pride's Purge? . . .[3]

Cromwell certainly trebled the county seats and slashed the borough seats, but if this was simply in the interests of decentralization, why did Richard Cromwell reverse the policy?[4] The Independents were not alone in wishing to decentralize education – so, too, did Richard Baxter, who was not of that party; and on the question of the peerage they were obviously divided. . . . If the Independents, again, were enthusiastic about reform and decentralization of the law, those in power in the Rump did not show it, and turned down even Cromwell's hardly radical proposals for law reform. And, if their party platform was against monopolies, why did the monopolists old Sir Henry Vane, Sir Henry Mildmay, Sir John Hippsley, Cornelius Holland and Lawrence Whitacre support it?[5]

In one important respect or another the programme outlined in Mr Trevor-Roper's thesis runs counter to the interests of every big group among the Independents. The London Independents, the conservative constitutionalists like Lord Say and Sele, or the Cromwellians striving for order and good government, or even the Rumper body, would each repudiate some big section of such a programme.

Exceptions do not, of course, invalidate the thesis, provided there was a solid core in the party giving substantial support to the programme. Big sections obviously did support substantial parts of it, and it is significant that it seems to fit most closely to the ideals of the two most classical Independents, Ireton and Peters, though I know of no evidence to suggest that they wanted decentralization of trade. But the evidence as to the aims of a solid core is still too scanty and uncertain for a final statement to be made. . . .

[*The Independents in the English Civil War*, Cambridge, 1958.]

Notes

1. Bastwick, *Independency not God's Ordinance* (1645), pp. 5–7.
2. M. P. Ashley, *Financial and Commercial Policy under the Cromwellian Protectorate*, p. 16.
3. See Yule, *The Independents*, pp. 52–3.
4. J. R. Tanner, *Constitutional Conflicts of the Seventeenth Century*, p. 203.
5. Monopolists according to 'The Legall Fundamentall Liberties of the People of England', *The Leveller Tracts 1647–1653*, ed. Haller, p. 431. See also Clement Walker, *History of Independency*, II, p. 147.

12 Critique of Yule

D. UNDERDOWN

. . . Yule examined the Independents in politics, in the process testing the two major recent theories about them: Hexter's contention that they were not necessarily committed to religious toleration, and Trevor-Roper's argument that they can be equated with the lesser or declining gentry. . . . The most Yule can say about the Independent party is that 'its early leaders and its later radical supporters . . . were Independents or favourers of toleration'.[1] Nor is he any more confident in his conclusions when he tests the other hypothesis – Trevor-Roper's case that the Independents represented the lesser or declining gentry and the forces of provincialism and decentralization. While rejecting Trevor-Roper, Yule takes refuge in the complexity of the evidence and comes to no sociological conclusions about the party at all.

Yule's negative generalizations rest on the evidence contained in an impressive biographical appendix, which provides notes on 233 'party supporters'. This appendix, he says, includes (1) 'all the important members of Parliament, and most of the others' who survived Pride's Purge, or later returned to the Rump; (2) all those who fled to the

Army during the Presbyterian coup of July–August 1647; (3) the regicides; and (4) 'a few others, active in the Barebones' or Protectorate Parliaments, who appear to have been Independents'. Thus there are four possible qualifications for inclusion in Yule's list of Independents. This sounds promising, but in fact there are several unsatisfactory features of the appendix, which makes it difficult to draw from it any valid or worthwhile conclusions. . . .

The most obvious criticism of Yule's appendix is methodological, concerning the principle of selection. There are two alternative ways of studying a group. One is to study the whole group, including all known members of that group, in which case it is vital to have some clear and objective principle of inclusive definition. The other is to take a sample, making no attempt at total inclusiveness, but here again some consistent principle of selection is required. Now it is obvious that Yule's list of 233 Independents is not intended to be a sample of all the known Independents in the country; it must therefore be a collection of all the known Independents (according to Yule's qualifications for Independency) in a unified group. Unfortunately Yule's four qualifications for inclusion do not in fact provide a unified group. The first and fourth qualifications both involve subjective criteria, which will probably, and in fact do, lead to prejudging the nature and composition of the party. If members of Parliament who survived Pride's Purge and sat in the Rump are to be included, surely it should be all such members of Parliament. Why only the 'important' ones, and why only 'most' of the others? If some members of the Barebones' and Protectorate Parliaments are to be included, why not all of them? . . .

It is admissible that if Yule's group had indeed been confined to M.P.s, if it had included all the M.P.s known to be Independents according to Yule's first three tests (the last one must be discarded as irrelevant to the Long Parliament) and *only* Independents who were M.P.s, then at least there would be a recognizable principle of selection. . . . But conclusions about Independent M.P.s may be seriously distorted if the statistics include twenty-nine people who are not M.P.s (almost $12\frac{1}{2}$ per cent of the total) and omit twenty-six (about 11 per cent) who are. Most of the twenty-nine interlopers are known to have been either sectaries or Independents in religion as well as politics. . . . In other words, Yule's case is misleadingly strengthened by both his apparently arbitrary inclusions and exclusions. . . .

Turning from methodological to historical questions, it may be asked whether Yule's 233 Independents (plus the others who deserve inclusion) were accepted by their contemporaries as a party to which they habitually gave the name Independent? Obviously some individuals, perhaps even the majority, were often so described, but this is not enough to label the whole group Independent. It is also true that there was a recognizable Independent party, commonly called by that name, in 1646–48; but this does not necessarily mean that there was one after 1648. It is very important for Yule (and for Brunton and Pennington) that there should have been, since a large number of their Independents have no other qualification for the title than having supported the Rump at some time after Pride's Purge. One can take comfort in observing that contemporaries were often as confused as present-day scholars are when they cast about for terms to describe men of apparently contradictory motives. After 1647 both Presbyterians and Independents divide into 'real' and 'royal' factions, distinctions are made between 'pure' and 'mixed' Independents, 'Presbyterial Republicans' appear and disappear, terms like Anabaptist, Fifth Monarchy man, Quaker and Vanist are abusively used with cheerful disregard of accuracy, and the climax of confusion is reached when the tearful General Fleetwood is agreeably labelled a Presbyterian Anabaptist. . . . Richard Baxter's analysis, quoted by Yule, distinguishes three factors: 'the Vanists, the Independents, and other sects, with the Democratical party'.[2] It seems, then, that contemporaries did not consistently describe all the revolutionaries of 1648 as Independents. It is equally clear that not all members of the Rump were regarded as belonging to a single Independent party. . . . What is one to make of a scheme of classification which puts the enigmatic Fairfax in the same category as revolutionaries like Vane, Harrison and Salway? . . .

To sum up, it seems clear that the term 'Independent' is worthless as a party name except in 1646–48, and that even then only the strictest definition will do. Outside this period it is justified neither by logic nor contemporary usage, and should be discarded along with much more of the debris of the Whig interpretation. Based as they are on a wide and therefore unsound definition of Independent, both Brunton and Pennington's and Yule's appendices are misleading, while the latter also contains serious errors of fact. Much detailed work remains to be done before there can be absolute certainty of the identities of the real Independent backbenchers in 1646–48, and perhaps the necessary evidence is irrecoverable. . . .

Instead of dismissing all members of the Rump as Independents, it might be better to follow the example of Denzil Holles, who a few years earlier divides the M.P.s into a 'moderate' and a 'violent' or revolutionary party. If this is done, some meaningful distinctions emerge which are blurred by the blanket inclusion of all 1647 Independents and all members of the Rump as Independents throughout. A rough count of the revolutionaries in the Commons can be obtained by adding together the regicides, the known supporters of the Purge, and those who took their seats without apparent hesitation shortly afterwards; altogether about 120 men. The group awaits thorough study, but even a cursory examination suggests two tentative conclusions. In the first place, there is about the same proportion of religious Independents among them, and the same high incidence of non-Independents, as Yule finds for his excessively broadly defined party. In the second place, granting all the hazards of categorizing members by social class, the insufficiency of the evidence and the well-known problems of definition, there does appear to be a significant difference between the revolutionaries and the rest of the Parliamentarians. By an admittedly crude and incomplete analysis, 63 of the 121 revolutionaries appear to be either lesser gentry (in which are included 'new' as well as 'declining' gentry) or townsmen (merchants and lawyers of urban rather than gentry origins): slightly over 52 per cent. . . . It does seem that a noticeably high proportion of the revolutionaries can be regarded as men from outside the normal political establishment. This is not in itself surprising, for such a displacement of leadership is a common feature of revolutions; however, since Brunton and Pennington's book appeared there has been a tendency to stress the absence of social differences in the two sides of 1648–49. So perhaps there is a case for renewed investigation.

Indeed, the whole subject needs fresh investigation, by historians willing to discard traditional categories and to ask more specific questions. For instance, is there any difference between the typical behavior of the solidly established gentry, the new upstarts and those of old family but declining fortune? Was there among the revolutionaries a higher proportion than among the moderates and Presbyterians of men with a material stake in the new regime, either through purchase of confiscated lands or through being creditors of the state for Civil War debts? Both Yule and Brunton and Pennington occasionally try to ask questions like these, but their answers are muddied by the excessive breadth of their categories, which obscure possibly important differences. . . .

Perhaps further evidence will appear that will confirm the religious–

political equation more convincingly than it is sustained by the records of the M.P.s. But alternatively, it may conceivably confirm some version of the now suspect 'social interpretation' of the Civil War. In that case it might be admitted that Tawney and Trevor-Roper, however inadequate their methods and questionable their conflicting conclusions, were not so far wrong after all, at least in the questions they asked. The problem of the Independents is still there: let scholars at least examine it afresh with open minds.

['The Independents Reconsidered', *Journal of British Studies*, III (1964).]

Notes

1. George Yule, *The Independents in the English Civil War* (Cambridge, 1958), p. 77.
2. Yule, *op. cit.*, p. 64. To treat this, as Yule does, as an analysis of a single Independent party, instead of a description of three distinct but overlapping groups, seems to me to be taking liberties with an important piece of evidence.

13 The Changing Composition of a County Committee

A. M. EVERITT

We know that the county was an important unit in seventeenth-century society; that the county gentry were the political nation; and that the organ of their vociferation was the parliament of Westminster. But not everyone realizes that between 1642 and 1650 there appeared forty other 'parliaments' in England; that their views did not necessarily coincide with those of Westminster; and that a study of them might help to elucidate those bewildering metamorphoses from royalist or parliamentarian to Cornish – or Kentish – men: and even to elucidate those changes from parliamentarian to royalist which produced the second civil war and the restoration. . . .

The common view of Kent as a society of transplanted courtiers and merchants, though based on Lambarde's aside that 'the gentry be not here (throughout) of so ancient stocks as elsewhere', is wide of the mark; for his qualifications have been ignored. The influence of mercantile wealth, in fact, was confined to a small area near London. The gentry elsewhere – and there were at least 700 of them – were largely indigenous to the county, and, as to their sources of wealth, deeply rooted in the land. In east Kent 85 per cent of the gentry were indigenous, in the Weald nearly 100 per cent. Most of them derived from the minor gentry of the fourteenth century, and they had risen much less by trade and the law than by careful estate management and careful marriage with Kentish heiresses. At least two-thirds of them in the seventeenth century married into Kentish families – among the minor gentry over 80 per cent – and these lateral connections ramified through the whole body of Kentish gentle society: whereas their links by blood and marriage with other counties were slight.

There was no single dominant family, like that of Derby in Lancashire; instead there was a group of twenty or thirty leading gentry, such as the Derings, Twysdens, Boyses, Finches, Honywoods, and Knatchbulls. Such families, headed by baronets and knights, with lands in half a dozen parishes, formed the 'county gentry'. They were essentially different from the hundreds of 'parochial gentry' of a single manor or less. Their origins in fourteenth-century freeholders were the same, but by 1640 they had risen in the world, and their sphere was different: it was the county instead of the parish. All of these county gentry were indigenous; most of them had several separate branches...

The initial division into parties in Kent was not a social cleavage, and with negligible exceptions all on the committee were gentle. Nevertheless, there was a notable change in its social composition. In February–March 1643, 22 per cent of the committeemen were baronets, 33 per cent knights and 45 per cent esquires; by December 1652 the proportion of baronets had fallen to 5 and knights to 6 per cent, whereas esquires had risen to 77 per cent, and 10 per cent were mere gentlemen. The tendencies should not be exaggerated, since some esquires were eldest sons of titled gentry, and some were later created knights or baronets. But not all: the figures undeniably indicate a gradual secession of county families and influx of parochial gentry. Equally important is the fact that, though committeemen were always inhabitants of Kent and the majority were of families long established in the county, the preponderance of indigenous families tended to diminish. In February 1643, 75 per cent of the members were of indigenous families (i.e. in Kent before 1485); in November nearly 70 per cent; in April–May 1649, 62 per cent. Newcomers (i.e. after 1603) were always few but increased slightly: at these dates 12, 14, 17 per cent. These two gradual changes in the social composition of the committee seem slight, and the dominance of well-to-do and solidly Kentish families throughout is undeniable; but they are significant, and for more interesting reasons than at first sight appears. It was not simply a class cleavage.

Parliament's problem was how to control the county. The essence of the difficulty – the lack of a single dominant family like the Barringtons in Essex – necessitated, as has been mentioned, rule through the county gentry, that is the group of twenty or thirty leading families of Kent. Charles I himself had found this. . . . Parliament never appointed a quorum to act as a 'standing committee' as in other counties; but, as was inevitable among sixty to seventy men, a distinct, though unofficial 'core' of people who guided committee policy soon emerged from the 'general body'. Let us first examine the core and then the general body of committeemen.

The composition of the core was highly unstable. At first, as committee letters and attendances show, it was composed entirely of members of the county gentry. Of sixty members only about twelve regularly attended the central committee; in a typical lathe – St Augustine – only four out of fifteen: Sir James Oxinden of Deane, John Boys of Trapham, senior, Sir Richard Hardres of Upper Hardres and Sir Edward Monins of Waldershare. The rest were lesser men; they attended rarely; and they merely followed the policy of the core. Led by their chief and eldest member, Sir Edward Hales, the core naturally reflected, in its early stages, the moderatism of the county gentry from whom it was drawn. But from the beginning there were a few discontented extremists within it: men of years and experience mostly, with a family tradition of opposition to the crown, like Sir Henry Heyman and Colonel Edwyn Sandys; or men always at the centre of local feuds, like Sir John Sedley of St Clere; or disappointed courtiers in economic difficulties, like Sir Thomas Walsingham; and combining nearly all these traits their leader, Sir Anthony Weldon, whose 'desire of rule brought hym to run with ye forwardest'.[1] Inevitably there was rivalry between this group and the moderates.

The theoretical and national basis of that rivalry, as far as there was one, turned on the absolute or qualified support that either group was prepared to accord the two Houses apart from the king. But for most men the basis was less theoretical and national than practical and local. The 'extremists', eager to sever the sheep from the goats, desired sequestration and imprisonment not only of all royalists but of all neuters, as they termed the king's inactive sympathizers. The 'moderates', on the other hand, wished to leave as many as possible, and in particular those numerous neuters, alone; for among neighbours they had no wish to sharpen discords and define divisions. . . .

Increasingly those like Sedley – one of the most influential of the county gentry – who thought in terms of county politics, were being forced from the core by those who, for various reasons, now looked to the state and thought nationally.[2] The core had now changed. Weldon, Livesey, Blount remained. But the milder men, the great men of the county gentry like Sir James Oxinden and Sir Edward Scott, do not appear as signatories of the remonstrance against Sedley. What sort of men supplanted them? Though all were armigerous, they were all 'parochial gentry'. . . . The majority of them – for since the New Model the core had come increasingly into line with national developments – were Independents. And among them were the three Kentish regicides – Livesey, Dixwell and Garland. The county gentry, county-mindedness and moderatism had vanished from the core of the committee together.

But the county gentry, county-mindedness and moderatism had not yet been forced from the general body of the committee, and the next developments came there. The reins of government were still held by Weldon and his confreres, but the wealth and influence of the county, represented by the county gentry, were now held by the general body. Hence the politics of the core now diverged from those of the county gentry. The latter, of indigenous families, moderate and still anglican, thought in terms of the county, and sought salvation there; the former, of newer families, extremist and puritan or Independent, looked more and more to parliament and army to secure their ideals. Only Sir Anthony Weldon, the chairman – of both core and county gentry – had kept the two divergent sections of the committee together; but with the exclusion of the county gentry from the core he could do so no longer. The greatest asset of the committee – the ramification of those families throughout Kentish society, bringing it into the sphere of the committee's rule – became its liability when they were excluded from the core and subjected to the influence of Royalism. . . .

Hence the explanation of the social changes in committee com-position is more complex than the mere influx of lesser families sug-gests. It denotes the supersession of the county gentry, the eclipse of moderatism, a blow to county-mindedness and a strong tendency to centralization. But would the new committee, with its parochial gentry and its newcomers, be able to hold the county? It would not. The way was prepared for the major-generals. . . .

Such was Kent and its county committee on the eve of rebellion in 1648 – that impossible rebellion, to contemporaries, which began the second civil war. . . .

The ancient, indigenous gentry like the Twysdens and Honywoods – rooted in their lands, moderate, anglican, county-minded – had been embittered by sequestration if they were royalists, and elbowed out of their natural leadership of Kentish society if parliamentarians. Control of the county committee had passed from these county gentry to other men. It had passed to the core of extremists, mainly of new and unpopular families like Sir Michael Livesey the regicide, national and Independent in outlook. But control of Kentish society had not passed to these extreme men, and when in 1648 the central knot of county gentry united as they had never done since 1640, nearly all Kentish society was drawn together in their following. Were they not all one family? Rebellion was not impossible; it was inevitable; and the dominant word was clear in their battle cry, 'For God, King Charles, and Kent'.

Before the national armies under Fairfax they failed. The county gentry were still excluded from the government of Kent; the new gentry remained the core of the reorganized county committee of the 'fifties; and the parochial gentry of the old accounts committee became its general body. But the problem of controlling Kentish society remained. The new gentry and the parochial families failed; the major-generals also failed. And when Cromwell had died, and in 1660 the people of Kent came down to Dover to greet Charles II, it was not only the king but the old families, the county gentry, that were restored.

[*The County Committee of Kent in the Civil War*, Department of English Local History Occasional Papers, No. 9, edited by H. P. R. Finberg (University College, Leicester, 1957).]

Notes

1. Sir Anthony Weldon, *The Court and Character of King James. Whereunto is added the Court of King Charles.*

2. Sedley did his utmost to regain favour, but having sowed the wind, he reaped the whirlwind: he was twice sequestered and at least once fined on the false allegation of assisting the 1648 rebellion.

III

Political Theory

14 James Harrington

J. SCHKLAR

It is well known that each age writes history anew to serve its own purposes and that the history of political ideas is no exception to this rule. The precise nature of these changes in perspective, however, bears investigation. For not only can their study help us to understand the past; it may also lead us to a better understanding of our own intellectual situation. In this quest the political theories of the seventeenth century and particularly of the English Civil War are especially rewarding. It was in those memorable years that all the major issues of modern political theory were first stated, and with the most perfect clarity. As we have come to reject the optimism of the eighteenth century, and the crude positivism of the nineteenth, we tend more and more to return to our origins in search of a new start. This involves a good deal of reinterpretation, as the intensity with which the writings of Hobbes and Locke, for instance, are being re-examined in England and America testify. These philosophical giants have, however, by the force of their ideas been able to limit the scope of interpretive license. A provocative minor writer, such as Harrington, may for this reason be more revealing. . . .

What is at stake here is the intrusion of ideology upon historical analysis. And ideology must be understood in three distinct senses. First of all there are simply the political convictions and preoccupations of later thinkers who read them into Harrington. Secondly, there was ideology, not as a mere matter of political preferences, but in its historicist, all-explaining form. Here the metaphors of historical explanation become personified entities, and catch-words like 'feudal', 'bourgeois' and 'revolution', dominate the stage entirely, while individual thinkers and events are used solely to prove the reality and necessity of these abstractions. Few writers have been exploited for this purpose more thoroughly than Harrington. Nor has this been entirely accidental. As one whose own main concern was with revolutions he was sure to become a center of interest for those ideologists whose thought is both the product of, and a continuous reflection upon, social conflict. It is this circumstance that makes Harrington such an excellent case-study for those who wish to examine the play of ideology upon history. . . .

That Marxists should concentrate on revolutions is hardly surprising – that *was* politics. And the Civil War as a part of the 'bourgeois revolution' was bound to come in for its share of analysis.[1] Harrington, moreover, had more to contribute to the 'bourgeois' than to the 'Puritan' revolution. Indeed, as historicism turned to economism in general, Marxists were not alone in noticing how remarkably modern it was of him to have discovered 'the principle that the economic elements in a State will determine its government'.[2] Now this is fair enough: Harrington too prided himself on the discovery of the principle of 'the balance', the idea that those who have the greatest share of property must rule. That power follows property was undeniably his belief. However, it was left to Eduard Bernstein to discover that this simple formula made him a precursor of historical materialism. There was, of course, Harrington's use of the word 'super-structure' to describe political institutions to justify this suggestion, but there was more. Harrington, Bernstein felt, had accurately diagnosed the class relationships prevailing in seventeenth-century England. Far from being mistaken about the impossibility of a restored monarchy, he had really foreseen that absolutism was impossible, and that the bourgeoisie must rule, as, in fact, it did after 1688. In short, Harrington had discovered the 'bourgeois revolution', not just 'the balance'. . . .[3]

R. H. Tawney has surely done more than anyone else to make that revolution intelligible, and he alone has given us a subtle and fascinating portrait of Harrington in the context of his age. He does not doubt that the decline of the nobility and the rise of capitalism were at the root of the Civil War, but at least we are told exactly who was rising and who was falling. According to Tawney's calculations, there emerged along with urban capitalists a class of rural ones, the gentry, who by benefiting from Tudor policies and by improving their estates, came to be part of the new bourgeois order that rose to challenge the Establishment.

If this is still the old bourgeois revolution it has at least been ruralized and we have been liberated from 1789, 1848 and 1917. For 'Tawney's country' is seventeenth-century England, his evidence is seventeenth-century evidence and the writers whom he quotes are seventeenth-century writers. Moreover, if the gentry had their Marx it was at least not a nineteenth-century Marx, but Harrington. . . . The only fault that Tawney can find in this prodigy is the weakness of all 'one key' explanations and the failure to grasp 'the dynamic power of religious conviction'.[4] It is, of course, the very charge he has for years brought against doctrinaire Marxism. What remains is impressive enough, and it has found many supporters. It is a persuasive picture because due weight is given to Harrington's limitations, his pre-occupation with peace and order, and his debts to earlier writers. However, it does not stand up. Poor Harrington simply cannot be made to bear the burdens of a twentieth-century social historian. . . .

To begin with, Harrington had no idea whatsoever of what we today call economic life. He never spoke of 'rents, sales or profits', only of property. Changes in ownership of property, not economic development, were his sole concern.[5] Now the political consequences of the amounts of property held by either a few or many persons were indeed a matter of 'necessity', but it was not 'historical necessity', not the logic of an historical situation at all. The necessity that Harrington had in mind was the universal need to eat. From this it follows that anyone who has the means to feed men, controls them. It also means that he has the power to maintain soldiers who depend on him. . . .

Happily the Tudor kings by statutes of alienation and by expropriating the clergy had enriched the people and destroyed the nobility. However, by depriving itself of the social and military support of the nobles the monarchy itself became impossible, for it was not a Turkish absolutism in which the king owned the balance of property. In England the people now held the balance, and it only remained for Englishmen to face the facts and set up political institutions compatible with this new order.

There is much that is ingenious in this account, but is it good modern social history? There is neither a notion of economics nor of class conflict in all this. Nor did Harrington ever claim to have said anything new. He merely repeated the accounts given by Bacon, Raleigh, Selden, and Henry Wotton. Not one of them spoke of the 'rise of the gentry', but all described the conflict that our textbooks have long spoken of as the end of feudalism and the rise of absolutism. . . . Harrington's only contribution to this history was to see the rise of the people as the consequence of Tudor policy and to explain the origins of the Civil War by that fact. The conflict itself had been one between absolutist legal institutions and a new economic–military balance of power. His originality was in the correlation of feudal history with the Polybian theory of constitutions. Had Tawney not insisted on treating Harrington's constitutional preoccupations as trivial, he would not have so distorted his ideas.

Against the traditionalists Harrington had to show only what conditions were necessary for the rule of law. He did not have to justify the inseparability of law and property, since their constitutional theory, too, rested on it. To refute Hobbes, however, he had to find a new answer to the question, 'What is law?' And it is here that his theory of 'interest' really comes to play its part. . . .[6]

Legitimacy is based solely on interest, on the balance of property. Effective law can only be made by those who possess the balance of property, and stability depends on law expressing their interests. It follows that the only legitimate government, the only government that *should* rule, is that which must in fact rule – that is, the government of the dominant 'interest'. An intelligent government will acquire authority, but its legitimacy rests on the interests that it represents. Against Hobbes's psychological account of the origins of law Harrington simply pitted an institutional one. It is an argument which, in rather less subtle form, still rages among political theorists. . . .

Tawney is perfectly right in attributing to Harrington a sense for the 'impersonal forces'. The trouble is that this came not from any historical sense, but from its total absence. One need only compare his account of the origins of the Civil War to Hobbes's. To Hobbes it was a war of ideologies. The doctrines of fanatical preachers, the seditious universities and the fantasies of those who, like Harrington, had derived exaggerated notions about Greek and Roman liberty from their youthful readings of classical authors, these were the causes of the disaster.[7] Hobbes was as sure as any post-Gardiner historian that it was a war of minorities. The people had merely followed prospects of pay and plunder. As for 'social factors', Hobbes noted the city merchants' disinclination to pay taxes, and the hopes of improvident gentlemen who were out to make their fortune in war; but these were minor points for him.[8] Ideas and the passions they produced were at the heart of the war. Now Harrington, having friends on both sides, was not, like Hobbes, inclined to deal out praise and blame. It was not the characters of the king or of the rebels that had caused the war, it was the nature of the situation.[9]

However, Harrington never gave the barest account of what that situation really was. He never described the interests at work. He is even less sociological than Hobbes, not to speak of Baxter. After repeating his predecessors' accounts of Tudor policy he tells us in one paragraph that the balance of property and power had shifted to the people and the Commons. Elizabeth had been able to charm them into acquiescence. The Stuarts, prompted by false counsellors, had ignored their demands, and, presumably lacking charm, were bound to fall. That is all he knew, that is all he had observed. Yet these were the crucial years during which the gentry is said to have been transformed. But Harrington had no interest in these events as such. He had read of republican institutions; he wanted them in England. His war was a very simple one between the monarchy and the people, a political war of institutions. There is no mention of the social or economic trends of his own age. He tells us nothing of the life of the towns, nor did he notice that the actual trend was toward the consolidation of estates. . . .

There is little left of Tawney's objective social historian; of the seventeenth-century Marx nothing remains at all. There is only a very ingenious defender of classical republicanism, an institutional historian who applied a modified version of Polybius to the history of England. . . .

Facing the 'rising gentry' is now a very different species of gentlemen. Trevor-Roper's gentry are far from prosperous. Stagnant economically, politically disgruntled, they are shopping for ideologies. . . .

Of this unattractive group, Trevor-Roper tells us, Cromwell was the incarnation, and Harrington the ideologue – still the Marx of the gentry here, but a very different gentry and a very different Marx. The science of society has been replaced by disastrous prophecy. Instead of giving his clients an accurate view of their prospects Harrington gave them a dream-picture of what they wished to be. . . .

It is an immensely persuasive picture. As Hexter says, we've seen these types before, and he mentions the Raubritter and Lord Eldon's entourage. But why stop there? Surely we have seen all this in our own day. As we have emerged from the twin myths of the eternal 'right' and 'left' and of the creativity of revolutionary movements, we have come to a new view of the nature of fanaticism and the forces that feed it.[10] And who knows more about the most ghoulish manifestations of nihilism than the author of *The Last Days of Hitler*?[11] The fact is that the picture of a group of socially displaced malcontents, animated by a pure wish to destroy the 'system', corresponds far more to our own experience than that of a sturdy, solid group of consciously 'rising' men, engaging in radical politics so as to assert the claims of their class against an order in which they are, after all, getting on. To which it might, of course, be very justly answered that we have not been living through the 'bourgeois revolution'. The impression remains that psychologically Trevor-Roper wins hands down. It has simply become difficult to envision a class-revolution of any kind. The work of nihilistic discontent, on the other hand, is not unfamiliar. . . .

But it is in the structure of government of *Oceana*, and in its policies, that Trevor-Roper's case finds its greatest support. Although it is an active state it has no taxes and no bureaucracy; administration is local, even if the traditional division of England has been replaced by a more symmetrical one. The 'owner at his plow' is the genius of this society. The city is to be curbed, since ancient history 'proves' that where city-life has had 'the stronger influence' in a republic it led to turbulence. The clergy and the lawyers, the natural deceivers of the people, are to be banished from political life. Indeed, one of the advantages of ending primogeniture was that it would end the flow of younger sons into these professions. . . . Here indeed is a 'pseudo-realistic utopia', a mixture of prophecy, historical speculation and exhortation that might well appeal to people like Trevor-Roper's rebellious hay-seeds.

Nevertheless, it is a false picture. Whatever may have been happening to the gentry, Harrington was not their Marx, and not their Lenin – neither a discoverer of the springs of history, nor a maker of ideology. All that Trevor-Roper has done is to turn Tawney's Harrington on his head, along with the 'rising-gentry' and the entire 'bourgeois revolution'. It is a procedure that does little to explain him. . . .

The first question is whether Harrington, in fact, provided the Cromwellian gentry with their operative political ideas. The second question is what light, if any, the ideology of the gentry can cast upon the character of Harrington's thought. For Trevor-Roper's Harrington depends not only upon a positive answer to the first question. It also assumes that this function of Harrington's thought, the role it played in gentry politics, corresponds exactly to Harrington's intentions. The present argument is that both these propositions are false. The first is a simple mistake in fact, the second a common, but extremely obvious, error in the art of historical interpretation. One need only recall how often Rousseau has been treated as if the Jacobins had *written*, rather than *quoted*, the *Social Contract*, to see, at once, what has happened to Harrington. In both cases the intellectual biography of a man has been distorted in the course of a far more general and complex argument about the 'nature' and 'causes' of a revolution. If Tawney is, perhaps, mistaken in his view of Harrington's purposes and methods, he at least has given us a portrait of a man, even if a rather impressionistic one. The same can hardly be said of Trevor-Roper's Harrington. What we get here is not a picture of a thinker, but a personificaion, an artificial assemblage of the various roles that his ideas *may* have played in gentry politics. This montage of their potential functions is then passed off as a genuine picture of Harrington's ideas. . . .

It is the habit of personifying events, ages, nations, classes and other groups, indeed history itself, that has led to the depersonalizing of individuals.[12] For it is now these abstract categories that have motives and intentions that must be uncovered and evaluated as one judges the behavior of individuals. Ideas are now rationalizations, deceptions practiced semi-consciously by groups, and the omniscient historian must expose them and grade them as 'ideology', 'utopia' or 'false consciousness', depending on their relation to the true standard – the course of 'real' history.[13] This has been the method of neo-Tories no less than of Marxists. According to the latter the 'virtue' of the seventeenth-century bourgeoisie was to have been 'progressive', that is, in line with the demands of history. Their error was to have thought that they were a 'universal' class, realizing general moral and religious values, not just their own aspirations; and this disguise must be pulled aside. Thus, too, the sin of Trevor-Roper's gentry is not that they were nasty, but that they attempted the impossible by vainly trying to interfere with the set course of England's historical development; and because they could not succeed their ideology was a mere cover for their impotence, 'false consciousness'. The terms of historical classification now become those of moral obloquy. Puritanism is 'really' only the 'veil of the bourgeoisie' or the 'false consciousness' of the declining gentry. Hobbes's philosophy was 'really' only 'bourgeois ideology'; Harrington's, that of an array of distempered 'mere' gentry. The revolution was 'really' caused by the rising classes, or it was 'really' caused by declining groups.

As has been well observed – and by a Marxist too – to describe Puritanism as the ideology of the declining gentry does little to explain the spiritual life of Milton or Vane.[14] To classify it as the rationalization of bourgeois aspirations does no better.[15] Nor does this distributing of identification disks throw much light upon Hobbes and Harrington. The only extenuating circumstance that excuses this rage for revealing the intimate secrets of groups and classes, and of history itself, is the political prudery of the Whigs, which was designed to bring out the worst in anyone. For to have said that the Civil War was 'really' about 'faith and freedom', not a 'social war' but 'a war of ideas', was to invite abuse.[16] Whatever else wars may be, they are social events in which organized groups of men fight each other. . . .

It remains to disentangle Harrington from the fortunes of the gentry and the 'real' causes of the Great Rebellion. To begin with, Trevor-Roper accepts Tawney's view that Harrington described the 'rise of the gentry', and in a way that was different from the earlier accounts of the decline of the nobility by Bacon, Raleigh and Selden. This, as we have seen, was not the case. If he appealed to the gentry this was not the reason for his popularity. However, the gentry did not in fact accept Harrington's ideas, and at no time did *Oceana* become the intellectual weapon, the verbal gunpowder, of the Independents. If they and Cromwell were the political leaders of the mere gentry, as Trevor-Roper claims, then Harrington never became their prophet. . . . Moreover, if Trevor-Roper were not so anxious to destroy Tawney's unreal Harrington he might well have asked himself who, in fact, did write Cromwell's propaganda, who answered his critics and rationalized his policies? It was not Harrington; it was Milton. The dying gasp of Independent ideology is the *Ready and Easy Way*. Here is the disillusion with 'the people', the call for the rule of the best, the best being the last Commonwealthmen. Here, too, is the religious fervor, the true note of seventeenth-century ideological combat. It is here that the Commonwealth is held up as the will of God, as toleration had earlier been defended as the way to help men to God. As for Cromwell's radical Republican opponents, they talked of rights, consent, the 'will of the nation' and 'the cause we fought for'. Whether the gentry was coming up or going down, these were the terms in which they, and the majority of their contemporaries, talked. It was not Harrington's manner any more than it was Hobbes's. That is why no one cared for them. . . .

['Ideology Hunting: the Case of James Harrington', *The American Political Science Review*, LIII (1959).]

Notes

1. C. Hill, 'The English Civil War Interpreted by Marx and Engels', *Science and Society*, vol. 12 (1948), pp. 130–56; L. Krieger, 'Marx and Engels as Historians', *Journal of the History of Ideas*, vol. 14 (1953), pp. 381–403.

2. J. Bonar, *Philosophy and Political Economy* (London, 1922), p. 895; H. F. Russell Smith, *James Harrington and his Oceana* (Cambridge, 1914), pp. 23–4 and 28.

3. E. Bernstein, *Sozialismus und Demokratie in der grossen englischen Revolution* (Stuttgart, 1919), pp. 259–67.

4. R. H. Tawney, 'The Rise of the Gentry', *Economic History Review*, vol. 11 (1941), pp. 36–7; 'Harrington's Interpretation of His Age', *Proceedings of the British Academy*, vol. 27 (1941), pp. 200, 204, 221.

5. I am very much indebted to the analysis of J. G. A. Pocock, *The Ancient Constitution and the Feudal Law* (Cambridge, 1957), pp. 128–30, and to his letter to *Encounter*, July 1958.

6. R. Polin, 'Economique et Politique au XVIIe Siècle: L'Oceana de James Harrington', *Revue Française de Science Politique*, vol. 2 (1952), pp. 27 and 30–1; F. D. Wormuth, *The Origins of Modern Constitutionalism* (New York, 1949), p. 135.

7. *Behemoth*, *English Works* (London, 1840), vol. VI, pp. 167–218, 362; *Leviathan*, pp. 140–1 and 214.

8. *Behemoth*, pp. 166–9.

9. *Oceana*, ed. S. B. Liljegren (Lund, 1924), p. 50. It was not, thus, that his friend Charles I had been *bad*, just helpless. *Works*, ed. John Tolland (London, 1771), p. 367.

10. See R. Aron, *The Opium of the Intellectuals*, tr. by T. Kilmartin (New York, 1957), *passim*, for a discussion both of the obsolescence of these ideas and the passions which they can stir among café-politicians.

11. I am happy to see that I am not alone in this suspicion, see M. Beloff, 'Another Fallen Idol?', *Encounter*, January 1959, p. 74.

12. Unlike Karl Popper, I do not regard the personification of historical categories as analogous to medieval realism. His own medieval nominalism would make the writing of any sort of history impossible. How little he has understood the real problems of historical explanation and especially those created by generalizations on different levels of abstractness can be seen by his claim that the First World War is an 'individual thing' just like Alexander the Great. *The Poverty of Historicism* (Boston, 1957), pp. 17–34, 76–83, 143–52.

13. Krieger, 'Marx and Engels', *loc. cit.*; K. Mannheim, *Ideology and Utopia* (Harvest Books, New York, n.d.), *passim* and pp. 56 and 93–7.

14. C. Hill, 'Recent Interpretations of the Civil War', *History* (n.s.), vol. 41 (1956), p. 74.

15. Bernstein, *op. cit.*, pp. 1–7; Hill, 'Marx and Engels', *loc. cit.*, pp. 132 and

154; *The English Revolution*, pp. 13 and 17; D. W. Petegorsky, *Left-Wing Democracy in the English Civil War* (London, 1940), pp. 22 and 25.

16. J. H. Hexter, 'Storm over the Gentry', *Encounter*, May 1958; see also C. Firth, *Cromwell and the Rule of the Puritans in England* (Oxford, 1953), p. 71, or G. M. Trevelyan, *England under the Stuarts* (London, 1922), pp. 195–6 and 228–31, where it is said, 'in motive it was a war not like the French or American of classes or of districts, but of ideas', p. 229.

Part Two
SELECT DOCUMENTS

I

Social Change

15 England in 1600

T. WILSON

Thomas Wilson (c. 1560–1629) was the younger son of a gentleman, who earned a rather precarious living in a great variety of positions from consul in the diplomatic service to government archivist, to the Master of a Cambridge College. His description of England was written in 1600, and reflects the prejudices of his class; but it is also the first attempt ever made at an analysis of English society on class lines with the use of statistical or pseudo-statistical information.

... It cannot be denied but [that] the common people are very rich, albeit they be much decayed from the states they were wont to have, for the gentlemen which were wont to addict themselves to the wars are now for the most part grown to become good husbands and know as well how to improve their lands to the uttermost as the farmer or countryman, so that they take their farms into their hands as the leases expire and either till themselves or else let them out to those who will give most; whereby the yeomanry of England is decayed and become servants to gentlemen, which were wont to be the glory of the country and good neighbourhood and hospitality; notwithstanding there are yet some store of those yeomen left who have long leases of such lands and lordships as they hold, yea, I know many yeomen in divers provinces in England which are able yearly to spend betwixt £300 and £500 yearly by their lands and leases, and some twice and some thrice as much; but my young masters, the sons of such, not contented with the states of their fathers' to be counted yeoman and called John or Robert (such a one), but must skip into his velvet breeches and silken doublet and, getting to be admitted into some Inn of Court or Chancery, must ever after think scorn to be called any other than gentleman; which gentlemen indeed, perceiving them unfit to do them that service that their fathers did, when their leases do expire turn them out of their lands (which was never wont to be done, the farmer accounting his state as good as inheritance in times past), and let them to such as are not by their bad pennyworths able to gentleman it as others have done.

Notwithstanding this that the great yeomanry is decayed, yet by this means the commonalty is increased, twenty now perhaps with their labour and diligence living well and wealthily off that land which our great yeoman held before, who did no other good but maintain beef and brews for such idle persons as would come and eat it, a fine daughter or two to be married after with £10,000 to some covetous mongrel gentleman. Of these yeomen of the richest sort which are able to lend the Queen money (as they do ordinarily upon her letters called privy seals whensoever she has any wars defensive or offensive or any other enterprise) there are accounted to be about 10,000 in country villages, besides citizens.

There are, moreover, of yeomen of meaner ability which are called Freeholders, for, that they are owners of lands which hold by no base service of any lord or superior, such as are able to keep 10 or 11 or 8 or 6 milch cows, 5 or 6 horses to till their ground, besides young beasts and sheep and are accounted to be worth each of them in all their substance and stock betwixt £300 and £500, more or less; of these, I say, there are reckoned to be in England and Wales about the number of 80,000, as I have seen in sheriffs' books.

The rest are copyholders and cottagers, as they call them, who hold some land and tenements of some other lord which is parcel of the demesne of his seigniory or manor, at the will of the Lord, and these are some of them men of as great ability as any of the rest; and some poor, and live chiefly upon country labour, working by the day for meat and drink and some small wages. . . .

[Citizens] by reason of the great privileges they enjoy, every city being as it were a commonwealth among themselves, no other officer of the Queen nor other having authority to intermeddle amongst them, must needs be exceeding well to pass. . . . And in Norwich I have known in my time twenty-four aldermen which were esteemed to be worth £20,000 apiece, some much more, and the better sort of citizens the half; but if we should speak of London and some other maritime places, we should find it much exceeding this rate. It is well known that at this time there are in London some merchants worth £100,000 and he is not accounted rich that cannot reach to £50,000 or near it. . . .

I have seen divers books, which have been collected by Secretaries and Counsellors of State, which did exactly show the several revenues of every nobleman, knights and gentlemen throughout the realm, and curiously collected by an uncle of mine which not long since was principal secretary to the Queen; but it were too long in this simple discourse to set down the particularities thereof, but comparing these books together I find great alterations almost every year, so mutable are worldly things and worldly men's affairs. . . . Earls some day decay, some increase according to the course of the world, but that which I have noted by perusing many of the said books, and of the later sort, is that still the total sum grows much to one reckoning, and that is to £100,000 rent yearly, accounting them all in gross to avoid prolixity. If a man would proportion this amongst nineteen Earls and a Marquis, it would be no great matter, to every one £5,000 rent, but as some exceed that much so many come short of it.

The thirty-nine Barons and two Viscounts do not much exceed that sum, their revenue is reckoned together to amount of £120,000 yearly.

The Bishops' revenues amount to about £22,500 yearly altogether, whereof three of them, viz. Canterbury, Winchester and Ely, receive rent per annum betwixt £2,000 and 3,000, the rest betwixt £1,000 and 500 and some less. . . .

. . . The state of the clergy is not altogether so bare as may perhaps be conjectured by the smallness of their revenue, for that they never raise nor rack their rents, nor put out tenants, as the noblemen and gentlemen do to the uttermost penny; but do let their lands as they were let 100 years since, reserving to themselves and their successors some commodities besides the bare rent, as corn, muttons, beef, poultry and suchlike; but to say the truth, their wings are well clipped of late by courtiers and noblemen and some quite cut away, both feather, flesh and bone.

These are the states of the nobility, both clergy and lay, which are called *nobilitas major*; there rests to touch those of the meaner nobility, which are termed *nobilitas minor* and are either knights, esquires, gentlemen, lawyers, professors and ministers, archdeacons, prebends and vicars.

There are accounted to be in England about the number of 500 knights as I have reckoned them, both by divers Commissions of several shire[s] remaining in the Chancery office for making of justices of [the] peace, of which commission all knights [tend] to be unless they be put by for religion or some particular disfavour. . . . These for the most part are men for living betwixt £1,000 and £2,000 yearly, and many of them equal the best barons and come not much behind many Earls, as I have divers, viz. Sir John Petre, Sir John Harington, Sir Nicholas Bacon and others, who are thought to be able to spend yearly betwixt £5,000 and £7,000 of good land.

Those which we call esquires are gentlemen whose ancestors are, or have been, knights, or else they are the heirs and eldest of their houses, and of some competent quantity of revenue fit to be called to office and authority in their county where they live; of these there are esteemed to be in England, as I have seen by the book of musters of every several shire, to the number of 16,000 or thereabouts, whereof there are of them in Commissions of the peace about 1,400 in every [county], in some forty, in some fifty, some thirty, more or less; these are men in living betwixt £1,000 and £500 rent. Especially about London and the counties adjoining, where their lands are set to the highest, he is not counted of any great reckoning unless he be betwixt 1,000 marks or £1,000, but northward and far off a gentleman of good reputation may be content with £300 and £400 yearly. These are the elder brothers.

I cannot speak of the number of younger brothers, albeit I be one of the number myself, but for their estate there is no man has better cause to know it, nor less cause to praise it; their state is of all stations for gentlemen most miserable, for if our fathers possess £1,000 or £2,000 yearly, at his death he cannot give a foot of land to his younger children in inheritance, unless it be by lease for twenty-one years or for three lives, . . . or else be purchased by himself and not descended, [in which case] he may demise as much as he thinks good to his younger children. But such a fever hectic has custom brought in and inured amongst fathers, and such fond desire they have to leave a great show of the stock of their house, though the branches be withered, that they will not do it, but my elder brother forsooth must be my master. He must have all, and all the [other brothers] that which the cat left on the malt-heap, perhaps some small annuity during his life or what please our elder brother's worship to bestow upon us, if we please him and my mistress his wife. This I must confess does us good someways, for it makes us industrious to apply ourselves to letters or to arms, whereby many times we become my master elder brothers' masters, or at least their betters in honour and reputation, while he lives at home like a mome and knows the sound of no other bell but his own.

[Common Lawyers:] within these forty or fifty years, since the practise of civil law has been as it were wholly banished and abrogated, and since the clergy has been trodden down by the taking away of church livings, and since the long continuance of peace has bred an inward canker and [un]rest in men's minds, the people doing nothing but jar and wrangle one with another, these lawyers by the ruins of neighbours' contentions are grown so great, so rich and so proud, that no other sort dare meddle with them; their number is so great now that, to say the truth, they can scarcely live one by another, the practice being drawn into a few hands of those which are most renowned, and all the rest live by pettifogging, seeking means to set their neighbours at variance whereby they may gain on both sides. This is one of the greatest inconveniences in the land, that the number of the lawyers are so great they undo the country people and buy up all the lands that are to be sold; so that young gentlemen or others newly coming to their livings, some of them prying into his evidence will find the means to set him at variance with some other, or some other with him, by some pretence or quidity, and when they have half consumed themselves in suits they are fain to sell their land to follow the process and pay their debts, and then that becomes a prey to lawyers.

For the greatness of some of them is incredible, not to speak of the twelve chief judges and the multitude of sergeants, which are most of them accounted men of £20,000 or £30,000 yearly; there is one at this day of a meaner degree, viz. the Queen's Attorney[-General], who within this ten years to my knowledge was not able to spend above £100 a year, and now by his own lands, his coins, and his office he may spend betwixt £12,000 and £14,000.

There are in number of Sergeants about thirty, Councillors about 2,000, and as many attorneys, besides solicitors and pettifoggers an infinite number, there being no province, city, town, nor scarce village free from them, unless the Isle of Anglesey, which boast they never had lawyers nor foxes.

[*The State of England 1600*, ed. F. J. Fisher, *Camden Miscellany*, XVI. *Camden Soc.*, LII (1936).]

16 The Increase of Gentry

T. SMITH

Sir Thomas Smith (1513–77) had a distinguished career as a scholar and a statesman, serving both as Regius Professor of Civil Law at Cambridge and as Secretary of State. His book, which was written in 1562–66, is regarded as a standard work on the late Tudor constitution.

... Ordinarily the king does only make knights and create barons or higher degrees; for, as for gentlemen, they be made good cheap in England. For whosoever studies the laws of the realm, who studies at the universities, who professes liberal sciences and to be short, who can live idly and without manual labour, and will bear the port, charge and countenance of a gentleman, he shall be called master, for that is the title men give to esquires and other gentlemen, and shall be taken for a gentleman ...; (and if need be) a king of heralds shall also give him for money, arms newly made and invented, the title whereof shall pretend to have been found by the said herald in perusing and viewing of old registers, where his ancestors in times past had been recorded to bear the same.

A man may make doubt and question whether this manner of making gentlemen is to be allowed or no, and for my part I am of that opinion that it is not amiss. For first the prince loses nothing by it, as he should do if it were as in France: for the yeoman or husbandman is no more subject to *taille* or tax in England than the gentleman. ... As for their outward show, a gentleman (if he will be so accounted) must go like a gentleman, a yeoman like a yeoman and a rascal like a rascal; and if he be called to the wars, he must and will (whatsoever it cost him) array himself and arm himself according to the vocation which he pretends: he must show also a more manly courage and tokens of a better education, higher stomach and bountifuller liberality than others, and keep about him idle servants who shall do nothing but wait on him. So that no man has hurt by it, but he himself, who hereby perchance will bear a bigger sail than he is able to maintain.

[*De Republica Anglorum*, ed. L. Alston (Cambridge, 1906).]

17 Evidence of Economic Growth

W. HARRISON

William Harrison (1534–93) was a country parson with an interest in topography and chronology. His Description of England, which was published in 1577, provides a vivid and on the whole convincing picture of the increasing material comforts of the upper levels of early Elizabethan society. His analysis of the evils of the day is perhaps more a product of conservative prejudice than of accurate observation.

. . . The ancient manors and houses of our gentlemen are yet, and for the most part, of strong timber, in framing whereof our carpenters have been and are worthily preferred before those of like science among all other nations. Howbeit such as be lately built are commonly either of brick or hard stone, or both; their rooms large and comely, and houses of office further distant from their lodgings. Those of the nobility are likewise wrought with brick and hard stone, as provision may best be made; but so magnificent and stately, as the basest hound of a baron does often match in our days with some honours of princes in old time. So that if ever curious building did flourish in England, it is in these our years, wherein our workmen excel. . . .

The furniture of our houses also exceeds, and is grown in manner even to passing delicacy; and herein I do not speak of the nobility and gentry only, but likewise of the lowest sort in most places of our south country, that have anything at all to take to. Certainly, in noblemen's houses it is not rare to see abundance of arras, rich hangings of tapestry, silver vessels and so much other plate, as may furnish sundry cupboards, to the sum oftentimes of £1,000 or £2,000 at the least; whereby the value of this and the rest of their stuff does grow to be almost inestimable. Likewise in the houses of knights, gentlemen, merchantmen and some other wealthy citizens, it is not [unusual] to behold generally their great provision of tapestry, Turkey work, pewter, brass, fine linen and thereto costly cupboards of plate, worth £500 or £600 or £1,000, to be deemed by estimation. But as herein all these sorts do far exceed their elders and predecessors, and in neatness and curiosity the merchant all other, so in time past, the costly furniture stayed there, whereas now it is descended yet lower, even unto the inferior artificers and many farmers, who by virtue of their old and not of their new leases have for the most part learnt also to garnish their cupboards with plate, their joined beds with tapestry and silk hangings, and their tables with carpets and fine napery, whereby the wealth of our country (God be praised therefore, and give us grace to employ it well) doth infinitely appear. Neither do I speak this in reproach of any man, God is my judge, but to show that I do rejoice rather to see how God hath blessed us with his good gifts; and whilst I behold how that in a time wherein all things are grown to most excessive prices, and what commodity so ever is to be had is daily plucked from the commonalty by such as look into every trade, we do yet find the means to obtain and achieve such furniture as heretofore has been impossible.

There are old men yet dwelling in the village where I remain, which have noted three things to be marvellously altered in England within their sound remembrance; and other three things [that] are too too much increased. One is the multitude of chimneys lately erected, whereas in their young days there were not above two or three, if so many, in most uplandish towns of the realm (the religious houses and manor places of their lords always excepted and peradventure some great personages), but each one made his fire against a reredos in the hall, where he dined and dressed his meat.

The second is the great (although not general) amendment of lodging, for (said they) our fathers (yea and we ourselves also) have lain full oft upon straw pallets, on rough mats covered only with a sheet, under coverlets made of dagswain or hopharlots (I use their own terms), and a good round log under their heads instead of a bolster or pillow. If it were so that our fathers or the good man of the house had within seven years after his marriage purchased a mattress or flock bed, and thereto a sack of chaff to rest his head upon, he thought himself to be as well lodged as the lord of the town, that peradventure lay seldom in a bed of down or whole feathers; so well were they contented, and with such base kind of furniture; which also is not very much amended as yet in some parts of Bedfordshire, and elsewhere further off from our southern parts. Pillows (said they) were thought meet only for women in childbed. As for servants, if they had any sheet above them, it was well, for seldom had they any under their bodies, to keep them from the pricking straws that ran oft through the canvas of the pallet, and razed their hardened hides.

The third thing they tell of, is the exchange of vessel, as of wooden platters into pewter, and wooden spoons into silver or tin. For so common were all sorts of wooden stuff in old time, that a man should hardly find four pieces of pewter (of which one was peradventure a salt) in a good farmer's house, and yet for all this frugality (if it so be justly called) they were scarce able to live and pay their rents at their days without selling of a cow, or a horse, or more, although they paid but four pounds at the uttermost by the year. Such also was their poverty that if some one odd farmer or husbandman had been at the alehouse, a thing greatly used in those days, amongst six or seven of his neighbours, and there in a bravery to show what store he had did cast down his purse, and therein a noble or six shillings in silver . . . (for few such men then cared for gold, because it was not so ready payment, and they were oft enforced to give a penny for the exchange of an angel), it was very likely that all the rest could not lay down so much against it; whereas in my time, although peradventure four pounds of old rent be improved to forty, fifty or a hundred pounds, yet will the farmer as another palm or date tree think his gains very small toward the end of his term, if he have not six or seven years' rent lying by him, therewith to purchase a new lease, besides a fair garnish of pewter on his cupboard, with so much more in odd vessells going about the house, three or four featherbeds, so many coverlets and carpets of tapestry, a silver salt, a bowl for wine (if not a whole nest) and a dozen of spoons to furnish up the suit. This also he takes to be his own clear; for what stock of money soever he gathers and lays up in all his years, it is often seen that the landlord will take such order with him for the same when he renews his lease, which is commonly eight or six years before the old be expired (since it is now grown almost to a custom that if he come not to his lord so long before, another shall step in for a reversion, and so defeat him outright), that it shall never trouble him more than the hair of his beard, when the barber has washed and shaved it from his chin.

And as they commend these, so (beside the decay of housekeeping whereby the poor have been relieved) they speak also of three things that are grown to be very grievous unto them, to wit the enhancing of rents, lately mentioned; the daily oppression of copyholders, whose lords seek to bring their poor tenants almost into plain servitude and misery, daily devising new means, and seeking up all the old, how to cut them shorter and shorter, doubling, trebling, and now and then seven times increasing their fines; driving them also for every trifle to lose and forfeit their tenures (by whom the greatest part of the realm does stand and is maintained) to the end they may fleece them yet more, which is a lamentable hearing. The third thing they talk of is usury, a trade brought in by the Jews, now perfectly practised almost by every christian, and so commonly that he is accounted but for a fool that does lend his money for nothing. . . . Forget not also such landlords as use to value their leases at a secret estimation given of the wealth and credit of the taker, whereby they seem (as it were) to eat them up, and deal with bondmen; so that if the lessee be thought to be worth £100, he shall pay no less for his term, or else another to enter with hard and doubtful covenants. I am sorry to report it, much more grieved to understand of the practice; but most sorrowful of all to understand that men of great port and countenance are so far from suffering their farmers to have any gain at all, that they themselves become graziers, butchers, tanners, sheepmasters, woodmen and *denique quod non*, thereby to enrich themselves, and bring all the wealth of the country into their own hands, leaving the commonalty weak, or as an idol with broken or feeble arms, which may in a time of peace have a plausible show, but when necessity shall enforce, have a heavy and bitter sequel.

[*Description of England* (New Shakespeare Society, 1908).]

18 Evidence of Social Mobility

T. FULLER

Thomas Fuller (1608-61) was a scholarly clergyman of conservative and Royalist views. He deplored the changes that he observed around him.

. . . Our English gentry, such who live southward near London (which for the lustre thereof I may fitly call the sun of our nation) in the warmth of wealth and plenty of pleasures, quickly strip and disrobe themselves of their estates and inheritance, whilst the gentry living in [Northumberland] . . . buckle their estates (as their armour) the closer unto them, and since have no less thriftily defended their patrimony in peace than formerly they valiantly maintained it in war. . . .

The gentry in Middlesex seem sojourners, rather than inhabitants therein. It is not strange that of the thirty-three fore-named families [in 1433] not three of them were extant in the shire 160 years after, in 1593. . . . I impute the brevity (as I may term it) of such gentry in this county to the vicinity of London to them, or rather of them to it. . . .

Hungry time has made a glutton's meal on this catalogue of gentry [of 1433 in Bedfordshire] and has left but a very little morsel for manners remaining, so few of these are found extant in this shire and fewer continuing in a gentle equipage. . . . The lands in Berkshire are very skittish, and often cast their owners. . . .

Let others render a reason why the ancient families in [Huntingdonshire] (more in proportion than elsewhere) are so decayed. This seems a probable cause why many new ones are seated herein, because Huntingdonshire being generally Abbey land . . . after the Dissolution many new purchasers planted themselves therein. . . .

This is a comfortable catalogue [of 1433, in Cumberland] for one delighting in ancient families. . . . Sure I am that northern gentry transplanted into the South, by marriage, purchase or otherwise, do languish and fade away within few generations. Whereas southern men on the like occasions removing northward acquire a settlement in their estates with long continuance. Some peevish natures (delighting to comment all things into the worst sense) impute this to the position of their country, as secured from sale by their distance from London (the staple place of pleasure), whilst I would willingly behold it as the effect and reward of their discreet thrift and moderate expense. Two-thirds of this catalogue of Cumberland, being still extant, and the third extinct for lack of issue, and not estate.

[*The Worthies of England* (1662).]

19 The Grumbles of a 'Mere Gentleman'

J. OGLANDER

Sir John Oglander (1585–1655) is the archetype of the disgruntled backwoods squire, for ever lamenting, often at the expense of logic and consistency, the deteriorating moral and economic condition of his times and his class. Despite his hostility to the Court, it is typical that his conservatism made him a resolute Royalist when Civil War came. What is not typical, however, is his geographical location in the Isle of Wight, whose economy was peculiarly dependent on privateering and supplying the Navy in times of war.

[1622] I do assure myself that my wife and I have lived at Nunwell for the space of fifteen years . . . as happily as our estate, as well and plentifully and in as good repute and fashion as any could, or would, desire. But true content thou must not expect in this world. . . .

The Isle of Wight, since my memory, is infinitely decayed by reason of so many attorneys that have of late made this their habitation and so by suits undone the country. Or else it is for want of the good bargains they were wont to buy from men-of-war, who also bought all our commodities at very high prices, and ready money was easy to be had for all things. Now Peace and Law have beggared us all, so that within living memory many of the gentlemen and almost all the yeomanry are undone. . . .

[1629] In Queen Elizabeth's time . . . the state was well ordered. We had, in a good manner, wars with Spain and peace with France, and the Low Countries' men were our servants and not our masters. Then it was insula fortunata – now infortunata. . . .

It is impossible for a mere country gentleman ever to grow rich or to raise his house. He must have some other vocation with his inheritance, as to be a courtier, lawyer, merchant or some other vocation. If he hath no other vocation let him get a ship and judiciously manage her, or buy some auditor's place or be vice-admiral in his country. By only following the plough he may keep his word and be upright, but will never increase his fortune. . . .[1]

[1642] I believe such times were never before seen in England, when the gentry were made slaves to the commonalty and in their power, not only to abuse but plunder any gentleman. . . .

O the tyrannical misery that the gentlemen of England did endure from July 1642 till April 1643, and how much longer the Lord knoweth! They could call nothing their own and lived in slavery and submission to the unruly base multitude. O tempora, o mores. . . .

From Anno Domini 1641 till Anno Domini 1646, in our unnatural wars, no man understanding the true grounds of it, most of the ancient gentry were either extinct or undone. The King's side were almost all the gentlemen and, of the Parliament's, few. . . .

This island was beyond compare, Anno Domini 1630. . . . It was the Paradise of England, and now, Anno Domini 1647, it is just like the other parts of the Kingdom, a melancholy, dejected, sad place. . . .

If thou desirest to live plentifully, out of debt, worshipfully and with the respect of thy neighbours and the inhabitants, settle thyself to live in the Island and roam not out of it. Learn not by thy grandfather and father, for both to their loss have repented it. . . .

If you will live plentifully and be in action to keep you from melancholy, keep in your hands land enough to fat beasts and sheep. . . .

Be sure, whatever misfortune befalls thee, sell not thy land, which was with much care and pain provided and kept for thee and hath continued so many ages in thy name. Rather feed on bread and water than be the confusion of thy house. . . . Observe this above all. . . .

I scorn base getting and unworthy penurious saving. . . .

Be sure to give all thy sons a vocation, and God will bless thee and them. Without this they will hardly live in this or the next world. Keep not thy children idly at home to be bird-catchers or dog-drivers, but be sure to settle them in a course of life – and that betimes, lest the name of gentry make them too high for it and so, in the end, bring them to beggary.

[*A Royalist's Notebook*, ed. F. Bamford, (1936).]

Notes

1. Sir John Oglander wrote this with his own blood, 25 June 1632, then aged forty-eight years.

20 Changing Styles of Building

R. REYCE

Robert Reyce (?–1638) was a native of Preston, Suffolk, a gentleman, and an antiquary in touch with other scholars like John Selden and Sir John Cotton. He wrote his description of Suffolk in 1618.

. . . And first of their buildings, among which sort I reckon their castles so often mentioned in the days of our forefathers, the ruins whereof are yet in many places extant, so that at this day here is in Suffolk no castle fully standing, or at leastwise none fortified or defensible. Such is the state and policy of this land at this day, and so far differing from former times, and the present administration of other countries, who think that the security of a commonwealth is impaired when such buildings are ruinated. . . .

The next sort of buildings are their mansions and dwelling houses, which by the traces of antiquity yet remaining, I find to be far differing from them of the former times, who used in the situation of their houses to regard profit more than pleasure, and safety more than wholesomeness of the air. From whence we find that all our ancientest houses, for their more security and quiet against all worldly accidents were ever so placed that they were ever environed with a broad and deep ditch or moat, and to that end for the most part they were enforced to the low valleys, that they might the more easily draw water from the next river to enclose their houses. These houses were always built low not with many rooms or above one or two stories, but these more in length than in largeness. Thick were their walls, of squared or rough stone, brick or strong timber, their windows small, their chimneys large, or instead of them to have round hearths in the midst of their great halls or rooms, with round holes or louvres aloft in the roof, which carried away the smoke never offending; whereas our building at this day is chiefly to place the houses where they may be furthest seen, have best prospect, sweetest air and greatest pleasure, their walls thin, whether with brick, stone or timber, their lights large, all for outward show, their rooms square, raised high commonly with three and often with four stories, their chimneys as many but small, their roofs square, and so slender that they are enforced often to repair. . . .

[*Breviary of Suffolk*, ed. Francis Lord Hervey, (1902).]

21 The Status of the Merchant

T. MUN

Thomas Mun (1571–1641) was a prominent London merchant who traded in the Mediterranean and was a director of the East India Company. The purpose of his book, which was written in about 1630 but not published till 1664, was to emphasize the importance of the merchant in increasing national prosperity.

. . . It is true indeed that many merchants here in England, finding less encouragement given to their profession than in other countries, and seeing themselves not so well esteemed as their noble vocation requires, and according to the great consequence of the same, do not therefore labour to attain unto the excellency of their profession; neither is it practised by the Nobility of this kingdom as it is in other states from the father to the son throughout their generations, to the great increase of their wealth and maintenance of their names and families. Whereas the memory of our richest merchants is suddenly extinguished; the son, being left rich, scorns the profession of his father, conceiving more honour to be a gentleman (although but in name), to consume his estate in dark ignorance and excess, than to follow the steps of his father as an industrious merchant to maintain and advance his fortunes.

[*England's Treasure by Forraign Trade* (Oxford, Basil Blackwell, 1933).]

22 Military Decay of the Aristocracy

W. RALEGH

Sir Walter Ralegh (c. 1552–1618) wrote a series of essays on politics during his long imprisonment in the Tower of London from 1603 to 1616. Though highly derivative from Machiavelli, they contain some shrewd observations about the English scene.

... Mysteries, or sophisms of state, are certain secret practices, either for the avoiding of danger or averting such effects as tend not to the preservation of the present state, as it is set or founded.

State mysteries are of two sorts.

1. General; that pertain to all states; as first, to provide by all means, that the same degree or part of the commonwealth do not exceed both in quantity and quality. In quantity, as that the number of the nobility, or of great persons, be not more than the state or common-wealth can bear. In quality, as that none grow in wealth, liberty, honours, etc. more than it is meet for that degree: for as in weights, the heavier weights bear down the scale; so in commonwealths, that part or degree that excels the rest in quality and quantity oversways the rest after it, whereof follow alterations, and conversions of state. Secondly, to provide by all means, that the middle sort of people exceed both the extremes, viz. of nobility and gentry, and the base rascal and beggarly sort. For this makes the state constant and firm, when both the extremes are tied together by a middle sort, as it were with a band; as for any conspiracy of the rich and beggarly sort together, it is not to be feared. To these two points the particular rules in sophisms of every commonwealth are to be applied. ...

The lords in former times were far stronger, more warlike, better followed, living in their countries, than now they are. Your lordship may remember in your reading that there were many earls could bring into the field a thousand barbed horses, many a baron five or six hundred barbed horses, whereas now very few of them can furnish twenty fit to serve the king. But to say the truth, my lord, the justices of peace in England have opposed the injustices of war in England; the king's writ runs over all, and the great seal of England, with that of the next constables, will serve the turn to affront the greatest lords in England, that shall move against the king. The force therefore by which our kings in former times were troubled is vanished away, but the necessities remain. The people therefore, in these latter ages, are no less to be pleased than the peers; for as the latter are become less, so by reason of the training through England, the commons have all the weapons in their hand.

— Was it not so ever?

— No, my good lord; for the noblemen had in their armouries [sufficient] to furnish some of them a thousand, some two thousand, some three thousand men, whereas now there are not many that can arm fifty. . . .

[*The Works of Sir Walter Ralegh*, ed. Thomas Birch (Oxford, 1829).]

23 Landlords and Tenants

J. SELDEN

John Selden (1584-1654) was the most distinguished legal historian and antiquary of his day. His Table Talk was noted down by his secretary and amanuensis, and published long after his death, in 1689.

. . . When men did let their lands under foot,[1] the tenants would fight for their landlords, so that way they had their retribution. But now they will do nothing for them, nay, be the first, if but a constable bid them, that shall lay the landlord by the heels; and therefore 'tis vanity and folly not to take the full value [in rent].

[*Table Talk of John Selden* (London, 1927).]

1. I.e. at nominal or easy rents.

24 Economic Decay of the Aristocracy

D. DEFOE

Daniel Defoe (c. 1661–1731) was a journalist, pamphleteer and novelist. He was a shrewd observer of the social scene, though there is reason to suppose that he is exaggerating in this comment. By 1727 the tide had been running the other way for over a generation.

... In former days the Nobility possessed great estates, and had powerful dependencies; the landed interest was theirs, and almost all the possession was their own; the Commons held under them either in vassalage or villeinage either as vassals, tenants, cottagers or servants. ...

But then two things are to be observed which have happened in England since that time: 1. the Commons have grown rich by industry and commerce; 2. the nobility are become poor or at least poorer; be it by sloth and luxury, I do not determine.

The consequence is this, that the nobility sell their estates and the Commons buy them. And so the landed interest is separated and the Commons possess, I believe, ten parts of twelve, hardly leaving the other two parts of the twelve to the better guided nobility.

[*A Treatise Concerning the Use and Abuse of the Marriage Bed* (1727).]

25 The Crown and the Aristocracy

F. BACON

In 1592 Francis Bacon was still only a promising lawyer and aspiring courtier with his way to make in the world. In this year he published a propaganda piece for the Government defending the achievements of Elizabeth's reign. Among other things he pointed to the growth of prosperity and to the new social role of the aristocracy.

... Now for arguments of the great wealth and plenty in all other respects, let the points following be considered.

There was never the like number of fair and stately houses as have been built and set up from the ground since her Majesty's reign; insomuch that there have been reckoned in one shire that is not great to the number of three and thirty, which have been all new built within that time; and whereof the meanest was never built for two thousand pounds.

There were never the like pleasures of goodly gardens and orchards, walks, pools and parks, as do adorn almost every mansion house.

There was never the like number of beautiful and costly tombs and monuments, which are erected in sundry churches in honourable memory of the dead.

There was never the like quantity of plate, jewels, sumptuous movables and stuff, as is now within the realm.

There was never the like quantity of waste and unprofitable ground inned, reclaimed and improved.

There was never the like husbanding of all sorts of grounds by fencing, manuring and all kinds of good husbandry.

The towns were never better built nor peopled; nor the principal fairs and markets never better customed nor frequented.

The commodities and eases of rivers cut by the hand and brought into a new channel, of piers that have been built, or waters that have been forced and brought against the ground, were never so many.

There was never so many excellent artificers, nor so many new handicrafts used and exercised, nor new commodities made within the realm; as sugar, paper, glass, copper, divers silks and the like.

There was never such complete and honourable provision of horse, armour, weapon, ordinance of the war.

The fifth blessing hath been the great Population and multitude of families increased within her Majesty's days. For which point I refer myself to the proclamations of restraint of building in London, the inhibition of inmates in sundry cities, the restraint of cottages by Act of Parliament and sundry other tokens of record of the surcharge of people. . . .

It is true that there have been in ages past noblemen (as I take it) both of greater possessions and of greater commandment and sway than any are at this day. One reason why the possessions are less I conceive to be, because certain sumptuous veins and humours of expense – as apparel, gaming, maintaining of a kind of followers and the like – do reign more than they did in times past. Another reason is, because noblemen nowadays do deal better with their younger sons than they were accustomed to do heretofore, whereby the principal house receives many abatements. Touching the commandment, which is not indeed so great as it hath been, I take it rather to be a commendation of the time than otherwise. For men were wont factiously to depend upon noblemen; whereof ensued many partialities and divisions, besides much interruption of justice, while the great ones did seek to bear out those that did depend upon them; so as the kings of this realm, finding long since that kind of commandment in noblemen unsafe unto their crown and inconvenient unto their people, thought meet to restrain the same by provision of laws; whereupon grew the statute of retainers; so as men now depend upon the prince and the laws and upon no other. A matter which has also a congruity with the nature of the time; as may be seen in other countries, namely in Spain, where their *grandees* are nothing so potent and so absolute as they have been in times past.

['Observations on a Libel' in *The Life and Letters of Francis Bacon*, ed. J. Spedding (1857–74).]

26 The Causes of Social Mobility

E. WATERHOUSE

Edward Waterhouse (1619–70) came from a gentry family. He spent the Civil War working away in the Bodleian Library at Oxford, and produced thereafter a flow of erudite works on early christianity, heraldry and genealogy Two years before he died, he took holy orders and became a 'fantastical preacher'. He was described by a contemporary as 'a cock-brained man', and his work gives some support to the accusation. He invented words with a freedom that is reminiscent of James Joyce, and his books are poorly organized. But his Gentleman's Monitor *(1665) is perhaps the first analytical study of social mobility ever to have been published. He can claim to be England's first sociologist.*

I. *Causes of Rise*

. . . To have money is to be master of every almost desirable adjustment to God's glory and men's good. Money then being thus prevalent, it cannot be denied to be a probable rise to men and in them to families.

Secondly, favour with the prince is the most undoubted step to honour, wealth and greatness. This I had placed first, but that money is the more general cause of rise, many coming thereby to honour and esteem who never see the prince, or transiently only, being added to by him. . . .

Those then that are favoured by the prince, as they are the better sort of subjects, so are they better dealt with in the shares and participations of their favours.... For theirs are the offices of revenue, the titles of honour, the embassies of credit, the matches of fortune, the disposal of trusts to bestow, or have undeniable influence upon....

For though riches, industry and frugality give many rounds to the ascents of men, yet the master caper, and the noblest capriole to advance, is the King's favour....

Frugality [is] a great advance to families, for though to live high and splendid makes a noise, filling the sails of a family with the air of applause; yet the purchase of that flourish is so chargeable, exhaustive and irreparable that wise men decline it as the sluice and sieve through which the increase of a family drains and passes....

I am no orator for narrow minds or penurious living. I thank God I have both a spirit above the one, and have ever had the mercy to be exempt from the necessity of the other. A free spirit and a free port suit well, and nothing beneath it become noblemen and gentlemen, where God give them fortunes to their degree, credit and wisdom, to do what is honest, seemly and prudent. But that which I defend in patronage to the fortune and generosity of a family is wisdom of practise to live within bounds, that is to live virtuously....

For no man can be truly worthy who contemns health, reputation, counsel, preservation, to satiate the rude importunity of a delicate palate, a wanton eye, an extravagant brain, a credulous humour and a costly levity; all which, as so many eager hounds gnaw upon the surprised carcass of an overdriven prodigal, whose transition of the modest bounds of virtue renders him a prey to the extorting usurer, the cunning broker, the harpy cook, the cozening tailor, the deluding steward, the fawning tenant, the crafty devil, till at last he become lord and master of nothing but a prison, and be denied pity when he himself is helpless....

The inconsideration of which πρόνοια, or wise forethought, in the practical use of it, is one of the main and to us known reasons of the unprovision that in many of the great families of England makes daughters and younger sons unhappy....

Nor have I ever in my experience seen so great estates raised by what has been gotten, as by what has been saved....

Callings of employment and income are great rises and enlargements to a family....

Nor would the great men of England know how to dispose of their younger children, or their families expatiate so, and by such alliances strengthen and embellish themselves as now they do, were it not for learned callings and employments of trade, which in the income of them are equivalent to lands and manors, and by exchange purchase them. . . . And what would have become of the younger brothers of England after the cessation of the Civil Wars by the union of York and Lancaster in Henry VII of happy memory; and after the dissolution of religious houses by Henry VIII, in both of which they were bestowed and from them supported, if sciences, trades and callings of civil request had not taken them up, is easy to say: either reason of state must have turned them to a foreign war, or they must have lived at home upon the prey either of their elder brothers or of the country. . . .

Though therefore there are no arts, callings or ways of life, but have and do yield estates and honours to those that are industrious and fortunated by God in them, . . . the rises of persons in [other] callings are not so great, nor so general, as those of law and trade are. . . .

[The lawyers] are the most knowing men in business of any profession, and they contrive settlements of purchase and marriage; these frame wills of bequests and disposition; these exhibit bills and petitions in courts of equity; these draw pleadings in courts of law; these are pleaders at the Bar, counsels in their chambers, officers in courts, attendants on circuits, stewards in manors, under-sheriffs in shires, judges in corporations, which shows their abilities and their possibilities to improve them to their enriching. . . . Hence come they to purchase the best seats, the noblest royalties, the best to be improved lands in the nation and to match their children with the least portions and to most advantage of any men.

Nor has the Law only been thus fertile of rise and honour to families but trade in cities and corporations, chiefly that of famous London. . . . There is no argument of God's blessing stronger to me than this, . . . that notwithstanding these hazards and infinite others, trade should be thus gainful, and in twenty years (for more than that few men have gainful times, their trade being to seek and settle till they are thirty years old, and their children breaking their stocks for breeding and portions when they are fifty), that, I say, in twenty years or some few more or less, there should be 10, 20, 30, 40, 60 or a 100 thousand pound clear estate and more raised. . . .

Ecclesiastical promotions and incomes are now a great rise to riches and honour. . . .

Another means to raise estates and thereby honour to families is trusts and agitation in and about great men's estates, ... especially if the pleasures of London seduce their master from their country residencies. ... For their lord's or master's absence and expenses in high diet, rich clothes, frequent treatments, fashionable equipage, added to by great gamings, lewd compotations, exhausting suretyships, perilous quarrels, amorous caressings, draining him of all exuberances, forces him to be more greedy upon his servant to return moneys, and more to accept him when he returns him money supplies. ...

Apt matches in marriage are helps to raise and advance families. ... Marriage must be a mercy, not as it is a bare conjunction of male and female, for that has ... made the married persons tetrical [sic] and deplorable in the sad effects of their unmeet and inconsiderate association. [This] occasions first undervaluation, then sourness, then neglect, then abhorrence and at last total alienation. ...

After fit matches in marriage, towardly children by them are great advantages to families, ... which commends to wise parents the method of ordering their sons aright, that they breed their eldest son to learning, if he be capable of it and the younger to trades, travels, wars and such courses of life as have employment and profit attending them, and are not distasteful to their addictions ...; and enfeoff them with the lustre and reward of such, which I believe to be notably seen in some families, wherein almost every heir or son, being complete in breeding, enamours a fortune and heir female, whereby he adds to his family land, landsworth [sic] and alliance, with armoreal accessions; when others precipitating do not in ages add anything by their marriages ...; and so they resting upon the single fortune of their ancestors, decrease every descent (as profuseness or multitude of children eats upon them); whereas those that have several fangs to fasten them, and accruements of marriages, to relieve their distresses and inevitable expenses upon, endure longest and bear the expensive accidents of life with less palpable injury and visible diminution. ...

II. *Causes of Decay*

Prodigality and ill conduct of life is a great worm to the flourishing gourd of an estate ... for estates are made up of savings as much as gettings; and so they are kept together when got. ...

He may be accounted as true a waster of his estate, who lets it have its own swing and minds it not; as he that by vain and costly living contracts debts upon it, and then is fain to sell it to pay them: for estates seldom stand at stay; if they increase not, they diminish. ...

Idleness, which brings nought home, is a great corrosive to a family for it makes a plenary waste of all ancestors' acquisitions. . . .

Vanity of gaming is another decay of estates. . . . There is nothing thought a genteeler pass of time than cards and dice. . . . I dare be prophetic of general eradication of virtue and good proof amongst the youth now breeding and hereafter to be bred, if gaming be not inhibited or moderated and restrained in a high degree. . . .

Pompous housekeeping and the equipage of it, is a great decay to families, and the persons of it; for it is a daily sluice to the estate, which is eaten and drunk out by it, or lies fallow in the costly furniture in it. . . . Multitude of acquaintance together with the consequence of it is a means to decay estates and families now. . . .

Immoderate flocking to and residing in London and Westminster and the precincts thereof from the several quarters of the country and nation, where the nobility and gentry reside and their seats are, is in my opinion, but if I err I crave pardon, a great danger to destroy persons of worth in their virtue and fortune, by drawing them from their retirements, where they may live thriftily and usefully to the King, Country and themselves, into the public, where they are taken off their local service and assaulted by delicacies and vices of cost and effeminacy, and inconsistence with all abode of Virtue.

[*The Gentleman's Monitor, or a sober Inspection into the Virtue, Vices, and ordinary means of the rise and decay of men and families* (1665).]

II

Family Histories

27 The Holles

G. HOLLES

Gervase Holles (1607–75) was a minor local gentleman, a notable antiquary and a devoted Royalist during the Civil War. He wrote the history of his family when he was living in exile abroad during the 1650s. It is distinguished both by a keen sense of personal involvement and by scholarly research into documentary evidence.

Outline Genealogy of the Holles Family

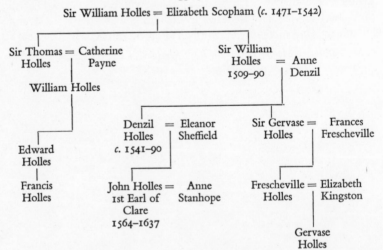

... Sir William Holles, the son of Thomas Holles of Stoke in the county of Warwick, was born in the reign of King Edward IV at Stoke aforesaid which is a village within a mile of Coventry ... and it seems was at man's estate before he was bound apprentice, which was not unusual in those days, ... to Robert Kervile, mercer of London, for ten years; but it seems he demeaned himself so well that he purchased his freedom by the way of redemption (as they call it in the City) at seven years' end. . . .

He had the good fortune both to serve in and be free of the society of the Mercers, which is the prime company in the City of London and enjoys beyond all the rest the greatest privileges. He was chosen Warden of that company in 1519, and Master Warden of the same company (which last office they call Master of the company) in 1529. . . . He was chosen Sheriff of Middlesex by the commonalty the nineteenth year of King Henry VIII. . . . The same year he was elected Alderman of the ward of Aldersgate on the last day of March following. . . . He received the order of knighthood in the twenty-fifth year of that king's reign. . . . About six years after . . . he was elected Mayor of London. . . . In his mayorality he caused the Moore ditch and all those ditches which annoyed the city to be scoured, which (as Stow observes) were never scoured but once before. . . .

Hence by the way I shall observe the dignity of the Mayor of London who, out of the city and his proper jurisdiction, was ranked amongst the Barons of England. . . . This value, in all ages, had the wisest and best sort of men for this worthy calling, and with reason enough. For no man conveys more advantages to the commonwealth than the merchant (I mean all this while the right merchant, not every pettyfogging fellow that usurps that title) transmitting both necessaries, wealth, intercourse and friendship to their own country from the places where they traffic. Neither is there any condition whatever that lives in more opulency, that are more able to oblige or commonly more obliging. . . . For my own part I shall ever esteem it more honour to be descended from a merchant (for so this worthy ancestor of mine was . . .) than from any civil profession whatever: all other having some alloys or other in them which impair their value and make them look less handsomely. . . .

His estate that he left behind him amongst his three sons was very great, I believe as great as ever Lord Mayor had before him; a good part of which he had either purchased in their names or assured upon them in his lifetime. . . .

I come with no little trouble to relate of Sir Thomas Holles who was a son of misfortune and by his lavishness and improvidence the ruin both of himself and his posterity. His father left him a very fair estate. Yet he lived to spend it all in effect and (as my grandfather has told me) to die in prison. This wasteful disposition it should seem his

father either saw or foresaw in him; for I observe in his last will that ...
he waives the trust of that to this his eldest son and places it upon his
lady or (in case of her decease) upon his second son, William. . . .

To force headlong his undoing the faster, he took himself a wife
from the Court (slips transplanted from that soil for the most part
make but ill proof in the country) ... who was a maid of honour to
Queen Catherine of Spain, the first wife of King Henry VIII. It is to
be thought that she brought not over much good housewifery from
thence. . . .

I ever thought he might be knighted at King Edward's coronation,
for I have it by tradition that he was present there with a retinue of
three-score and ten followers. This spacious port he kept (as I have
heard) so long as he was anyways able, and like a well-spread oak
carried a great shade even then when he was spent at the heart, not
lessening, like a huge willow, by degrees, but sinking in effect all in one
moment. . . .

William Holles the only son of Sir Thomas Holles was born in the
lifetime of his grandfather. . . . Nothing more hath come to my knowledge concerning him save that he followed his father's steps and
utterly consumed what his father left of that estate. . . .

His son, Edward Holles, I do remember, for he came when I was a
boy to see my father, indeed to desire something from him, for he was
then in a very wanting condition. He was of a middle stature, lean and
slender, and something high-nosed. I guessed him then to be near fifty
years of age. In his youth he had been a soldier and trailed a pike for
some years in the Netherlands. After that he returned into England
and married a Lancashire gentlewoman named Anne Bradshaw, who
I have heard was a very good woman and much beloved of the first
Countess of Clare. . . .

Francis Holles, his son, whilst he was yet a little boy, had lost both
his father and mother and was exposed unto the most wretched condition, had he had years to have understood it, that any poor child
could be, for he was forced to beg his bread in the streets amongst other
poor children.

In this condition as he was playing in the street one day amongst
poor boys it chanced the 1st Earl of Clare to pass by him, and one of
his servants, knowing him, told his lord who he was. The Earl passed
on a little, and then (nature and peradventure shame too working upon
him) he stopped and bid that servant go carry him into his house
which was hard by in Westminster and let him abide there until his

return, which he did. He was then in a leather-patched hose and doublet, and the other servants seeing him in the Hall and not knowing him, would have put him out, but he telling them it was the Earl's pleasure he should stay until his return, they put him into the kitchen and bid him turn a spit, which he did. In this posture and equipage I found him a little after (being stepped into the kitchen to take a pipe of tobacco) and seeing a pretty boy at that employment (indeed he had a very good face and a pure complexion) I asked his name; he told me it was Francis Holles, that he was Mr Edward Holles' son, and that the Earl had sent him thither. I was then very angry with the cook and removed him from that exercise. The Earl after his return caused him to be handsomely clad and sent down into the country to Houghton, where he gave order to have him taught to read and write and speak French, and bred him up his page for some years. We shall hardly find in any family a greater example of fortune's mutability. For we see this poor boy (then the chief of an Earl's family) whose great-grandfather had a revenue descended upon him from his father at this day worth at least £10,000 *per annum*, and had been seen sometimes followed by a train of three-score and ten servants of his own; here, I say, we see this boy, the direct heir of this ancestor, clad in patches, turning a spit, begging in the streets. . . .

He bound him apprentice to a jeweller (one Pancefoot) in Foster Lane, with whom he abode some years, till at length, debauched by a neighbour apprentice, they watched their opportunity when their masters and mistresses were gone out of London in a long vacation, robbed their trunks and ran away, and for these seventeen years hath not been seen that I could hear of; most likely dead, else these late troubles in England would probably have brought him abroad again. Thus I have pursued the first branch of Sir William Holles from its cradle to its grave.

It appears by what hath been said that Sir William Holles the father, like a wise merchant, had not adventured all his stock in one bottom nor entrusted the prosperity of his posterity upon the management of an eldest son only; for he left both his other sons very fair revenues, and particularly to his son William, the manor of Houghton with [fifteen manors in Notts and Lincs]; and his lands and tenements in the parishes of St Clement Danes, St Giles, St Pancras and Kentish Town in the county of Middlesex, which lands of Middlesex by the improvement and building upon them yield his heir at the present a revenue of about £3,000 *per annum*, and when the leases are expired they may treble that value. Besides he had in his father's lifetime the moiety of Denzil's estate with his wife. . . . We see by this that though the first branch withered and decayed to nothing, yet there remained a flourishing estate in the hands of the second, both to yield a present lustre and found a future greatness; which how well and worthy it was placed we shall see in the following relation.

Sir William Holles (second son of Sir William Holles Kt by Dame Elizabeth his wife) was born in London in the first year of King Henry VIII as I find it set down under my grandfather's hand. He married in his father's lifetime Anne the eldest daughter and co-heir of John Denzil of Denzil in the County of Cornwall, serjeant at law. . . .

George Lord Clifford, that brave and active Earl of Cumberland, fell exceedingly in love with his daughter, whom after Walter Stanley married (who indeed was very handsome as appears by the picture which I have of her) and made his application to Sir William Holles desiring her for his wife, but could by no means draw him to admit of it; and when Sir William's friends did most passionately persuade him to it, telling what an honour it would be to his family, and what an advancement to his daughter to have her matched to a person so highly noble he answered 'Sake of God' (that was his usual word of asseveration) 'I do not like to stand with my cap in hand to my son-in-law; I will see her married to an honest gentleman with whom I may have friendship and conversation'; which accordingly he did to Mr Stanley upon the 20th day of January 1578. This relation may seem very strange to such as are strangers to his memory; but such as have received a true account of the plainness of his heart and the freedom of his soul will not so much wonder at it. The truth is he ever did affect a freedom of life, and to be loved and honoured at home amongst his neighbours, which he attained to beyond others his concurrents by his honesty, humanity and hospitality.

This last was so great and so constant all his life that it was even to a wonder. He always began his Christmas at All Hallowtide and continued until Candlemas, during which time any man was permitted freely to stay three days without being asked from whence he came or what he was, as I have been assured by several old people. Sir Percival Willoughby, in a letter of his to my grandfather (which I have), gives this testimony of it: 'I can never forget your noble father, the wonder of this county for a settled house and constant hospitality.' And I have heard that his proportion, which he allowed during the twelve days of Christmas, was a fat ox every day, with sheep and other provision answerable. Besides it was certain with him never to sit down to dinner till after one of the clock; and being asked the reason why he always dined so late he answered that for ought he knew there might a friend come twenty miles to dine with him, and he would be loth he should lose his labour. This liberal hospitality of his caused the 1st Earl of Clare to let fall once an unbecoming word, that his grandfather sent all his revenues down the privy house.

It will not be amiss to remember (because even in those times unusual amongst the greatest subjects) that he always kept a company of stage players of his own which presented him masques and plays at festival times and upon days of solemnity. In the summer time they usually acted abroad in the country. . . .

Sir William Holles died at Houghton 18 January 1590 . . . being the fourscore and third year of his age current. . . . He was of so noble a nature and so good a disposition that even to these days (amongst the country people) he is mentioned by the addition of 'good Sir William' and 'the good Lord of Houghton'. . . . His retinue was always (answerable to his hospitality) very great and (according to the magnificence of those days) far more than necessary. At King Edward VI's coronation he appeared with fifty followers in their blue coats and badges, and I have heard divers affirm (that knew him) how he would not come to Retford sessions without thirty proper fellows of his own at his heels. To his servants he was very bountiful, whereof some (of the more thriving dispositions) made very good use. For the father of Sir Gervase Helwys (that Sir Gervase who was Lieutenant of the Tower and ended so unfortunately) and the ancestor of Sir Thomas Williamson of Markham (now a Baronet of great possessions) were both his servants (stewards or bailiffs) and under him laid the foundation of their posterity's growth and present condition. In short, he was (as one very well expressed him) like a good planet that did fortunate and make happy all over whom he was predominant. . . .

In his own country[1] he did most especially honour and maintain the strictest friendship with the Earl of Shrewsbury and Sir Gervase Clifton (sirnamed The Gentle) whose grandchild during his lifetime his younger son married. He had notwithstanding a general kindness for all the gentry of his country[1] as likewise for his neighbours of inferior quality, and received from them a reciprocal return; whence he would often say that the whole country[1] was his garden, for if there was anything in it rare or delicate he was sure to have it presented to him.

As for his own private estate, he advanced it nothing save only by the addition of his first wife's inheritance. He would say that good deeds was the best good husbandry and that the honour of living nobly and to the benefit of others was the best improvement he could make of his private fortune. . . .

Denzil Holles was the eldest son of Sir William Holles by dame Anne his wife. . . . Certain it is he was born before the death of Sir William Holles his grandfather, who died in the year 1542. . . . He married Eleanor daughter of Edmund Lord Sheffield of Butterwick, the first Baron of that race. The time of their marriage seems to be near the close of Queen Mary's reign. . . . His lot falling, by his father's appointment, in Lincolnshire he seated himself at Irby (four miles distant from Great Grimsby) lying at the entrance upon the Wolds, a place happy in the sweetness of the air and very delectable by the pleasant hills and dales where there are dry and inviting walks both summer and winter, with a welcome prospect towards the sea, affording withal as good hawking and hunting and as good convenience for training and airing of young horses as is anywhere else to be found. . . .

After he had purchased my grandfather Kingston's lands in Irby he made it his next care to improve the lordship, which he did by enclosing it, much to the advantage both of himself and tenants; for he divided into so many farms and laid all the lands he apportioned to each apart by themselves, which he fenced with quickset hedges, which are now the handsomest and best thriving that I know in all the country,[1] which has added much both to the beauty of the place and convenience of the inhabitants. Besides he had this just care with him to leave the commons very large (indeed far beyond the proportion of any of their neighbours near about them) and all these together have been the cause that I never knew in the township any tenant that was not thriving. . . .

His whole life (for the most part) he spent in Lincolnshire, where he had seated himself. And that life was most spent in civil affairs, he being in the Commission of the Peace for that county. Yet he had something of martial employment, for in the rebellion of the Earls of Northumberland and Westmorland in 1569 I find in a list which I have of the army marching against them (under the command of Ambrose Dudley, Earl of Warwick and Edward Lord Clinton) that he was captain of a company of 252 footmen. But the rebels were scattered before that army could have the advantage to engage with them. . . .

I shall now give you his description as truly as I can from those relations which I have received. . . . He was not unlearned, having been seasoned therewith in the University of Cambridge. He was of a great spirit – indeed a very stout and valiant man. I have been told from old Mr Townrow that he has seen him several times upon the bench confront Henry Earl of Lincoln (who was a great tyrant amongst the gentry of that county) and carry businesses against him, as it were in despite of his teeth; and the truth is he might better do it than any other gentleman of his country[1] having so good a back as his wife's nephew the Lord Sheffield who was then in great favour with Queen Elizabeth. It well appears that had he lived to inherit his father's estate he had improved it, for we may observe that notwithstanding the great charge of children, he had purchased lands both in Irby and Bernaby out of that proportion which his father had given him. It is plain too that he was a good landlord from his care in his last will for the good usage of his tenants, and of a charitable disposition to the poor by that house which he had built in Irby for their behoof.

These were his virtues, and with these he had his weakness too, which was an immoderate love to women, and from which neither the virtues nor fertility of a noble wife could at all reclaim him. In a Pasquill made in those days of the Lincolnshire gentlemen I found these rhymes of him –

> 'Holles hit in every hole
> And Denzil drives through all their dints.
> He gets his neighbours' wives with foal,
> And yet they say the man but mints.'

And I remember that walking once in Irby grounds with the Earl of Clare he showed me a good handsome farmhouse, telling me that that house his father built to please a foolish woman; the truth is he was seldom without one or other in it, for his private use and pleasure. One base daughter (whose name was Susan) he left behind him, who was first married to Thomas Whittingham and after to George Bradley of Retford.

He died at Irby 22 April 1590, being then about fifty-two years of age (near nine months before his father) after he had been much afflicted both with the stone and gout; and lies buried in the chancel of that church under a gravestone without any inscription.

Thus far by God's favour and permission I have proceeded and have finished what I had to say of him that first raised our family to opulency, of him that made it specious by his scarce equalled hospitality, of those that ennobled it by their military glory. And now my discourse must relate to him who first advanced it from the lesser to the greater nobility, which was Sir John Holles, Lord Houghton and Earl of Clare. . . .

He was the eldest son of Denzil Holles by his wife Eleanor, daughter of Edmund Lord Sheffield. He was born at Houghton in the county of Nottingham near the beginning of Queen Elizabeth's reign. . . . From his childhood he expressed an extraordinary towardliness, beyond most others his [contemporaries]; his understanding and apprehension being quick and his judgement sound and ripe even in the morning of his life; which yet (though contrary to common observation) continued vivid and vigorous even to his last, not deceiving the world at all of those excellent fruits which these early hopes (conceived of him) did so fairly and largely promise.

To Cambridge he was sent very young (being not thirteen years of age) but so well fitted for the University that the Master of the College posing him at his first coming both in grammar and Greek, and receiving from those years unexpected satisfaction to every question, he caught him up in his arms, and kissing him, to those that were by, said, 'This child (if he lives) will prove a singular honour and ornament to this kingdom.'

From the University he was by his father sent to Gray's Inn, that by the study of the laws he might be the better fitted for the service of the Commonwealth. There he continued some years which he spent not fruitlessly (as most of our Inns of Court gallants do) but took good impressions there of such notions as were necessary both for the management of his private estate and the performance of public offices. And this I must affirm (and the whole country[1] where he lived will witness with me) that it never had in it a more upright or a more able justiciar.

Those excellent materials which nature had so liberally bestowed upon him thus far polished by the arts (the Muses and the Graces conspiring as it were to make him every way exactly accomplished), his years and endowments made him now appear fulsomed for a further flight, and the Court (the most glorious then of the Christian world whether we regard the prince or the servants) invited him to it to add to its former lustre; where he was chosen by that unparalleled Queen Elizabeth one of her Pensioners.

The trade of a soldier he first entered into in the Netherlands, serving there some time as a volunteer under his kinsman Sir Francis Vere. I have heard him say that he was the first that put a pike into the hands of Sir Edward Vere (who was then very young), Sir Francis saying to him, 'You will make that scurvy boy but over proud.'

He served in that famous sea fight of '88 (and being then but a young gentleman and not having any command) was called to be present at all their councils of war, so great an opinion there was of him then. And particularly he was present at that great debate whether they should fight the Spanish fleet or no; which was with difficulty carried upon the affirmative especially by the sound and resolute arguments of Sir Martin Frobisher. I have heard him relate that he was then of so able and active a body that (being heavily armed at all pieces) he would without difficulty climb to the top of the tallest ship that was then in the fleet.

In the year 1590 he lost his father and then his grandfather, by whose decease there devolved upon him a very fair and opulent inheritance and with it the care of divers brothers and sisters. His brothers he sent to the University of Cambridge, from whence the elder made a sally (as the younger not long after did from the Inns of Court) into the Netherlands, where they both became brave and eminent commanders.

Shortly after his grandfather's death, namely in May 1591, he married Anne, the only daughter of Sir Thomas Stanhope of Shelford in the county of Nottingham, Knight, he being then twenty-six years of age. This marriage, though it brought him all the happiness that could be hoped for in a wife, yet it conveyed him withal a deep and lasting animosity from a great and potent neighbour (the son of his grandfather's especial friend) Gilbert Earl of Shrewsbury. It seems (and so I have heard) that there had been a treaty between the old Earl and Sir William Holles concerning a marriage betwixt him [Sir John] and a niece or kinswoman of the Earl's; to which motion (whether he meant it in earnest or pretended it only for fear of displeasing his grandfather) he seemed not unwilling, so that everyone thought it would have proceeded. But after the decease of them both (for George Earl of Shrewsbury and Sir William Holles died both in one year), liking, it seems, Mistress Stanhope better, he relinquished the Earl's kinswoman and married her; which the Earl took as the greatest affront in the world, the rather because Sir Thomas Stanhope and the Earl were great enemies. The process of this difference cost a great deal of trouble and some men's lives. . . .

There was contracted against him a great deal of envy and animosity and a strong combination even in his own country.[1] For diversion of which, and to indulge his own inclination which strongly affected knowledge and actions of honour (as those things which would make him most serviceable and considerable to his country) he made several sallies out of the kingdom and spent several years either in travel or military employments; and that after his marriage to a lady who both deserved and had from him a very great and hearty affection. Some of which time he spent in Ireland under the then Deputy, Sir William Fitzwilliam, where, accompanying Sir Henry Norris in an expedition he made against the Irish rebels and carrying himself in that service with a great deal of courage and gallantry he received from the Deputy at his return, as a reward of his merit, the honour of knighthood.

He served likewise about two years in Hungary against the Turk, and in his passage to and fro viewed and observed the best parts of France and Italy, both which languages he was master of, and reasonably well of the Spanish. I have heard him say that whilst he served in Hungary he was grown so perfect in that tongue that he might have passed for a native. . . .

[In 1597] he dashed upon a rock which probably might have sunk him and indeed threatened more danger than all those sharp enmities which he had encountered with before: which was a sharp difference with the Lord Burghley, Treasurer of England, who was then (and long before) of great power with the Queen. What the ground of this difference was is not certainly known (though some have imagined it to be the very much familiarity that Sir John Holles had with the Lady Hatton, the Treasurer's grandchild), but certain it is that the Treasurer during the preparation for this expedition inveighed bitterly against him (with little arguments of that gravity and wisdom he had formerly expressed) in the Exchequer Chamber. . . . But Sir John sailed out of reach and the Treasurer's death followed so seasonably after that this danger vanished.

Neither did this cast him at all (as his enemies hoped it would) into the Queen's disfavour. For that brave Queen did never steer her opinion of any man by the passions or affections of others but by her own judgement. So she continued to afford him that gracious favour she was accustomed even unto her death which happened about five years after the time we speak of. . . .

This bright star set, the face of the scene at Court was strangely altered. For though King James entered with the greatest expectations and acclamations that any prince could do (such as his wisdom and virtues well merited) yet he brought along with him a crew of necessitous and hungry Scots, and (as his natural affection to his countrymen might reasonably persuade them) filled every corner of the Court with these beggarly blue caps. This was that which first darkened the glory of the English Court which Queen Elizabeth had ever maintained in so great a lustre. I have heard the Earl of Clare say that when he was Pensioner to the Queen he did not know a worse man of the whole band than himself, and that all the world knew he had an inheritance worth five thousand pounds a year. For it was the constant custom of the Queen to call out of all counties of the Kingdom the gentlemen of greatest hopes and of the best fortunes and families, and with those to fill the most honourable rooms of her household servants; by which she honoured them, obliged their kindred and allegiance, and fortified herself. But when most of those rooms were possessed by such trotting companions, the better sort of the gentry declined the Court as scorning their fellowship. Hence it followed that in a little time the Court was in a manner wholly composed of these Scots and such inconsiderable persons as favourites preferred or money introduced. This caused Sir John Holles for that time to retire himself into the country and to tend his estate, which to do until then he had very little leisure.

As concerning his estate, he had sold lands of a good value both in Lincolnshire and Derbyshire after his grandfather's decease, but those he recompensed again by a far better improvement. . . . He likewise purchased the one half of Prince's Street by Drury Lane. And he caused to be erected those edifices called Lowches Buildings, with the most part of Clements Inn Lane, Blackamore Street by Drury Lane and a part of Clement's Inn Fields. So that by these purchases and improvements he advanced his estate before his death to near £8,000 *per annum*. He likewise enlarged very much Thurland House (now called Clare House) in Nottingham and new built the house at Houghton and had several platforms[2] drawn of it, resolving for to have seated it upon higher ground above the barns. But that charge was like to be so great that he thought it better to consider of it than to undertake it.

Three great suits of law he was engaged in during his life. The first was about the wardship of Robert Sutton, now Lord Lexington, whose manor of Averham was held of his manor of Houghton by fealty and knight's service, which had ever been performed by the ancestors of

Mr Sutton to the ancestors and predecessors of Sir John Holles, and their wardships accordingly accrued when any of those Suttons died, his heir within age. But when this last fell, a trick was found to entitle the King, for whom judgement was given in the Court of Wards against Sir John Holles. The second was with the society of that Inn of Chancery called Clement's Inn. . . . Both these causes were carried against him with all the injustice that might be, the first by the power of the King, and the next by the partiality of the lawyers. In the third though he had a worse cause, yet he found a more favourable success. . . .

The loss of Mr Sutton's wardship (as some have thought) made him much averse to King James, for whom living he had little kindness, nor indeed was he a friend to his memory. I have heard him say 'that he came to govern a people that he knew he was not worthy of, and then was ruled himself by two beggars and a base fellow, Suffolk, Northampton and Salisbury'. And at any time when he mentioned anything which he thought an error in that King, he would ever give his discourse this severe close 'which now he feels'.

Yet when Prince Henry was created Prince of Wales (which was in 1610) and shortly after settled his household, Sir John Holles was by the King appointed to that Household the Comptroller; the King well understanding his great abilities and judging it very requisite to have him near about his son's person. In this office he continued during the prince's life, which was about two years and a half after. The prince expressed ever a very great love to him and value of him; insomuch that once he took a progress to his house at Houghton in Nottinghamshire where the prince continued with him many days and found an entertainment answerable to his greatness. And I may well question (had that prince lived to be King) whether any subject had found greater arguments of his love or received higher marks of his favour. But in the year 1612 upon the 6th day of November Prince Henry died: a prince of so great expectation that not only the eyes of all England but all Christendom were upon him. . . .

With the life of his brave master all his favour at Court vanished, and he lay open and exposed to the malice of his adversaries. And some three years after the Prince's death (or thereabouts) there was a bill filed in Star Chamber against him stuffed with several trivial allegations: viz. his private conference with two Jesuits (Jervis and Garret) at their execution; that in all his leases to his tenants he inserted a condition that they should not go to law one with another but should make him the umpire of all their differences; with other charges as

inconsiderable. These misdemeanours (for so they must then be understood) were notably pressed and amplified against him by Sir Edward
Coke, then Chief Justice, who bore a particular spleen against him for
the familarity which Sir John Holles had with his then wife the Lady
Elizabeth Hatton. . . . Though he made his defence to the great satisfaction of the hearers, who were not a little pleased with his eloquence,
yet he was committed to the Fleet, where he continued a prisoner some
weeks, until at the last he came out a Baron of England, being created
so upon 9 July in the fourteenth year of King James as appears by his
patent. . . . For this dignity he paid the then favourite (the Duke of
Buckingham) £10,000 sterling. For after the entrance of King James
the sale of honours was become a trade at Court; and while that Duke
lived, scarce any man acquired any honour but such as were either his
kindred or had the fortune (or misfortune) to marry with his kindred
or mistresses, or paid a round sum of money for it. Nor indeed did that
way of merchandise cease all the reign of our last martyred King,
which was one cause (and not the least) of his misfortunes. I have
heard the Earl of Clare (I now treat of) often inveigh bitterly against it,
and he would usually call it temporal simony. I remember I once took
the liberty (hearing him so earnest upon that subject) to ask him why
he would purchase himself, seeing he condemned the King for selling.
He answered 'that he observed merit to be no medium to an honorary
reward, that he saw divers persons who he thought deserved it as little
as he (either in their persons or estates) by that means leap over his
head, and therefore seeing the market open and finding his purse not
unfurnished for it he was persuaded to ware his money as other men
had done. . . .'

Certain it is that much about this time he (in a manner) wholly
withdrew himself from Court, though for what reason principally I
am ignorant. . . . But I am of opinion that his perpetual averseness to
the Duke of Buckingham was the main thing that choked up his way
to preferment; for it is certain that he could never be drawn to comply
with the Duke, although often endeavoured on the Duke's part.

Yet could he [the Duke] be content to do him unprofitable offices for
his own advantage; and upon that score was a means about eight years
after his creation of Baron (for the sum of £5,000 sterling) to procure
his advancement in honour one step higher, namely to the Earldom of
Clare. . . .

He had now acquired the highest dignity of honour that in reason
he could aspire to; which may be reckoned amongst the felicities of

his life. Yet this was accompanied with several near and pressing afflictions, the death of many of his children, and the downfall of some of his nearest friends. For between and about the times of his several creations he buried four of his youngest sons and two daughters, and saw the ruin of the Earl of Somerset and the beheading of Sir Walter Raleigh. The Earl's person he loved well (though his crime he abhorred), having ever received from him in his most flourishing condition a singular esteem and affection; which he never failed to return even when the Earl was lost and underfoot. Sir Walter Raleigh and he had been much bred together, both in court and camp, fellow servants and fellow soldiers. And being both of choice parts and spirits easily took impressions of firm friendship. . . .

King James (a little before his close) discovered an intention of making the Earl of Clare Lord Treasurer of England, which was so generally believed that divers made suit and means for places under him. And this was the more likely (notwithstanding his former dryness towards him) because about the same time he betrayed some jealousies and weariness of the Duke of Buckingham and an inclination to introduce again into favour the Earl of Somerset. But his death (which followed immediately upon it) made frustrate both these intentions. . . .

Before this time he had altogether estranged himself from Court, nor did he much repair to the city but lived for the most part in the country sometimes at his manor of Houghton and sometimes at his house in Nottingham, cherishing more quiet and contented thoughts in a retired life. . . . He delivered his soul into the hands of God in his house at Nottingham the 4th October 1637 being the seventy-third year of his age and was interred in the place he himself appointed. . . .
He was naturally just, but nothing liberal, no man living more ready to oblige by his interest and endeavours, but not at all by his purse; which I have often fancied to be the reason why our modern writers are so silent concerning him. For it is not merit so much as munificence that stuffs history with so many commendable characters, and writers (for the most part) remember not so willingly who deserve well as who deserves well of them.

[*Memorials of the Holles Family 1493–1656*, ed. A. C. Wood, *Camden Soc.*, 3rd ser., LV (1937).]

Notes

1. I.e. county or locality.
2. I.e. plans.

28 The Owners of Longford Castle

H. PELATE

*This extract, taken from a family history written by the family chaplain in
1678, provides a perfect example of the Trevor-Roper thesis: the old declining
gentry family of the Cervingtons is ruined and ejected by the new merchant,
John Webb, Mayor of Salisbury, whose executors in turn sell the property
to a family of old small gentry newly enriched by Court service and marriage,
the Gorges. Ruined in turn by rash business speculation and extravagance,
the Gorges sell to the Hares, a family enriched by trade, law and government
service. Hugh Hare was the son of John Hare, Bencher of the Middle Temple,
seventh son of John Hare of Stow Bardolf, mercer of London; he was co-heir
of his uncle, Hugh Hare, Master of the Court of Wards (Blomefield, Norfolk,
VII, p. 440).*

*In the story of Richard Grobham is illustrated the possibility of rise as an
official in the household of a great family. The history is a true one, but is
enriched by legendary, not necessarily apocryphal, stories. Longford Castle still
stands today, much as it was in Sir Thomas Gorges' time. It was not based on
Uraniborg, but it may well have owed something to Gripsholm.*

... Joan de Bohun 20 Edw. II (1326) grants her manor of Langford to
Oliver de Sevyngton or Cevynton.... It descended to Nicholas
Cervynton, living in 1547, with whom this ancient family began to
decay, till it came to John Cervyngton, Esq., who, by his fondness for
gaming and other extravagance, brought it to complete ruin. He
mortgaged it to Mr John Webb, of Sarum, who foreclosed on him
16 Eliz. (1573). He resisted the legal process by violence till the Sheriff
interfered, and, forcibly ejecting him, put Webb in possession.

This John Cervynton, the last of the family, spent the latter part
of his life in great grief for his former extravagance, and in absolute
poverty, wandering about the domains which had once been his own
and occasionally subsisting on the charity of Sir Thomas Gorges, who
had purchased the estate of the Webbs. It is said that, being flouted
from the door by servants, he demanded an audience with their
master; and, forcing his way into the house, he complained to Sir
Thomas of the treatment he had met with, and added that Sir Thomas
must know that John Cervyngton was as good a gentleman as himself.
In pity to his distress, and perhaps also commiserating his state of

mind, which seems to have been shaken by misfortune, Sir Thomas gave orders that he should be treated kindly and respectfully as often as he chose to call. He continued to haunt the grounds as the troubled spectre of their former master, and at length, worn out with misery, laid himself down and died under an elm tree in the [rabbit-warren]. . . .

The manor of Langford was sold by the guardian of John, son of John Webb of Sarum above mentioned, to Sir Thomas Gorges, fifth son of Sir Edward Gorges of Wroxhall, co. Somt. This Sir Thomas was a favoured courtier of Queen Elizabeth and married Helena Snachenburgh, daughter of Wolfgangus a noble Swede, who was the young widow of Thomas Parr, Earl of Northampton. She came over from Sweden in the train of King Eric, who courted Elizabeth, to whom she became maid of honour. . . . It was at the instigation of this lady that Sir Thomas pulled down the old mansion of the Cervingtons and began another on the plan of the Castle of Uraniberg, built by Tycho Brahe. . . .

[The editor, R. C. Hoare, continues the story:]

The writer [Pelate] adds that, so great was the expense in driving piles etc. that Sir Thomas nearly sunk his fortune in the foundation. During the threat of the Spanish Armada he was made Governor of Hurst Castle, and a Spanish galleon having been wrecked near it, his wife begged the hull of the Queen, in which were found bars of silver and other treasure to an immense amount, which not only served to complete their pile at Longford but also to enrich their steward Richard Grobham, who chiefly managed their business, procured a knighthood and left a fortune almost equal to his master's. . . .

Edward, the second Lord Gorges, engaging in some expensive and unprosperous projects, of draining fens, and living too carelessly, involved himself in great debts, which obliged him to sell Longford to Hugh Hare, Baron of Coleraine in Ireland.

[R. C. Hoare, *The History of Modern Wiltshire, the Hundred of Cawden* (1835).]

29 The Reresbys

J. RERESBY

John Reresby wrote this unpublished account of his old gentry family in the late seventeenth century. The causes of his great-grandfather's decline are typical of many of his generation.

... Thomas [Reresby], the eldest son and heir, married Mary Monson, daughter of Sir John Monson of South Carleton, Com. Lincs, as appears by the deed of settlement upon the marriage dated the 30 March anno 30 Elizabeth, whereby it is covenanted that she should have for portion £1,200. ...

This Sir Thomas (for he was knighted about the fortieth year of the Queen, when Honour was rarely bestowed) entered to the greatest and freest estate both real and personal of any heir of the family to that day, to which he added also considerably in the beginning of his time by several purchases. ... This addition to the paternal estate had been a great estate had he kept it entire, but he lived to sell more than he bought and left the remainder much encumbered, as hereafter appears. ... The reasons given for Sir Thomas his great expenses and debts were his following the Court without any other recompense than empty knighthood, though very rare and consequently of great honour in those days; an expensive wife; his accompanying my Lord Zouche sent anno 1593 Ambassador into Scotland; an humour to live high at the first, which he did not abate as his fortune decreased; his quarrel with Sir William Wentworth and his giving a box on the ear at Rotherham sessions upon the Bench; and his buildings: first he built the tower to the east of Thriburgh Hall, wainscotted the gallery and boarded it, with several other rooms there. He built Estwood Hall at Ashover of freestone and leaded the roof, which cost him above £2,000 only to live in that year that [he] was Sheriff of Derbyshire, which office he is reported to have performed at too prodigal a rate in the year 1613. ... Another great occasion of his expenses was his great charge of children and great attendance, he seldom going to church or from home without a great many followers in blue coats and badges, and beyond the usual number for one of his quality and fortune.

[British Museum, Additional MSS 29442, ff. 44-7.]

30 The Berkeleys

J. SMYTH

John Smyth (1567–1640) entered the service of the Berkeleys in 1584 and served them until his death. He acted as land agent for the Berkeleys, and the value of his family history lies in the intimate knowledge it displays both of the lords and their wives and of the accumulation of papers preserved in Berkeley Castle. The book was written between 1618 and 1628 for the information of the young George Lord Berkeley. The section on his grandfather Lord Henry was intended as a warning – alas, in vain – on how not to manage an estate.

... Edward VI being dead in July 1553 and Queen Mary settled in the Crown, her marriage was concluded upon with Philip prince of Spain, during which time this lord [Henry, Lord Berkeley]'s mother was busied in regaining her son's Barony and possessions, and Sir Thomas Wyatt and his Kentish accomplices in raising arms against that foreign marriage and the entry of strangers into the land. Brett and others of the Queen's captains and subjects then also falling unto Wyatt from their own faith and her allegiance, the Queen, diffident of many of her nobility, resolved amongst others (partly out of the correspondence of this lord's mother with herself in religion, and partly out of the bounty she then had and was empowering upon her son then but nineteen years of age), to trust him more than many others more aged and experienced: Whereupon she sends her letters to him together with her commission in January in the first year of her reign (he then at Yate in Gloucestershire) forthwith to arm 500 of his trustiest tenants and servants and with all possible diligence to attend her person then at Whitehall. This lord, to his great charges, readily prepares, arms and apparels that number, all of them drawn out of the parts about Yate and Berkeley; for help whereto he obtained a loan of money from his tenants from 40s. to £20 apiece, and gave bills of repayment, in like resemblance as kings by their privy seals borrow of their subjects; and for further supply pawned his mother's and ancestors' plate (much of which was never after redeemed) and having conducted those 500 men about half the way towards London (with many of whom I since have talked) the Queen's letters met this lord upon his way in the beginning of the next month, signifying that Wyatt was taken and prisoner in the Tower, and his accomplices dispersed, willing them to return into his country and with his utmost care and industry to keep the same in quiet: 200 or more of which armours yet remain in Berkeley Castle, rather as memorials of this intended service than fit for any modern use. . . .

Not long after (like a young lord left too much to the oversight of his own education) he came to London, settled at Tower hill, frequented the Court and spent all his time at tennis, bowls, cards, dice and in the company of his huntsmen and falconers, delights that drew on greater totals of his accounts at the year's end than his revenue would support, especially [with] two jointures of his father's and grandfather's widows draining a third part thereout. . . .

And what through the company of many gentlemen of the Inns of Court and others of lower condition that daily accompanied him, and what through the fame amongst those students of his [law suits]; and what through his marriage in one of the greatest families then of favour and observation, and of his 150 servants in livery that daily then attended him in their tawny coats, and the opinion of his mother's virtue and chastity then the only solicitor of her sex in her own person, in her own and her son's causes, he was of as great note and hope as any of his age and of that time. But how long that height of opinion held, and how by degrees it waned, the rest of his life will tell his posterity. . . .

In September in the second [year] of Queen Mary this lord married the lady Katherine Howard, at the Duke her grandfather's house in Norfolk. . . . And thus up and down all the time of Queen Mary removed this lord and his wife, with seldom less (often more) than 150 servants in livery, between Yate, Mangottesfield, London, Callowdon and other places: and used to hawk as he travelled those ways, making his removes from those places to London eight days at the least, and as many back again.

Having in his first four years after his marriage much overrun his purse, he in the last of Queen Mary and somewhat before, sojourned with the Countess of Surrey, his wife's mother, at Rising in Norfolk, himself and his lady at 10s. the week, her gentlewomen at 4s., and their gentlemen and yeomen at 3s. the week, . . . whither when he had brought his wife, he in few days after returned to London, and living with his mother at her said house in Shoe Lane, spent most of his time at cards, dice, tennis, bowling-alley, and hawking and hunting near that City.

In July in the first [year] of Queen Elizabeth he returned to Rising, and from thence with his wife and family by the ways of Newmarket, Cambridge and Northampton, came to Callowdon by Coventry, where the first work done was the sending for his buckhounds to Yate in Gloucestershire. His hounds being come, away goes he and his wife a progress of buck hunting to the parks of Barkewell, Groby, Bradgate, Leicester forest, Toley and others on that side [of] his house. And after a small repose, then to the parks of Kenilworth, Ashby, Wedgenock and others, on the other side. . . . And this was the course of this lord (more or less) for the thirty next summers at least, not omitting his own at Callowdon and in the county of Gloucester. And his wife being of like honour and youth, from this first [year] of Queen Elizabeth to the beheading of her brother the Duke of Norfolk thirteen years after, gave herself to like delights as the country usually affords, wherein she often went with her husband part of those hunting journeys, delighting [in] her cross-bow, kept commonly a cast or two of merlins, which sometimes she mewed in her own chamber, which falconry cost her husband each year one or two gowns and kirtles spoiled by their mutings; used her longbow, and was in those days amongst her servants so good an archer at butts as her side by her was not the weaker; whose bows, arrows, glove, bracer, scarf and other ladylike accommodations I have seen and heard also herself speak of them in her elder years; which partly by the death of that noble prince her brother, and partly by the troubles that then invaded her husband's estate were broken off and much discontinued.

And thus lived this lord and his wife between London, the Duke's houses in Norfolk, Callowdon and Berkeley, never long at one place, the first thirteen years of Queen Elizabeth. In which their travels (if both together) they were seldom or never attended with fewer than 150 servants in their tawny cloth coats in summer, with the badge of the white lion rampant embroidered on the left sleeve; and in coats of white frieze lined with crimson taffeta in the winter, this lord allowing only cloth, buttons and badge; amongst whom many were gentlemen and esquires of remarkable families and descent, and of alliance to this house, many of whom I lived to see and know and to talk of these times; and have with some of them then in nearest relation and place of his revenue, expostulated why they would suffer their young lord and lady his wife to run yearly £1,500 at least into expense above their utmost income, each year (or second at least) shortening the same by sale of a manor, having no suits in law, nor daughters then married away, foreign embassies, domestic services in court or country, nor any other extraordinary causes of expense in the world. . . . But most sure it is that in the time of Queen Mary when this lord Henry entered upon his lands descended to him from his father, and also upon his barony of Berkeley and those manors which reverted to him after the death of King Edward VI, that he had many flatterers and sycophants, as well of his own family as out of London: captains, scholars, poets, cast courtiers and the like, that for their private ends humoured him and his wife, making them to conceive that their estate and yearly revenue was greater than that they could exceed it; which would afford an expense at pleasure, and to give without fear of want, whereto they listening with too open an ear, for *facile credimus quod volumus*, it came to pass that within two or three years they were unknowingly cast into a great debt, ere they came to discern their estate. And to take off the same (after borrowing upon mortgages, Statues and pawns) this lord began to sell his land, a course he overlong after continued in, expending one year with another all that time of Queen Mary and divers years after £1,500 per annum at least, as by the medium (which I with some hours' expense drew out of his officers' accounts of those times) appears, above his ordinary revenue, and the fines and other casualties that his estate presented. . . .

His Christmas (as most part of this second year of Queen Elizabeth) he kept at Yate with great port and solemnity, as the extraordinary gilded dishes, the vanities of cooks' arts (having none other guests but the gentlemen and ruralty of the country) served to the table on Twelfth Night well declare, whereof one was a whole boar inclosed in a pale workmanly gilt by a cook hired from Bristol, as the clerk of the kitchen's book declares. . . .

Thus slept this title[1] (whatever it was) in the Crown, quietly without awaking till Thomas Duke of Norfolk (whose sister Katherine was wife to this lord) was at the King's Bench bar condemned for treason, 16 January in the fourteenth year of Queen Elizabeth, whose fall, whether furthered by the policy of that prudent statesman Robert Dudley Earl of Leicester son of the Duke of Northumberland (as some have written) or not, I have not to determine. But when that great and affectionate friend and brother-in-law of this lord's was so cast down (and his head taken off 2 June after) forthwith came in the next term an information of intrusion into the Exchequer against this lord (long before plotted and prepared) for intruding into the said manors of Wotton and Symondsall and for taking the profits thereof since the first of her reign. Wherein after pleading and issue joined, a trial was [held] by jury at the Exchequer bar, whereat the Earl of Leicester was present in person as the promoter and follower of that suit, who now like a storm amongst weakened waves wrought high, and all too be-ruffled this family into a foam of fury, bringing with him divers other courtiers of eminency to countenance the cause, he at this time having a private promise in writing under the Queen's hand and signet to have this land, which I after met withal and is now in Berkeley Castle. The verdict passed against this lord [Berkeley]. . . .

And at last for £500 paid into the receipt, [he] obtained from the Queen a pardon for the same, dated 23 June in the 16th [year] of Elizabeth. And, as I have heard this lord himself report, this court suit cost him in the means he used £1,800 in ten weeks. In one passage about which pardon, his lordship added to me, that what time his wife was upon her knees before the Queen delivering a petition touching these arrears, her Majesty replied, 'No, no, my lady Berkeley, we know you will never love us for the death of your brother,' meaning the Duke of Norfolk beheaded about two years before . . .

This lord and his lady lay at Ivybridge, at that time commanded by Queen Elizabeth to attend the coming of Monsieur out of France, an attendance which in thirteen weeks cost this lord and lady £2,500. . . .

Having ended the long title of law suits, I now return to a shorter but worse, the sale of lands; too soon begun and too long continued. . . . And in place of all these manors and lands thus sold for £41,399 13s., he purchased of Mr Beconsale in the thirteenth year of Elizabeth the little poor manor of Canonbury, of the value of £5 11s. 8d. per annum. . . .

The hours may seem too many which this lord spent in his best ages at bowls, tennis, cock-pit, shove-groat, cards and dice, especially when he liked the company. And I will, without blemish to his honour, tell his posterity that his long and slender lady-like hand knew a die as well, and how to handle it, as any of his rank and time. . . . But his chief delights, wherein he spent near three parts of the year, were, to his great charges, in hunting the hare, fox and deer, red and fallow, not wanting choice of as good hunting horses as yearly he could buy at fairs in the North; and in hawking both at river and at land. And as his hounds were held inferior to no man's (through the great choice of whelps, which with much care he yearly bred of his choicest brachs,[2] and his continual huntings) so were his hawks of several sorts, which if he sent not a man to fetch from beyond seas, as three or four times I remember he did, yet had he the choice as soon as they were brought over into England, keeping a man lodging in London, in some years [for] a month or more, to be sure of his choice at their first landing; especially for his haggard falcons for the river, wherein he had two that fell in one after the other, and lasted twelve or more years, the one called Stella and the other Kate, that were famous with all great falconers in many counties, and prized at excessive rates, esteemed for high and round flying, free stooping and all other good conditions, inferior to none in Christendom, whom myself in my younger years, waiting upon his son Thomas, then not twelve years old, at Binly Brook, have in the height of their pitch, lost the sight of, in a clear evening. . . .

What household port this noble lord for his first twenty years after full age, that is till the beheading of his brother-in-law the Duke of Norfolk . . . has kept has before appeared. About which time the tide began to turn with this family, and their full sea ebbed, especially when the power of Robert Dudley Earl of Leicester, under his Court greatness and Queen Elizabeth's title, and the sale of eight or more manors by that time sold away, had drained so great a portion of their possessions, from which time, upon this lord's return from sojourning with Sir Thomas Russell at Strensham, the checkroll of his servants was shortened [by] forty persons at the least, and many unuseful people pared off. Howbeit the sail this family still bore for the next twelve years or near thereabouts seemed full and the gale fair. And his hospitality much renowned in all the neighbourhoods of his abodes. But then about the twenty-sixth [year] of Elizabeth, upon the second recovery of Arlingham with the other manors and lands . . . and the further sales of seven or eight other manors that had in that time been done away, upon this lord's returning from sojourning with Sir John Savage of Baraper, the former checkroll of his household servants was again further shortened [by] twenty persons at the least, and a second paring of unuseful drones. Howbeit, removing from Baraper to the White Friars at Coventry, and myself at that time first becoming a member of that household, I well remember the number then was about three-score and ten of all sorts. In which condition it continued till within a year or two before his wife the Lady Katherine died, and the marriage of his eldest son to the daughter and heir of George Lord Hunsdon. . . .

His rewards to servants: I will not come too near the heels of this title nor draw a needless envy from the sons and survivors of such

whom the bounty of this lord Henry raised and rewarded in the first
ten years after his full age and restitution to his barony of Berkeley,
what times the least deserving of twenty or more then in relation to
this family in the several counties of Gloucester, Somerset, Leicester,
Derby, Huntingdon and Sussex, had their barren fields watered from
this lord's bounty, some for years, others for lives, with the value of
£60, £80, £100, £150, £200 and £300 apiece by the year and
more, above the rents reserved upon such leases, some of which determined not till within three years now past, the most of them rather
bred to drink, sport and play, than for merit or employments. Neither
grew this lord's bounty much drier to sundry others in the riper part
of his life. . . .

As touching this lord's alms to the poor, it was three days in the
week wherein the poor of four, five and six country parishes and
villages next adjoining to Callowdon were relieved, with each of them
a mess of wholesome potage with a piece of beef or mutton therein,
half a cheat [wheat] loaf and a can of beer, besides the private alms that
daily went out of his purse, never without eight or ten shillings in
single money, of 2d., 3d. and groats, and besides his Maundy each
Thursday before Easter day, wherein many poor men and women
were clothed by the liberality of this lord and his first wife, whilst they
lived; and besides 20 marks or £20 or more, which thrice each year
against the feasts of Christmas, Easter and Whitsuntide was sent by this
lord to two or three of the chiefest inhabitants of those villages, and of
Gosford Street at Coventry, to be distributed amongst their poor
according to their discretions. . . .

In his last day's journey to Berkeley I have often attended, when I
have observed him met by the way and accompanied with 300, 400
and 500 horse of his kindred, friends and tenants, ere he came to
Berkeley town, though he usually set forth from Callowdon with
seldom above fourteen or sixteen, which confluence of train, how it
daily does and is more like to degenerate, let his posterity observe and
declare to their generations. . . .

I do ascertain [to] this noble lord's posterity that I spent a month
and more in tumbling over all such books of officers' and ministers'
accounts as might inform me and I them, what the total sum was of all
moneys which came to this lord's hands and were raised in rents, fines,
heriots, sales of coppice woods and of timber, and in the sales of the
lands he made, in the benevolences of his tenants thrice given him, and
loans (never repaid) and in the aids he had from his freeholders, moneys

paid for confirmation of customs of Bosham, Auconbury and Fenny-
stanton manors, and for such wardships, releases and other casualties as
happened and came to his coffers and were put into account, from the
first [year] of Queen Mary to his death in the eleventh [year] of King
James, the space of three-score years, and that the total thereof comes to
£260,500. . . .

[*Lives of the Berkeleys*, ed. J. Maclean, (Gloucester, 1883).]

Notes

1. A legal claim to some of the Berkeley estates.
2. Hound bitch.

III

Social Class and Civil War

31 Royalists and Parliamentarians

R. BAXTER

Richard Baxter (1615–91) was a Presbyterian divine whose writings have formed the main quarry for those seeking to demonstrate a link between puritanism and capitalism.

... It is of very great moment here to understand the quality of the persons which adhered to the King and to the Parliament, with their reasons.

A great part of the Lords forsook the Parliament, and so did many of the House of Commons, and came to the King; but that was, for the most of them, after Edgehill fight, when the King was at Oxford. A very great part of the knights and gentlemen of England in the several counties (who were not Parliament-men) adhered to the King. ... And most of the tenants of these gentlemen, and also most of the poorest of the people, whom the other call the rabble, did follow the gentry and were for the King.

On the Parliament's side were (besides themselves) the smaller part (as some thought) of the gentry in most of the counties, and the greatest part of the tradesmen and freeholders and the middle sort of men, especially in those corporations and counties which depend on clothing and such manufactures. ...

But though it must be confessed that the public safety and liberty wrought very much with most, especially with the nobility and gentry who adhered to the Parliament, yet was it principally the differences about religious matter that filled up the Parliament's armies and put the resolution and valour into their soldiers, which carried them on in another manner than mercenary soldiers are carried on. Not that the matter of bishops or no bishops was the main thing (for thousands that wished for good bishops were on the Parliament's side), though many called it *bellum episcopale* (and with the Scots that was a greater part of the controversy). But the generality of the people through the land (I say not *all*, or *everyone*) who were then called Puritans, precisians, religious persons, that used to talk of God and heaven, and Scripture and holiness . . ., I say, the main body of this sort of men, both preachers and people, adhered to the Parliament. And on the other side, the gentry that were not so precise and strict against an oath, or gaming, or plays, or drinking, nor troubled themselves so much about the matters of God and the world to come, and the ministers and people that were for the [Prayer] Book, for dancing and recreations on the Lord's days and those that made not so great a matter every sin, but went to church and heard Common Prayer, and were glad to hear a sermon which lashed the puritans. . . .

If you ask how this came to pass, it requires a longer answer than I think fit here to give; but briefly, actions spring from natural dispositions and interest. There is somewhat in the nature of all worldly men which makes them earnestly desirous of riches and honours in the world. . . . Yet conscience must be quieted and reputation preserved, which can neither of them be done without some religion. Therefore such a religion is necessary to such, as is consistent with a worldly mind, which outside-formality, lip-service and hypocrisy is, but seriousness, sincerity and spirituality is not.

On the other side, there is that in the new nature of a spiritual believer which inclines him to things above, and causes him to look at worldly grandeur and riches as things more dangerous than desirable; and he is dead to the world, and the world to him, by the Cross of Christ. . . . And the laws of Christ, to which they are so devoted, are of such a stream as cannot suit with carnal interest. . . .

And thus the interest of the diocesans and of the profane and ignorant sort of people were unhappily twisted together in England. . . .

And abundance of the ignorant sort of the country, who were civil, did flock in to the Parliament, and filled up their armies afterward, merely because they heard men *swear* for the Common Prayer and bishops, and heard others *pray* that were against them; and because they heard the King's soldiers with horrid oaths abuse the name os God, and saw them live in debauchery, and the Parliament's soldierf flock to sermons and talking of religion, and praying and singing Psalms together on their guards. And all the sober men that I was acquainted with, who were against the Parliament, were wont to say: 'The King has the better cause, but the Parliament has the better men.'

[*Autobiography of Richard Baxter* (Everyman ed., Dent, 1931).]

32 Royalists and Parliamentarians

THE EARL OF CLARENDON

Edward Hyde, Earl of Clarendon (1609–74) was a Parliamentary opponent of Crown policies up to 1641, but veered round to the Royalist side as the Parliamentary leaders began to threaten major change in religion and the Constitution. His History of the Rebellion is a great, but prejudiced, work, which seeks to justify the Royalist cause.

. . . [In 1642, training as volunteers for Parliament] began to be practised in many places of the kingdom, but only in those corporations and by those inferior people who were notorious for faction and schism in religion. . . . The people generally (except in great towns and corporations where, beside the natural malignity, the factious lecturers and emissaries from Parliament had poisoned the affections), and especially those of quality, were loyally inclined. . . .

[In Somerset, the Parliament leaders were] for the most part clothiers, and men who, though they were rich, had not been before of power or reputation there. . . . Though the gentlemen of ancient families and estates in that country were for the most part well affected to the King, . . . yet there were a people of an inferior degree who by good husbandry, clothing and other thriving arts had gotten very great fortunes, and by degrees getting themselves into the gentlemen's estates, were angry that they found not themselves in the same esteem and reputation with those whose estates they had; and therefore with more industry than the other, studied all ways to make themselves considerable. These from the beginning were fast friends to the Parliament. . . .

[In Lancashire,] men of no name and contemned interest, by the mere credit of Parliament and frenzy of the people on a sudden snatched that large and populous county from their devotion to the great Earl of Derby. . . . The town of Manchester had from the beginning (out of that factious humour which possessed most corporations and pride of their wealth) opposed the King and declared magisterially for the Parliament. . . .

[In the West] though most of the gentry were engaged against [the Parliamentarians], as they were in truth throughout the Kingdom, yet the common people, especially in the clothing parts of Somerset-shire, were generally too much inclined to them. . . .

[In Gloucestershire, it was] the yeomanry, who had been most forward and seditious, being very wealthy. . . .

[In Yorkshire,] besides the Lord Fairfax, there were in truth few of good reputation and fortune who ran that way. . . . Leeds, Halifax and Bradford, three very populous and rich towns (which depending wholly upon clothiers naturally maligned the gentry) were wholly at their disposition. Upon publishing this last monstrous Declaration of No Addresses in 1648, most of those persons of condition, who, as has been said before, had been seduced to do [the Parliamentarians] service throughout the kingdom, declined to appear longer in so detestable an employment; and now a more inferior sort of the common people succeeded in those employments, who thereby exercised so great insolence over those who were in quality above them, and who always had a power over them, that was very grievous; and for this, let the circumstances be what they would, no redress could ever be obtained, all distinction of quality being renounced. And they who were not above the condition of ordinary inferior constables six or seven years before, were now the justices of people, sequestrators and commissioners; who executed the commands of the Parliament in all the counties of the kingdom with such rigour and tyranny as was natural for such persons to use over and towards those upon whom they had formerly looked at such a distance. But let their sufferings be never so great, and the murmur and discontent never so general, there was no shadow of hope by which they might discern any possible relief; so that they who had struggled as long as they were able submitted patiently to the yoke, with the more satisfaction in that they saw many of those who had been the principal contrivers of all the mischiefs, to satisfy their own ambition and that they might govern over others, reduced now to almost as ill a condition as themselves, at least to as little power and authority and security; while the whole government of the nation remained, upon the matter, wholly in their hands who in the beginning of the Parliament were scarce ever heard of, or their names known but in the places where they inhabited.

[*The History of the Rebellion and Civil Wars in England*, ed. W. D. Macray (Oxford, 1888).]

33 The Crown and the Aristocracy
THE MARQUIS OF NEWCASTLE

William Cavendish, Marquis of Newcastle (1592–1676), was one of the wealthiest peers of the realm, and one of the most active in the Royalist cause during the Civil War. While in exile abroad during the 1650s, he sent the young Charles II a lengthy memorandum on how to manage his kingdom after the Restoration. It is a very conservative, indeed reactionary document, and reflects many of the ideas of the Marquis's protégé, the philosopher Thomas Hobbes.

... It was neither the Church nor the Law that kept up the King so long, but part of the nobility and gentry, therefore your Majesty's wisdom will cherish them. It is true wise kings heretofore took as much power from the nobility as they could, because of the Barons' wars, and put more to the Commons, wherein they committed a very great error, for the worst in the nobility is but to pull down one king and set up another, so that they are always for monarchy, but the Commons pulls down root and branch and utterly destroys monarchy. So that your Majesty will be pleased to stick to your nobility and gentry and they will stick to you, being no great danger, as long as your Majesty has the force in your hands, being divided into so many hands of your nobility which is as many lords as there are counties, which is fifty-two; and certainly all those are not likely to agree at one time against you. ... When the ceremony and order of noblemen were pulled down, which is the foundation of monarchy, monarchy soon after fell. ... Therefore, Sir, keep up your nobility for your own sake.

[S. A. Strong, *A Catalogue of . . . Documents at Welbeck* (1903).]

IV
Political Theory

34 The Theory of the Balance
J. HARRINGTON

James Harrington (1611–77) was the eldest son of a knight. He was neutral in the Civil War, but after it, perhaps under the influence of his friend Henry Neville, he developed strong republican leanings. His Oceana *was published in 1656, and his other writings – defending, expanding, and abstracting the ideas it contained – are all the work of the one year 1659, when political chaos reigned and Harrington saw his chance to frame a new constitution for England. His ideas were eagerly discussed at the weekly meetings of an intellectual club, the* Rota, *but his hopes were dashed by the Restoration.*

... The reason why a single person, or the nobility that has 100,000 men or half so many at command, will have the Government, is that the estate in land, whereby they are able to maintain so many, in any European territory, must over-balance the rest that remains to the people, at least three parts in four, by which means they [the latter] are no more able to dispute the Government with him or them, than your servant is with you. Now for the same reason, if the people hold three parts in four of the territory, it is plain there can neither be any single person nor nobility able to dispute the Government with them; in this case therefore, except force be interposed, they govern themselves. So by this computation of the balance of property or dominion in land, you have, according to the three-fold foundation of property, the root or generation of the three-fold kind of government or empire.

If one man be sole landlord of a territory, or over-balance the whole people three parts in four, or thereabouts, he is Grand Signior; for so the Turk, nor from his empire, but his property is called; and the empire in this case is absolute monarchy.

If the few, or a nobility, or a nobility with a clergy, be landlords to such a proportion as over-balances the people in the like manner, they may make whom they please King; or if they be not pleased with their

King, down with him, and set up whom they like better; a Henry IV or Henry VII, a Guise, a Montfort, a Nevil or a Porter, should they find that best for their own ends and purposes; for as [it is] not the balance of the King, but that of the nobility in this case [which] is the cause of the government, so [it is] not the estate and riches of the prince or captain, but his virtue or ability, or fitness for the ends of the nobility, [that] acquires that command or office. This for aristocracy or mixed monarchy. But if the whole people be landlords, or hold the land so divided among them, that no one man or number of men within the compass of the few, or aristocracy, over-balance them, it is a commonwealth. Such is the branch in the root, or the balance of property naturally producing empire; which not confuted, no man shall be able to batter my superstructures, and which confuted, I lay down my arms. Till then, if the cause necessarily precede the effect, property must have a being before empire, or beginning with it, must be still first in order.

Property comes to have a being before empire or government [in] two ways, either by a natural or violent revolution. Natural revolution happens from within, or by commerce, as when a government erected upon one balance, that for example of a nobility or a clergy, through the decay of their estates comes to alter to another balance; which alteration in the root of property, leaves all to confusion, or produces a new branch or government, according to the kind or nature of the root. Violent revolution happens from without, or by arms, as when upon conquest there follows confiscation. . . .

The balance in money may be as good or better than that of land in three cases. First where there is no property of land yet introduced, as in Greece during the time of her ancient imbecillity; whence as is noted by Thucydides, the meaner sort through a desire of gain underwent the servitude of the mighty. Secondly, in cities of small territory and great trade, as Holland and Genoa, the land, not being able to feed the people, who must live upon traffic, is over-balanced by the means of that traffic, which is money. Thirdly, in a narrow country where the lots are at a low scantling, as among the Israelites, if care be not had of money in the regulation of the same, it will eat out the balance of land. . . . Usury is of such a nature as, not forbidden in the like cases, must devour the Government. . . . But in a territory of such extent as Spain or England, the land being not to be overbalanced by money, there needs no forbidding of money or usury. . . .

Henry VII, though he missed of the Indies, in which for my part I think him happy, was the richest in money of English princes. Nevertheless, this accession of revenue did not at all preponderate on the King's part, nor change the balance.

The monarchy of Spain, since the silver of Potosi sailed up the Guadalquivir, which in English is since that King had the Indies, stands upon the same balance in the lands of the nobility on which it always stood. . . .

It is true, there is not only such a thing in nature as health, but sickness too; nor do I deny that there is such a thing as a government against the balance. But look about, seek, find where it stood, how it was named, how liked or how long it lasted. Otherwise the comical proposition comes to this: It is not to be doubted but that violence may be permanent or durable. What other construction can be made of these words? It is not to be doubted, but a revenue sufficient to maintain a force able to beat down all opposition (that is a force able to raise such a revenue) does equally conduce to empire; that is, as much as could any natural balance of the same. . . .

The strength whereby this effect can be expected consists not in a pair of fists, but in an army; and an army is a beast with a great belly, which subsists not without very large pastures: so if one man has sufficient pasture, he may feed such a beast; if a few have the pasture, they must feed the beast, and the beast is theirs that feed it. But if a people be the sheep of their own pastures, they are not only a flock of sheep, but an army of lions, though by some accidents, as I contest before, they be for a season confinable to their dens. So the advantage or increase of strength depends also upon the balance. . . .

The balance of empire that is national, as it is stated in the former chapter, stands in a regulated or mixed monarchy upon the property or native interest of the nobility; in a commonwealth, upon the property or native interest of the people; so these are very natural. But the balance of absolute monarchy, partaking of force as well as nature, is a mixed thing, and not much different from the balance of provincial empire, or the manner of holding a province or conquered country. . . . Wherefore if the King of Spain by his war against the commons altered the balance of Aragon, it must have been one of two ways, either by strengthening the balance of the nobility, and governing the Aragonian people by them, in which case their balance, though altered, remained yet national; or by holding both nobility and people by a provincial governor and an army, in which case his empire in that kingdom is provincial. There is no third way. . . .

The land in possession of the nobility and clergy of England till Henry VII cannot be esteemed to have over-balanced those held by the people less than four to one. Whereas in our days, the clergy being destroyed, the lands in possession of the people over-balance those held by the nobility, at least nine in ten. . . . But Henry VII being conscious of infirmity in his title, yet finding with what strength and vigour he was brought in by the nobility, conceived jealousies of the like power in case of a decay or change of affections. *Nondum orbis adoraverat Romam.* The Lords yet led country lives, their houses were open to retainers, men experienced in military affairs, and capable of commanding; their hospitality was the delight of their tenants, who by their tenures or dependence were obliged to follow their lords in arms. So that, this being the militia of the nation, a few noblemen discontented could at any time levy a great army; the effect whereof, both in the Barons' Wars and those of York and Lancaster, had been well known to divers Kings. This state of affairs was that which enabled Henry VII to make his advantage of troublesome times, and the frequent unruliness of retainers; while under the pretence of curbing riots, he obtained the passing of such laws as did cut off these retainers, whereby the nobility wholly lost their officers. Then, whereas the dependance of the people upon their lords was of a strict tie or nature, he found means to loosen this also by laws, which he obtained upon as fair a pretence, even that of population. Thus farms were so brought to a standard, that the houses being kept up, each of them did of necessity enforce a dweller; and the proportion of land laid to each house did of necessity enforce that dweller not to be a beggar or cottager, but a man able to keep servants, and set the plough on going. By which means a great part of the lands of this nation came in effect to be amortised to the hold of the yeomanry, or middle people, whereof consisted the main body of the militia, hereby incredibly advanced; and which henceforth, like cleaner underwood less choked by their staddles, began to grow exceedingly. But the nobility, who by the former laws had lost their offices, by this lost their soldiery. Yet remained to them their estates, till the same prince introducing the Statutes for Alienations, these also became loose; and the Lords less taken (for the reasons shown) with their country lives, where their trains were clipped, by degrees became more resident at Court, where greater pomp and expense by the Statute of Alienations began to plume them of their estates. The Court was yet at Bridewell, nor reached London any farther than Temple Bar. The later growth of this

City, and in that the declining of the balance to popularity, derives from the decay of the nobility and of the clergy. In the reign of the succeeding King were. Abbeys (than which nothing more dwarfs a people) demolished. . . .

The growth of the people of England, since the ruins mentioned of the nobility and the clergy, came in the reign of Queen Elizabeth to more than stood with the interest, or indeed the nature or possibility of a well-founded or durable monarchy; as was prudently perceived, but withal temporized by her Council, who (if the truth of her government be rightly weighed) seem rather to have put her upon the exercise of principality in a commonwealth, than of sovereign power in a monarchy. Certain it is that she courted not her nobility, nor gave her mind (as do monarchs seated upon the like foundation) to balance her great men, or reflect upon their power now inconsiderable; but ruled wholly, with an art she had to high perfection, by humouring and blessing her people. For this mere shadow of a commonwealth is she yet famous, and shall ever be so; though had she introduced the full perfection of the orders requisite to popular government, her fame had been greater. . . .

To this Queen succeeded King James, who likewise regardless of this point (into which nevertheless he saw so far as not seldom to prophesy sad things to his successors) neither his new peerage, which in abundance he created, nor the old availed him anything against that dread wherein, more freely than prudently, he discovered himself to stand of Parliaments, as now mere popular councils, and running to popularity of government like a bowl down a hill; not so much, I may say, of malice [aforethought], as by natural instinct, whereof the Petition of Right, well considered, is a sufficient testimony. All persuasion of court eloquence, all patience for such as but looked that way, was now lost. There remained nothing to the destruction of a monarchy, retaining but the name, more than a prince who by contending should make the people to feel those advantages which they could not see. And this happened in the next King, who, too secure in that undoubted right whereby he was advanced to a throne which had no foundation, dared to put this to an unseasonable trial; on whom therefore fell the Tower in Siloh. . . .

Fixation of the balance of property is not to be provided for but by laws; and the laws, whereby such a provision is made, are commonly called agrarian laws. Now as governments, through the divers balance of property, are of divers or contrary natures, that is monarchical or popular, so are such laws. Monarchy requires of the standard of property, that it be vast or great; and of agrarian laws, that they hinder recess or diminution, at least in so much as is thereby entailed upon honour; but popular government requires that the standard be moderate and that its agrarian [laws] prevent accumulation. In a territory not exceeding England in revenue, if the balance be in more hands than three hundred, it is declining from monarchy; and if it be in fewer than 5,000 hands, it is swerving from a commonwealth; which as to this point may suffice at present. . . .

If a prince, by easing his nobility of taxes, and feeding them with such as are extorted from the people, can so accommodate their ambition and avarice with great offices and commands that, a party rebelling, he can over-balance and reduce them by a greater part of their own order, he may have greater power and less security, as at present in France.

The safer way of this government is by orders; and the orders proper to it especially consist of an hereditary senate of the nobility, admitting also of the clergy, and of a representative of the people made up of the Lords' menial servants, or such as by tenure and for livelihood have immediate dependence upon them, as formerly in England. . . .

It is very reasonable that, in the proposition of a commonwealth, we begin with a fixation of the balance in property; and this being not otherwise to be done than by some such laws as have been commonly called Agrarian, it is proposed:

That everyone holding above £2,000 a year in land, lying within the proper territory of the commonwealth, leave the said land equally divided among his sons; or else so near equally that there remain to the eldest of them not above £2,000 a year in land so lying. That this proposition be so understood, as not to concern any parent having no more than one son, but the next heir only that shall have more sons; in such sort, as nothing be hereby taken from any man, or from his posterity, but that fatherly affection be at all points extended as formerly, except only that it be with more piety, and less partiality. And that the same proposition, in such families where there are no sons, concern the daughter or daughters in the like manner. That no daughter, being neither heir nor co-heir, have above £1,500 in portion, or for her preferment in marriage. . . .

That these propositions prevent the growing of a monarchical nobility, is their peculiar end. . . .

That to Agrairan laws some standard is necessary, appears plainly enough. . . . But why yet must this standard of land in the present case be neither more nor less than just £2,000 a year? . . .

Let the dry rent of England (that is, at the rate a man may have for his land without sweating) be computed at ten millions. This presumed, if you set the standard at £10,000 a year, the whole territory can come into no fewer than 1,000 hands. If you set it at £5,000 a year, it can come into no fewer than 2,000 hands; and if you set it at £2,000 a year, it can come into no fewer than 5,000 hands. It will be said, in which way you please it will never come into so few hands as are capable of having it, which is certain; yet, because the effects in their approaches would be such as may be measured by their extremes, I shall pitch upon these as the readiest way to guide my computation. The balance in a thousand hands might affect the Government with a hankering after monarchy; in two thousand hands it might usurp it, as did the Roman nobility, and thereby occasion a feud between the Senate and the people.

[*The Oceana of James Harrington and his Other Works,* ed. John Toland (Dublin, 1737.)]

35 The Theory of the Balance

H. NEVILLE

Henry Neville (1620–94) was the younger son of a knight. An active M.P. in Parliament 1645–53, and again in 1659, he was a strong republican and close friend of James Harrington. Plato Redivivus was not published till 1681, but represents the author's ideas formulated in the late 1650s. It should be noted that in 1675 he published a translation of the works of Machiavelli.

. . . I will not trouble myself nor you to search into the particular causes of this change which has been made in the possessions here in England; but it is visible that the fortieth part of the lands which were at the beginning in the hands of the peers and church, is not there now; besides that not only all villeinage is long since abolished, but the other tenures are so altered and qualified that they signify nothing towards making the yeomanry depend upon the lords. The consequence is, that the natural part of our government, which is power, is by means of property in the hands of the people, whilst the artificial part, or the parchment in which the form of government is written, remains the same. Now art is a very good servant and help to nature, but very weak and inconsiderable, when she opposes her and fights with her; it would be a very *impar congressus* between parchment and power. This alone is the cause of all the disorder you heard of, and now see in England, and of which every man gives a reason according to his own fancy, whilst few hit the right cause: some impute all to the decay of trade, others to the growth of popery; which are both great calamities, but they are effects, and not causes. . . . In our ancestor's times most of the Members of our House of Commons thought it an honour to retain to some great lord, and to wear his blue coat; and when they had made up their lord's train, and waited upon him from his own house to the Lords' House, and made a lane for him to enter, and departed to sit themselves in the Lower House of Parliament as it was then (and very justly) called: can you think that anything could pass in such a Parliament that was not ordered by the Lords? Besides, these Lords were the King's great Council in the intervals of Parliament, and were called to advise of peace and war; and the latter was seldom made without the consent of the major part; if it were not, they would not send their tenants, which was all the militia of England (besides the King's tenth part). Can it be believed that in those days the Commons should dislike anything the Lords did in the intervals, or that they would have disputed their right to receive appeals from courts of equity, if they had pretended to it in those days, or to mend money-bills? And what is the reason, but because the Lords themselves at that time represented all their tenants (that is, all the people) in some sort? And although the House of Commons did assemble to present their grievances, yet all great affairs of high importance concerning the Government was transacted by the Lords; and the war which was made to preserve it, was called the Baron's Wars, not the War of both Houses. . . . Now if this property, which is gone out of the peerage into the Commons, had passed into the King's hands, as it did in Egypt in the time of Joseph, as was before said, the prince had had a very easy and peaceable reign over his own vassals and might either have refused, justly, to have assembled the Parliament any more; or if he had pleased to do it, might have for ever managed it as he thought fit. But our princes have wanted a Joseph, that is a wise councillor; and instead of saving their revenue, which was very great, and their expenses small, and buying in those purchases which the vast expenses and luxury of the Lords made ready for them, they have alienated their own inheritance; so that now the Crown lands that is the public patrimony is come to make up the interest of the Commons, whilst the King must have a precarious revenue out of the people's purses, and be beholden to the Parliament for his bread in time of peace; whereas the Kings their predecessors never asked aid of his subjects, but in time of war and invasion; and this alone (though there were no other decay in the Government) is enough to make the King depend upon his people, which is no very good condition for a monarchy. . . .

Now the Commons succeeding, as was said, in the property of the peers and church (whose lands five parts of six have been alienated, and mostly is come into the same hands with those of the King and peers) have inherited likewise, according to the course of nature, their power. . . . I cannot say that the greater part of the people do know this their condition, but they find very plainly that they want something which they ought to have; and this makes them lay often the blame of their unsettledness upon wrong causes; but, however, are altogether unquiet and restless in the intervals of Parliament; and when the King pleases to assemble one, spend all their time in complaints of the inexecution of the law, of the multiplication of an infinity of grievances, of mis-spending the public moneys, of the danger our religion is in by practices to undermine it, and the State by endeavours to bring in arbitrary power, and in questioning great officers of State, as the causers and promoters of all these abuses; inasmuch as every Parliament seems a perfect state of war, wherein the Commons are tugging and contending for their right, very justly and very honourably, yet without coming to a point; so that the court sends them packing and governs still worse and worse in the vacancies, being necessitated thereunto by their despair of doing any good in Parliament; and therefore are forced to use horrid shifts to subsist without it, and to keep it off; without ever considering that if these counsellors understood their trade, they might bring the Prince and People to such an agreement in Parliament, as might repair the broken and shipwrecked government of England; and in this secure the peace, quiet and prosperity of the people, the greatness and happiness of the King, and be themselves not only out of present danger (which no other course can exempt them from) but be renowned to all posterity. . . .

Our war did not begin upon a point of right, but upon a matter of fact: for without going to lawyers or casuists to be resolved, those of the people who believed that the King did intend to destroy our liberties, joined with the Parliament; and those who were of opinion that the prevailing party in Parliament did intend to destroy the King or dethrone him, assisted vigorously His Majesty with their lives and fortunes.

[*Plato Redivivus*, published in *The Works of James Harrington*, ed. J. Toland (Dublin, 1737).]

Bibliography

This bibliography is arranged in two sections. First comes a list of books and articles, numbered consecutively. There follows a section with topical headings, under each of which is listed the relevant numbers from section I.

Section I

Unless otherwise stated, the place of publication is London.

1. G. ANSTRUTHER. *Vaux of Harrowden, a recusant family.* Newport: R. H. Johns, 1953.
2. G. E. AYLMER. *The King's Servants: The Civil Service of Charles I, 1625–42.* Routledge: 1961.
3. G. E. AYLMER. 'Office-holding as a Factor in English History, 1625–42', *History*, XLIV, 1959.
4. F. BACON. 'Observations on a Libel', *Life and Letters of Sir Francis Bacon*, ed. J. Spedding. 1857–74.
5. F. BAMFORD. *A Royalist's Notebook.* Constable, 1936.
6. T. G. BARNES. *Somerset, 1625–1640.* Cambridge, Mass.: Harvard University Press, 1961.
7. G. R. BATHO. 'The Finances of an Elizabethan Nobleman: Henry Percy, 9th Earl of Northumberland', *Economic History Review*, 2nd ser., IX, 1957.
8. G. R. BATHO. The Household Accounts of Henry Percy, 9th Earl of Northumberland (unpublished London M.A. thesis, 1953).
9. RICHARD BAXTER. *Autobiography.* Dent, 1931 (Everyman edn.).
10. T. BIRCH, ed. *The Works of Sir Walter Ralegh.* 1751.
11. D. BRUNTON and D. H. PENNINGTON. *Members of the Long Parliament.* Allen and Unwin, 1954.
12. M. CAMPBELL. *The English Yeoman under Elizabeth and the Early Stuarts.* New Haven, 1942; new edn. Merlin, 1960.
13. *Memoirs of Robert Cary Earl of Monmouth*, ed. G. H. Powell. 1905.
14. *Memoirs of Sir Hugh Cholmley.* 1787.
15. Earl of CLARENDON. *History of the Rebellion and Civil Wars in England.* Oxford, 1704.
16. J. T. CLIFFE. The Yorkshire Gentry on the Eve of the Civil War (unpublished London Ph.D. thesis, 1960).
17. J. P. COOPER. 'The Counting of Manors', *Economic History Review*, 2nd ser., VIII, 1956.
18. J. P. COOPER. Letter in *Encounter*, XI, 1958, iii, p. 73.
19. M. C. CROSS. The Career of Henry Hastings 3rd Earl of Huntingdon, 1536–95 (unpublished Cambridge D. Phil. thesis, 1959).

20. W. R. EMERSON. The Economic Development of the Estates of the Petre Family in Essex in the 16th and 17th centuries (unpublished Oxford D.Phil. thesis, 1951).

21. A. M. EVERITT. *The County Committee of Kent in the Civil War.* Leicester: University Press, 1957.

22. M. E. FINCH. *The Wealth of Five Northamptonshire families, 1540–1640.* Northants. Record Society Publications, XIX, 1955.

23. C. H. FIRTH. *The House of Lords in the Great Civil War.* London, 1910.

24. F. J. FISHER. 'The Sixteenth and Seventeenth Centuries: the Dark Ages in English Economic History?', *Economica*, n.s., XXIV, 1957.

25. F. J. FISHER. 'London as a Centre of Conspicuous Consumption in the Sixteenth and Seventeenth Centuries', *Transactions of the Royal Historical Society*, 4th ser., XXX, 1948.

26. F. J. FISHER, ed. *T. Wilson's State of England in 1600.* Camden Society, 3rd ser., LII, *Miscellany*, XVI, 1936.

27. T. FULLER. *The Worthies of England.* 1662.

28. E. F. GAY. 'The Temples of Stow', *Huntington Library Quarterly*, II, 1939.

29. I. GRIMBLE. *The Harington Family.* Cape, 1958.

30. G. B. HARRISON, ed. *Instructions to his Son by Henry Percy 9th Earl of Northumberland.* Benn, 1930.

31. W. HARRISON. *Description of England.* 1577.

32. J. H. HEXTER. *Reappraisals in History.* Longmans, 1961.

33. C. HILL. *The Century of Revolution, 1603–1714.* Edinburgh: Nelson, 1961.

34. C. HILL. 'Recent Interpretations of the Civil War', in *Puritanism and Revolution.* Secker, 1958.

35. C. HILL. 'La Révolution Anglaise du XVIIe siècle (Essai d'Interprétation), *Revue Historique*, CCXXI, 1959.

36. C. HILL. *Society and Puritanism in Pre-Revolutionary England.* Secker, 1964.

37. E. HOPKINS. The Bridgwater Estates in North Shropshire in the first half of the seventeenth century (unpublished London M.A. thesis, 1956).

38. E. HOPKINS. 'The Re-leasing of the Ellesmere Estates, 1637–42', *Agricultu ra History Review*, X, 1962.

39. W. G. HOSKINS. 'The Estates of the Caroline Gentry', in *Devonshire Studies*, ed. W. G. Hoskins and H. P. R. Finberg. Cape, 1952.

40. W. G. HOSKINS. 'The Rebuilding of rural England, 1570–1640', *Past and Present*, 4, 1953.

41. M. E. JAMES. 'The Estate Accounts of the Earls of Northumberland, 1562–1637', *Surtees Soc.*, CLXIII, Durham, 1955.

42. M. F. KEELER. *The Long Parliament, 1640–41.* Philadelphia: American Philosophical Society, 1954.

43. E. KERRIDGE. 'The Movement of Rent, 1540–1640', *Economic History Review*, 2nd ser., VI, 1953.

44. E. KERRIDGE, ed. 'Surveys of the Manors of Philip First Earl of Pembroke and Montgomery, 1631–2', *Wilts. Record Soc.*, IX, 1953.

45. W. MACCAFFERY. 'Place and Patronage in Elizabethan Politics', in *Elizabethan Government and Society*, ed. S. T. Bindoff *et al*. Athlone Press, 1961.

46. D. MATHEW. *The Age of Charles I*. Eyre and Spottiswoode, 1951.

47. D. MATHEW. *The Social Structure in Caroline England*. Oxford: University Press, 1948.

48. J. E. NEALE. *The Elizabethan House of Commons*. Cape, 1949.

49. J. E. NEALE. 'The Elizabethan Political Scene,' *Essays in Elizabethan History*. Cape, 1958.

50. DUDLEY LORD NORTH. *Observations and Advices Oeconomical*. 1669.

51. J. U. NEF. *Industry and Government in France and England, 1540-1640*. Philadelphia: American Philosophical Society, 1940.

52. J. U. NEF. 'The Progress of Technology and the Growth of large scale industry in Great Britain, 1540-1640', *Economic History Review*, V, 1934.

53. V. PEARL. *London and the Outbreak of the Puritan Revolution*. Oxford: University Press, 1961.

54. E. H. PHELPSBROWN and S. V. HOPKINS. 'Wage-Rates and Prices: Evidence for Population Pressure in the Sixteenth Century', *Economica*, n.s., XXIV, 1957.

55. C. J. PHILLIPS. *History of the Sackville Family*. Cassell, 1930.

56. G. D. RAMSAY. 'Isham's Account Book', *Northants. Record Society Publications*, 1962.

57. P. RAMSEY. *Tudor Economic Problems*. Gollancz, 1963.

58. R. REYCE. *Breviary of Suffolk*, ed. Francis Lord Hervey. 1902.

59. W. R. B. ROBINSON. The Earls of Worcester and their Estates, 1526-1642 (unpublished Oxford B.Litt. thesis, 1959).

60. J. SELDEN. *Table Talk*, ed. F. Pollock. Quaritch, 1927.

61. J. SHKLAR. 'Ideology Hunting: the Case of James Harrington', *American Political Science Review*, LIII, 1959.

62. A. SIMPSON. *The Wealth of the Gentry, 1540-1660*. Chicago University Press, 1961.

63. T. SMITH. *The Commonwealth of England*. 1583.

64. J. SMYTH. *The Lives of the Berkeleys*, ed. J. Maclean. Gloucester, 1883.

65. H. SPELMAN. *The History and Fate of Sacrilege*. 1698.

66. R. T. SPENCE. The Cliffords Earls of Cumberland, 1579-1646 (unpublished London Ph.D. thesis, 1959).

67. L. STONE. 'The Anatomy of the Elizabethan Aristocracy', *Economic History Review*, XVIII, 1948.

68. L. STONE. *The Crisis of the Aristocracy, 1558-1641*. Oxford: University Press, 1965.

69. L. STONE. 'The Educational Revolution, 1560-1640', *Past and Present*, 28, 1964.

70. L. STONE. 'The Elizabethan Aristocracy: A Restatement', *Economic History Review*, 2nd ser., IV, 1952.

71. L. STONE. 'The Fruits of Office: the Case of Robert Cecil, First Earl of Salisbury', *Essays in the Social and Economic History of Tudor and Early Stuart England*, ed. F. J. Fisher. Cambridge University Press, 1961.

72. C. C. STOPES. *Henry 3rd Earl of Southampton*. Cambridge University Press, 1922.

73. R. H. TAWNEY. *The Agrarian Problem in the Sixteenth Century*. 1912.

74. R. H. TAWNEY. *Business and Politics under James I*. Cambridge University Press, 1958.

75. R. H. TAWNEY. 'Harrington's Interpretation of his Age', *Proceedings of the British Academy*, XXVII, 1941.

76. R. H. TAWNEY. *Religion and the Rise of Capitalism*. Murray, 1926.

77. R. H. TAWNEY. 'The Rise of the Gentry, 1558–1640', *Economic History Review*, XI, 1941.

78. R. H. TAWNEY. 'The Rise of the Gentry: a Postscript', *Economic History Review*, 2nd ser., VII, 1954.

79. R. H. TAWNEY, ed. *T. Wilson's Discourse upon Usury* ... (1572). Bell, 1925.

80. J. THIRSK. 'The Restoration Land Settlement', *Journal of Modern History*, XXVI, 1954.

81. J. THIRSK. 'The Sales of Royalist Land during the Interregnum', *Economic History Review*, 2nd ser., V, 1952.

82. H. R. TREVOR-ROPER. 'The Bishopric of Durham and the Capitalist Reformation', *Durham University Journal*, XXXVIII, 1946.

83. H. R. TREVOR-ROPER. 'The Elizabethan Aristocracy: an Anatomy Anatomised', *Economic History Review*, 2nd ser., III, 1951.

84. H. R. TREVOR-ROPER. 'The General Crisis of the Seventeenth Century', *Past and Present*, 16, 1959; 18, 1960.

85. H. R. TREVOR-ROPER. *The Gentry, 1540–1640, Economic History Review Supplement*, I, 1953.

86. H. R. TREVOR-ROPER. 'Oliver Cromwell and his Parliaments', in *Essays presented to Sir Lewis Namier*, ed. R. Pares and A. J. P. Taylor. Macmillan, 1956.

87. H. R. TREVOR-ROPER. 'La Révolution Anglaise de Cromwell', *Annales: Economies, Sociétés, Civilisations*, 10, 1955.

88. D. UNDERDOWN. 'The Independents Reconsidered', *Journal of British Studies*, III, 1964.

89. SIR EDWARD WALKER. *Historical Discourses*. 1705.

90. B. M. WARD. *The 17th Earl of Oxford, 1550–1604*. Murray, 1928.

91. E. WATERHOUSE. *The Gentleman's Monitor, or a sober Inspection into the Virtues, Vices, and Ordinary Means of the Rise and Decay of Men and Families*. 1665.

92. C. V. WEDGWOOD. Letter in *Encounter*, XI, 1958, V, p. 81.

93. G. C. WILLIAMSON. *George 3rd Earl of Cumberland, 1558–1605*. Cambridge University Press, 1920.

94. A. C. WOOD, ed. 'Memorials of the Holles Family, 1493–1656', *Camden Society*, 3rd ser., LV, 1937.

95. L. B. WRIGHT. *Middle Class Culture in Elizabethan England.* Chapel Hill, 1935; Methuen, 1959.

96. G. YULE. *The Independents in the English Civil War.* Cambridge University Press, 1958.

97. P. ZAGORIN. 'The English Revolution, 1640–1660', *Cahiers d' Histoire Mondiale*, II, 1955.

98. P. ZAGORIN. 'The Social Interpretations of the English Revolution', *Journal of Economic History*, XIX, 1959.

Section II

1. *The Main Debate*
   In chronological order: 75, 77, 67, 83, 70, 85, 78, 87, 17, 32, 18, 92, 98, 61, 68

2. *Particular Studies*
   (i) *Families:* (a) *Contemporary:* 5, 13, 14, 30, 64, 94
   　　　　　　　(b) *Secondary:* 1, 7, 8, 19, 20, 28, 29, 37, 38, 41, 42, 44, 55, 56, 59, 66, 71, 72, 74, 90, 93
   (ii) *Areas:* 6, 16, 21, 22, 62

3. *Contemporary Comment*
   4, 9, 10, 15, 26, 27, 31, 39, 50, 58, 60, 63, 65, 79, 89, 91

4. *General Economic and Social Background*
   12, 24, 25, 32, 33, 40, 43, 46, 47, 48, 51, 52, 54, 57, 68, 69, 73, 76, 79, 82, 95

5. *Court and Office*
   2, 3, 45, 46, 47, 49, 71, 74, 84, 85

6. *The Revolution, 1640–60*
   11, 21, 23, 33, 34, 35, 36, 42, 53, 80, 81, 86, 87, 88, 96, 97

Note. The following appeared too late to be included in this bibliography:

C. HILL. *Intellectual Origins of the English Revolution.* Oxford University Press, 1965.

A. EVERITT. *The Community of Kent and the Great Rebellion 1640–60.* Leicester University Press, 1966.

L. STONE. 'Social Mobility in England, 1500–1700', *Past and Present*, 33, 1966.

A. EVERITT. 'Social Mobility in Early Modern England', *Past and Present*, 33, 1966.

INDEX

INDEX

Marx, Karl, xxii–xxiv, 40, 51
Marxist view of history, xiii, xx–xxi,
104–5, 107, 109–10
Merchants, 5, 7, 12–13, 15, 51, 66, 71,
87–9, 93, 97, 116, 126, 128–9, 135,
139, 153, 164, 166–7
Milton, John, 110

Namier, Sir Lewis, xiii, 90
Neville, Henry, 17, 30, 65, 169, 175
New Model Army, 29, 37, 48–9, 55,
62, 101
Newcastle, Earl of, *see* Cavendish

Office-holders, 21–4, 81–6, 134, 153
Oglander, Sir John, 25, 57, 125–7

Parliament, 28; Commons, House of,
38–9, 54, 61, 77, 176; Long
Parliament, 16, 38, 44, 47–8, 54,
86–90; Lords, House of, 15, 29, 61,
78, 176; Rump, 30, 48, 86–7, 91–8
Parliamentarians, 49, 51–2, 55–6, 61,
85–90, 126, 164–7
Patronage, 24, 41–3
Peerage, 4, 20–1, 26, 32, 36, 51, 60,
63–7, 72–3, 83–4, 117, 121, 130–3,
168, 176
Pennington, D. H., *see* Brunton, D.
Presbyterians, xviii, 47, 56, 62, 86,
91–3, 96–7

Puritanism, 25–6, 28, 53, 57, 92, 165;
see also Calvinism

Ralegh (Raleigh), Sir Walter, 24,
28–9, 41, 60, 105, 110, 129, 152
Republicanism, 4, 29–30, 90, 92–3, 96,
107, 110, 169, 175
Royalists, 47, 49, 51–2, 55–7, 61, 66,
85–90, 125–6, 164–7
Rump, see Parliament

Selden, John, 41, 105, 110, 127, 130
Social Mobility, xi–xvi, xxi, 6–10,
12–13, 49–50, 66–7, 70–1, 83,
98–9, 133–7, 140–1, 143, 153–4
Spain, xxii, 23, 27, 29, 56, 77
Stone, L., xi–xv, xx, 32–4, 39–40

Tawney, R. H., xi–xiii, xv–xvi,
xix–xx, xxiv, 19–22, 25–6, 30–1,
33–45, 47, 50, 60, 67, 74, 83, 98,
104–10
Trevor-Roper, H. R., xi–xiv, xx–
xxiv, 33–49, 53, 60, 83, 91, 93–4,
98, 107–10, 153

Villiers, George, Duke of Buckingham, 75–7; family, 21, 66

Walker, Sir Edward, 17, 66
Wardship, 27, 29, 91, 149–50